MISCARRIAGE

A DOCTOR'S GUIDE TO THE FACTS

MISCARRIAGE

Why It Happens and How Best to Reduce Your Risks

Henry M. Lerner, M.D., OB/GYN

With contributions by Alice Domar, Ph.D.
Introduction by Robert Barbieri, M.D.

PERSEUS
PUBLISHING

A Member of the Perseus Books Group

Many of the designations used by manufacturers and sellers to distinguish their products are claimed as trademarks. Where those designations appear in this book and Perseus Publishing was aware of a trademark claim, the designations have been printed in initial capital letters.

Copyright © 2003 by Henry M. Lerner

Library of Congress Control Number: 2002114586
ISBN 0–7382–0634–2

Perseus Publishing is a Member of the Perseus Books Group.
Find us on the World Wide Web at http://www.perseuspublishing.com
Perseus Publishing books are available at special discounts for bulk purchases in the U.S. by corporations, institutions, and other organizations. For more information, please contact the Special Markets Department at the Perseus Books Group, 11 Cambridge Center, Cambridge, MA 02142, or call (800) 255–1514 or (617)252–5298, or e-mail j.mccrary@perseusbooks.com.

Text design by Brent Wilcox
Set in 11-point Goudy by the Perseus Books Group

First printing, February 2003
3 4 5 6 7 8 9 10—06 05 04 03

To my parents, Ira and Shirley Lerner, who have shown
by their lives what a handicap is *not*.

Contents

Introduction

Why did I miscarry? What can be done to prevent it from happening again? Millions of women have suffered a miscarriage, and these questions are almost always quick to follow. This book answers these and many other questions. Indeed, if you are looking for the best book on the problem of pregnancy loss, this is the book for you. It authoritatively interprets the best available scientific information in a sympathetic manner, and it never strays from a commitment to present the real, scientific facts. Yet it consistently recognizes and respects the emotional pain of miscarriage.

Acting as your scientific guide, Dr. Lerner presents a clear picture of what causes miscarriage and what can be done to prevent and treat this problem. He deals clearly with issues such as the role of age, anatomy, hormones, genetics, lifestyle, and environment on the risk of miscarriage. He has masterfully, and without bias, cut through all the false claims that have made it difficult to understand miscarriage. This scientific achievement alone makes the book essential reading for women who have experienced or who are worried about miscarriage.

But what makes this book special—and unique in the literature—is that Dr. Lerner has written it with a uniform focus on your needs. Complete with a chapter by Dr. Alice Domar, the world's foremost authority on the relationship between emotion and pregnancy problems, this comprehensive guide provides recommendations on how to approach recovery from the sorrow of miscarriage and, for many, the emotions that occur with the next positive pregnancy test. In his writing, as in his practice, Dr. Lerner has made caring for you, the patient, the primary purpose of the medical care experience. Simply put, this is the best book on miscarriage available.

ROBERT BARBIERI, M.D.
Professor and Chairman of the Department of Obstetrics
and Gynecology at Brigham and Women's Hospital
and Harvard Medical School

Acknowledgments

I would like to thank the following people for their help in the preparation, writing, and publishing of *Miscarriage: Why It Happens and How Best to Reduce Your Risk*.

My patients, especially the ones who themselves have gone through the ordeal of miscarriage.

Marnie Cochran, my editor at Perseus, for her patience, insight, and excellent suggestions for improving the content and language of the book.

Kristin Wainwright, my agent, for helping the book find a home.

Alice Domar and Alice Kelly, who produced so valuable a chapter and made working with them so easy.

Sharon Carlton, for helping me organize my ideas for the book proposal.

John Harrington and Melissa Sanford for their skillful and enlightening illustrations.

Megan Butler for her help in the late stages of publication.

My office staff at Newton-Wellesley Obstetrics & Gynecology who have done such a wonderful job over the years helping and nurturing our patients and keeping the doctors in line.

My friends and colleagues who were kind enough to read my initial manuscript and offer many helpful suggestions and corrections: Merle Berger, M.D., Patricia Robertson, M.D., and Ian Hardy, M.D.

Dr. Robert Barbieri for his graciousness in agreeing to write the foreword.

Kathy Larson for her years of wonderful collegiality and her early encouragement of this book.

Patricia Barylick, my office manager and friend of many years, to whom I owe a great debt of gratitude for her help, her support, and her efficient organization of my practice and other projects.

My partners Eugene Aron, M.D., Heidi Angle, M.D., Elaine Metcalf, M.D., and Elizabeth Konig, M.D., for their teamwork and for all that we learn from each other.

My brother Fred Lerner, the family librarian, for his help and suggestions all through the project.

My parents for their love, support, and inspiration through the years.

And most of all, my family:

My children Addie, Hilary, and Ross whose curious minds are a delight to behold.

My wonderful and beloved wife, Phyllis Scherr—herself a gynecologist—for her love, companionship, and integral support throughout the entire planning and writing of this book. Her perceptive insights, superb comments, and masterful editing during the project have been invaluable.

CHAPTER 1

What Is a Miscarriage?

LAURA AND TOM HAD BEEN TRYING TO CONCEIVE FOR TWO years. When it finally happened and Laura's pregnancy test was positive, they were overjoyed. They called their parents to share their happy news and they began to tell their closest friends. They started thinking about how they would convert their guest room to the baby's room, and they talked about names for their already cherished child.

Then Laura began to bleed.

Laura called my office, and I asked her to come right in. An ultrasound examination confirmed that Laura was having a miscarriage.

When I met with Laura in the office after the ultrasound, her first question to me was, "Why I am miscarrying? What's causing me to lose my baby?"

As gently as I could, I explained to her that miscarriages are common, natural events. I told her that usually miscarriages happen because the chromosomes of the egg and sperm did not fuse correctly at the time of conception. Because the chromosomes contain the genes that direct all growth, this incorrect fusion leaves the embryo without the proper "blueprints" for development. At some point in the early weeks of pregnancy, the fetus dies.

Thus began a long conversation with Laura and Tom—a conversation of the sort that led me to write this book. For the scenario described above occurs in one form or another approximately 800,000 times every year in the United States. Miscarriages are the most common form of personal tragedy that couples go through in their early years of marriage. Most often a miscarriage comes as a tremendous shock because it occurs so unexpectedly. It is a subject rarely talked about and about which most people know very little. Yet miscarriage is and always has been a very common event, occurring in fully one out of five of all pregnancies.

My goal in *Miscarriage* is to answer the questions that most women and men who have been through a miscarriage ask and that you yourself may well have wondered about:

What will happen to me during my miscarriage?
Why do miscarriages occur?
What happens afterward?
What forms of evaluation and testing are appropriate following the miscarriage?
What treatments are available to help prevent me from having another miscarriage?
Do they work?

In *Miscarriage*, I will also discuss the intense and varied emotional responses that most people experience as they go through a miscarriage. Along with Alice Domar, a nationally known psychologist who has worked for many years in the field of women's reproductive issues, I will talk about the pain, anger, grief, and guilt that you may have felt if you have lost an early pregnancy. Together we will explore the ways by which you can find the emotional support you need to get through the trauma of a miscarriage and, if you wish, to move on and become pregnant again.

First, though, let's talk more specifically about what a miscarriage is and what happens when one occurs.

What Exactly Is a Miscarriage?

A miscarriage is officially defined as the spontaneous end of a pregnancy during the first or early second trimester. Most commonly, however, miscarriages occur within the first twelve weeks of pregnancy.

Physicians generally use the technical term *spontaneous abortion* when talking about miscarriages. This term makes some people uncomfortable because they confuse it with the term *therapeutic abortion*, which is an *induced* termination of pregnancy. In fact, in the medical world the word *abortion* means *any* pregnancy that doesn't progress beyond twenty weeks from the last menstrual period. The loss of a fetus that is older than twenty weeks is considered a *stillbirth*. Thus, a woman who loses her pregnancy in the third month has a *miscarriage*, or a *spontaneous abortion*. If a woman experiences the death of her fetus in the sixth month of her pregnancy, she will deliver a *stillborn*. Stillbirths are much rarer than abortions and generally occur for different reasons.

The usual course of a miscarriage is that, for one of many reasons that I will discuss in subsequent chapters, an embryo or fetus dies. The level of pregnancy hormone in the pregnant woman's body, which had been rising since the onset of the pregnancy, begins to fall. The pregnancy tissues begin to break down. These tissues—called *products of conception*—are expelled by the uterus over the next one to three weeks.

Sometimes a miscarriage occurs when a fetus is still living, but this is a rare event. When it does happen, the cervix, weakened either from developmental abnormality or through surgery, is unable to hold in the increasing weight of a growing pregnancy. It dilates prematurely and the fetus is expelled. Because of extreme prematurity, the fetuses thus born almost never survive. This situation is called *cervical incompetence*.

As I have already mentioned, miscarriages are extremely common. They occur in fully 20% of all known pregnancies. The percentage is even higher if one counts the miscarriages that occur before a woman even knows she is pregnant. Therefore, if you are currently suffering through a miscarriage—or have had one in the past—it is important to keep in mind the following fact: Miscarriages are *spontaneous, frequent,* and *normal* reproductive events—even if extremely disappointing and sad ones. Your loss is real and wrenching—but you are not alone in having gone through this experience. And, as you will see, your chances for having a healthy pregnancy in the future are excellent.

HOW PREGNANCIES ARE DATED

In this book I will use such terms as *gestational age, fetal age,* and *time from conception* in describing the age of a fetus. What exactly is meant by each of these terms?

On average, it takes 266 days—thirty-eight weeks—from the moment of conception to the delivery of a full-term baby. Some pregnancies last longer than this, some end earlier, but the average length of time it takes a baby to grow is 266 days.

The length of a pregnancy from the time of conception is called the *fetal age.* This is the form of measurement that an embryologist, concerned mainly about fetal development, would use in describing the duration of a pregnancy.

When obstetrics was first developing as a science, a woman rarely knew the exact date on which she conceived. Because a woman did usually know when she had her last period, it became customary for doctors to measure the length of a pregnancy from the date of the last menstrual period.

If you have regular cycles, you will generally ovulate (make an egg) at mid-cycle, two weeks after your last period and two weeks before your next one. It is at the time of ovulation that you can become pregnant. Thus, if you count the beginning of your pregnancy from the first day of your last menstrual period—instead of from conception—you have to add two weeks to the fetal age to determine how far along your pregnancy is. Using this method, an average pregnancy lasts not thirty-eight weeks but forty weeks. This method of counting the duration of a pregnancy is called the *gestational age.* It is the method you and your doctor will use to keep track of pregnancy events and timing. Here are the differences between fetal age and gestational age:

	Gestational Age	Fetal Age
Conception	2 wks	0 wks
Pregnancy visible on U/S	6 wks	4 wks
First fetal movement felt	20 wks	18 wks
Term (due date)	40 wks	38 wks

The *due date* is the average time it takes a fetus to develop. Statistical analysis has shown that 90% of women will go into labor from between ten days before until up to ten days after their due date. This is the normal length of time for a pregnancy to last.

Many women feel that when they reach their due date they are "late." In fact, at that point a woman has just reached the fiftieth percentile—the average time—when she might expect her baby to arrive. She will not truly be late—outside the biological norm for delivery—until ten days after her due date.

There is a simple way to approximate your due date without having to look at a calendar: It is called *Nagel's rule* and it works like this: If you add seven days to the date of the beginning of your last menstrual period and then subtract three months from that date, the date so derived will be your approximate due date.

Terms You May Hear

Below is a list of terms you may hear or read about while you are going through a miscarriage:

- *Blighted ovum:* A very early miscarriage that occurs before definite fetal structures can be seen on ultrasound. This term describes a fertilized egg—a very early embryo—that has died shortly after conception. It does *not* mean that there was something wrong, or "blighted," about the egg.
- *Ectopic pregnancy:* An embryo that does not implant as it should in the thickened lining tissue of the uterus, but implants instead in the fallopian tube, ovary, or some other part of the abdomen. Since these other organs are not designed to hold a growing fetus, at some point the structure containing the pregnancy ruptures, causing potentially dangerous bleeding.
- *Molar pregnancy:* An abnormality of placental growth in which normal placental tissues change into grape-like clusters of soft cysts that fill the uterus. It is extremely rare for a normal fetus to be present in a molar pregnancy.
- *Chemical pregnancy:* A pregnancy that does not progress beyond its very earliest stages. The sperm and egg have just fused into an early embryo and the embryo has just started making pregnancy hormone—but the embryo dies before significant growth can occur. The pregnancy hormone measured in the mother's blood is the only evidence that a pregnancy had occurred.
- *Clinical pregnancy:* A pregnancy that reaches the point of having "clinical" symptoms. The mother may experience nausea or breast tenderness, and the physician who is examining her may find that she has an enlarged uterus. An ultrasound exam will show a fetal heartbeat and fetal structures.

Different Types of Miscarriage

- *Complete abortion:* When, after a miscarriage, all the pregnancy tissue is spontaneously passed from the uterus.

- *Incomplete abortion:* This is the most common type of miscarriage. Not all the pregnancy tissue has passed from the uterus, and often there is heavy vaginal bleeding and painful uterine cramping. The tissue often needs to be removed by a procedure called dilatation and curettage (D&C) (see below).
- *Threatened abortion:* A woman and her doctor see evidence—such as slight spotting or marked uterine cramping—that a miscarriage *might* occur.
- *Inevitable abortion:* Either symptoms, conclusive laboratory tests, or an ultrasound show that the pregnancy will not survive and a miscarriage is bound to happen, even if bleeding and cramping have not yet occurred.
- *Early miscarriage:* Miscarriage that occurs before the twelfth week of pregnancy.
- *Late miscarriage:* Miscarriage that occurs between thirteen and twenty weeks of pregnancy. (Pregnancy losses after twenty weeks are considered stillbirths.)
- *Recurrent miscarriage:* Three or more miscarriages, either occurring consecutively or interspersed between full-term pregnancies. (Some experts feel that two or more miscarriages should qualify as recurrent miscarriage. This issue is discussed further in Chapter 7.)

Determining Whether You Are Having a Miscarriage

Usually vaginal bleeding, with or without cramping, is the first sign that you might be having a miscarriage. This bleeding may be just a little bit of spotting, may be flow equal to your normal menstrual period, or may evolve into massive hemorrhaging. The amount of bleeding you have depends on how far along your pregnancy is. In an early miscarriage, you do not have much tissue to pass because only a small amount has developed inside your uterus. In contrast, if your pregnancy is more advanced when a miscarriage occurs, you have more tissue to expel.

The bleeding from a miscarriage is usually, but not always, accompanied by cramping. The cramping may range from mild "uterine irritability" akin to menstrual cramps to intensely painful uterine contractions. The cramping occurs when the uterus attempts to squeeze out pregnancy tissue and the blood that accumulates when the placenta separates from the uterine wall.

If you are experiencing cramping without bleeding—don't worry! *Cramping without bleeding in early pregnancy is normal* and does not mean that the pregnancy is at risk for miscarriage. This cramping is usually caused by the expansion of the uterine walls, the stretching of the round ligaments, and the general anatomic changes a growing uterus produces in the pelvis.

Moreover, even bleeding during early pregnancy does not always mean that a miscarriage is going to occur. Although such bleeding can be frightening, it's important to remember that some bleeding in early pregnancy is very common. It occurs in from 20 to 40% of all pregnancies. Although bleeding in early pregnancy is followed by a miscarriage 50% of the time, the other half of these pregnancies proceed normally.

I am often asked whether early pregnancy bleeding, even if the pregnancy continues, means that the baby is at higher risk for problems later on. Fortunately, multiple studies have shown that there is no increased risk of birth defects in such pregnancies. There does, however, seem to be a higher rate of preterm labor in the third trimester of those pregnancies in which first trimester bleeding has occurred.

If I'm Not Having a Miscarriage, Why Am I Bleeding?

The most common cause of bleeding during early pregnancy is *marginal abruption of the placenta.* What is this?

The placenta is a mass of blood vessels and supporting tissues. This mass, in the shape of a round, flat disk, is attached to the inner wall of the uterus. If a bit of the placental edge lifts up from its attachment to the uterus wall, small blood vessels are torn open and bleeding occurs. This is similar to what happens when you bump a scab and the edge bleeds. Fortunately, unless a large part of the placenta is dislodged, the slightly detached placental edge almost always reattaches itself over a few days and the bleeding stops.

The term *abruption* means the separation of the placenta from the uterus. The term *marginal* indicates that the separation is minimal and limited to the edge of the placenta. If there is only a small separation of the placenta from the uterine wall, then the placenta's ability to nourish the fetus and exchange oxygen is not compromised. If, however, more than about 40% of the placenta separates, the placenta's ability to sustain the pregnancy is lost and a miscarriage will almost always occur.

Although most marginal abruptions are small and usually do not result in miscarriage, the anxiety-producing spotting and bleeding they cause can continue for several weeks in the first and early second trimesters. I have seen many patients who have had to endure weeks of such bleeding without knowing for certain whether their pregnancies would survive. Fortunately, in the majority of these cases, the bleeding did eventually stop and the pregnancies proceeded normally.

There are other reasons why you might experience bleeding in early pregnancy:

- As the placenta "puts down roots"—that is, as parts of the placental tissue dig into the uterine wall and begin to exchange nutrients with the uterine blood vessels—the placental tissue sometimes penetrates these blood vessels. This sort of bleeding is common and is usually short-lived. It almost always stops on its own, the pregnancy continuing on unaffected.
- Inflammation, infection, or the hormonal changes of pregnancy can cause bleeding of the cervix.
- Endocervical polyps are small, soft pieces of reddish tissue that originate just inside the opening of the cervix. These polyps can protrude out of the cervix into the vagina. They are filled with small blood vessels and bleed easily, either spontaneously because of overstimulation by pregnancy hormones or because of direct contact during intercourse or vaginal examination.
- Another potential—but rare—cause of vaginal bleeding in early pregnancy occurs when one fetus of a twin or triplet pregnancy miscarries while the overall pregnancy continues with the surviving fetus or fetuses intact.

Loss of Normal Pregnancy Symptoms

Very often, just before a miscarriage occurs, pregnancy symptoms such as nausea, vomiting, breast tenderness, and fatigue suddenly stop. These symptoms are related to the level of pregnancy hormone in a woman's blood.

The blood level of pregnancy hormone, known as human chorionic gonadotropin (HCG), increases rapidly during the first ten weeks of pregnancy. However, when a miscarriage begins, the placenta stops producing HCG and its level in the blood quickly falls. This hormonal decline causes the pregnancy symptoms listed above to go away, either abruptly or slowly, over several days. If you have been pregnant before you may well note this change and be concerned about it. If this is your first pregnancy, you may simply feel relieved that your uncomfortable symptoms are gone, not fully understanding the potential implications of this change.

In a normal pregnancy, you will generally feel these early pregnancy symptoms at around six or seven weeks from the date of your last period. They increase in intensity, duration, and frequency until they peak at ten weeks' gestation when HCG reaches its highest level. Usually these symptoms gradually resolve over the next two or three weeks until, by the thirteenth week of your pregnancy, you no longer notice them.

Not all women have these pregnancy symptoms, and those who do experience them in varying degrees. Nevertheless, my patients often tell me that these symptoms, which had developed over the first weeks of their pregnancy, suddenly went away just before they realized they were miscarrying.

What You Should Do If You Think You Are Having a Miscarriage

Although vaginal bleeding, cramping, and the loss of pregnancy symptoms can all be caused by conditions other than miscarriage, you should contact your doctor's office immediately if you experience any of these things or if for any reason you think you are having a miscarriage. All physicians and midwives who care for pregnant women have twenty-four-hour emergency coverage, so a call to your health care provider's answering service at any time of day or night should result in a prompt return call. If you are bleeding heavily or cannot reach your physician, go the nearest hospital emergency room. Until a physician has evaluated you, stop all exercise and physical activity and don't insert anything into your vagina. If you are bleeding, use pads instead of tampons. It is also best that you do not eat or drink anything at this point so that your stomach will be empty in the event a procedure requiring anesthesia is necessary.

If tissue has passed and it is possible to retrieve it, put it into a small plastic bag and refrigerate it until you can bring it to your doctor's office or the hospital. The tissue can then undergo laboratory evaluation. Such an evaluation may provide information that will be useful to your doctor in confirming the diagnosis of your miscarriage.

Evaluating for Possible Miscarriage

How will your doctor determine whether you are having a miscarriage?

Medical History

The first thing that will happen when you reach your doctor's office is that he or she will inquire about your medical history and will ask you what symptoms you are having. Your physician will want to know when your bleeding or cramping started and whether you have had any other problems with your pregnancy. You will be asked about ongoing medical conditions you might have (diabetes, high blood pressure, etc.), previous surgical procedures you have undergone, and medications you may be taking. Your menstrual history and the date of your last period are especially important. Also, if you have a hereditary disorder that may be relevant, such as a tendency toward excessive bleeding, it is important that you tell your doctor about it.

Pelvic Examination

Next, your physician will perform a physical examination, including an internal exam. He or she will be looking for these symptoms:

- *Signs of severe blood loss* as reflected in your blood pressure, pulse, and respiratory rate.
- *The location and degree of abdominal or pelvic pain.* This information will help your doctor determine whether your symptoms are being caused by normal early pregnancy discomfort, a miscarriage, or some

other disorder such as tubal pregnancy, appendicitis, or a ruptured ovarian cyst.

- *The amount of blood or tissue in the vagina,* if any.
- *Changes in the normally thick, firm cervix.* In miscarriages, the cervix often opens slightly as the uterus attempts to expel the pregnancy tissue.
- *The size of the uterus.* Your doctor will check to see whether your uterus is the size it is supposed to be for a given gestational age—a good sign that your pregnancy is proceeding normally—or whether your uterus is smaller than would be expected—a sign that the growth of your pregnancy has stopped, likely due to a miscarriage.
- *Marked discomfort or enlargement in the area of the fallopian tubes and ovaries.* Either of these findings could indicate that you have a tubal pregnancy, an ovarian cyst, or a pelvic infection.

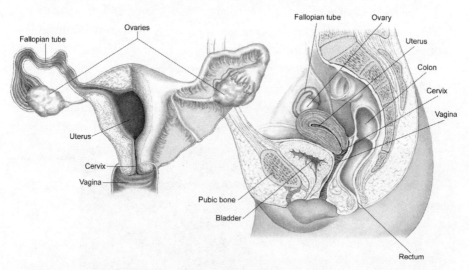

FIGURE 1.1   Normal Female Pelvic Anatomy

Laboratory Tests

Your doctor will likely also order laboratory tests. Your blood will be checked to see whether you are anemic—have a low blood level—either chronically (longstanding) or acutely (caused by recent bleeding). He or she will also perform a blood pregnancy test to determine the presence or absence of HCG in your blood. If HCG is present, its level may be either normal for the gestational age of your pregnancy or lower than expected. The latter result may indicate a miscarriage or a tubal pregnancy. If the HCG level is much higher than expected, your pregnancy may be further along than you thought, you may have a multiple pregnancy (twins, triplets) or—extremely rare—you may have a molar pregnancy.

Finally, your blood type will be checked. Some fetal red blood cells always enter the mother's body during pregnancy. Depending on the blood type a fetus inherits from its mother and father, these fetal blood cells that enter the mother may cause her to develop antibodies against them. Antibodies are blood components that can cause damage to tissues. If such antibodies form in the mother they can be harmful, even fatal, to the current pregnancy or to future pregnancies. They can also make it difficult for a woman to receive blood transfusions should that ever be necessary.

If your blood type is such that you are at risk of this happening, you will be given a shot of a special medicine called Rhogam following your miscarriage. One shot of Rhogam will prevent you from making these potentially dangerous antibodies.

Ultrasound

Once your doctor has performed a physical examination and taken blood for testing, he or she will likely order a pelvic ultrasound. If your bleed-

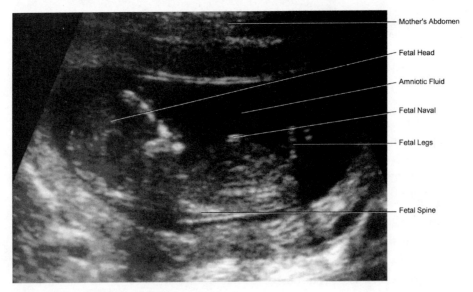

FIGURE 1.2   Ultrasound of Early Fetus

ing is heavy, your cramping severe, or tissue is passing from your uterus, then ultrasound may not be necessary to confirm that a miscarriage is occurring. However, if there is any question as to whether your pregnancy is still viable or whether it is located in the uterus (as opposed to the fallopian tubes or some other location), an ultrasound can provide important information.

In a viable pregnancy, the gestational sac—the outline of the growing pregnancy inside the uterus—should be identifiable on ultrasound examination after five weeks from the last menstrual period. Fetal structures can usually be seen as early as five and one-half weeks, and a fetal heartbeat in six or six and one-half weeks. If these features are *not* seen on ultrasound by these stages of gestation—and your pregnancy dates are accurately known—it is likely that either a miscarriage or (more rarely) an ectopic pregnancy is taking place. This may be so even if you have not yet experienced vaginal bleeding or cramping.

Often bleeding occurs at such an early stage (before five and one-half weeks' gestation) that the fetal heart will not yet be visible on ultrasound. In these situations it cannot be determined immediately whether you are having a miscarriage. In such cases you and your doctor can only wait and watch to see whether, over the next one or two weeks, your HCG levels rise appropriately. After this time your pregnancy will be far enough along so that the status of your fetus can be determined by ultrasound.

After a Miscarriage Is Diagnosed

If after evaluating you your doctor has determined that you are in fact having a miscarriage, the main concern becomes whether your uterus will pass the pregnancy tissue on its own relatively gently or whether severe bleeding and cramping will occur.

If the miscarriage occurs at an early stage of pregnancy—before approximately eight weeks' gestation—or if most of the pregnancy tissue has already passed, your uterus will feel small and firm when your doctor performs a physical examination. If this is the case it is likely that nothing further will need to be done. If fragments of tissue or blood remain in the uterus, they will usually pass on their own over the next few days.

However, if you are experiencing heavy bleeding or cramping or the physical examination and ultrasound show that there may be a significant quantity of tissue remaining inside your uterus, a procedure called *dilatation and curettage* (D&C) will likely be necessary.

Dilatation and Curettage (D&C)

Dilatation refers to the stretching of the cervix to allow instruments to be passed into the uterus. Curettage is the surgical scraping out of tissue—the "products of conception"—from the uterus. This procedure is also sometimes referred to as a "D&E," which stands for "dilatation and evacuation." The instrument most often used to empty the uterus is a suction curette—an approximately ten-inch-long sterile plastic tube that is attached to a suction machine and through which tissue remaining in the uterus is emptied.

If most of the tissue has already passed on its own, there will be no need to perform a D&C. If, on the other hand, you are experiencing heavy bleeding and cramping, a D&C is the quickest and surest way to empty your uterus and stop the bleeding.

In the in-between situation in which bleeding and cramping are not of great severity and only a moderate amount of tissue remains inside the uterus, the choice of treatment is not clear-cut. On the one hand, you might pass this remaining tissue on your own with minimal difficulty. On the other hand, the bleeding and cramping may persist unless a D&C is done to remove the tissue still inside the uterus. Since it cannot be predicted with certainty what will happen in any given case, there is often no one "right" way for you to proceed.

When faced with this situation, I generally allow my patients to decide how they would like to proceed. Here are the pros and cons I discuss with them:

Benefits of a D&C

- A D&C provides immediate relief and a quick end to the miscarriage episode. It stops the bleeding and cramping promptly and thus allows you to begin the process of letting your life move on.

- A D&C eliminates the potential for significant bleeding and cramping to recur in the weeks to come, perhaps necessitating a D&C under emergency circumstances.

Arguments Against a D&C

- It's always best to avoid surgery if possible.
- Although a D&C is a minor surgical procedure that is performed thousands of times every day, in 1 or 2% of patients having this procedure complications occur. These might be infection, persistent bleeding, scarring of the inside of the uterus, or even—rarely—a perforation of the uterus by the suction curette. Such a perforation can damage adjacent pelvic organs.
- A D&C procedure can be anxiety provoking and uncomfortable.

In these in-between situations, my patients usually make their decision based on what they wish to avoid more: a surgical procedure or the risk of having ongoing bleeding and cramping along with the possibility of needing a D&C over the next several days anyway.

What Can I Expect If a D&C Is Necessary?

A D&C may be performed in a doctor's office, in an outpatient clinic, or in an operating room. An overnight stay usually isn't necessary. You will be asked to refrain from eating or drinking anything for six or eight hours beforehand. Fasting decreases your risk of vomiting during the procedure.

The procedure is brief and straightforward. Your doctor will first "prep" your vagina and cervix—wash them with an antiseptic solution. He or she will then perform a pelvic examination to assess the exact size and position of your uterus. Following this you will be given medication to reduce the discomfort of the procedure. In a doctor's office or in a clinic, this medication will likely be given "locally" by injecting a Novocain-like solution into the vaginal wall where the nerves run into the cervix. In an operating room, it is more probable that intravenous or even general anesthesia will be used with or without the addition of a local anesthetic.

Once anesthesia has been administered, your cervix will be evaluated to see whether it is sufficiently open for the D&C procedure to be performed. If it is not, your doctor will stretch it open with "dilators," a set of sterile metal rods of graduated size. A suction curette will then be inserted into your uterus. The curette will be attached via plastic tubing to a suction machine. The tissue or blood clots remaining in your uterus will then be suctioned out.

If your miscarriage is diagnosed before you experience bleeding and cramping—a "missed" spontaneous abortion—your cervix may be too thick to allow a D&C to be performed safely. In this situation, your doctor may decide to dilate your cervix gradually with *laminaria* rather than the dilators that are generally used for this purpose. Laminaria are thin sticks from two to three inches long made of compressed seaweed. They absorb water slowly, expanding and thickening as they do so. Your doctor will place one or more of these laminaria into the opening of your cervix and leave them in overnight. By the time a D&C is performed the next day, the thin laminaria will have thickened to five times their previous size and will have stretched the cervix open.

After the D&C, you will be observed to make sure that the bleeding subsides, the cramping stops, and that you fully wake up from the anesthesia you received. Generally, your cramping will diminish quickly—usually within ten to thirty minutes. You may be given prescriptions to take home with you: an antibiotic to help prevent infection and a medication called ergonovine (Methergine) to help the uterus compress itself back to its normal nonpregnant size. This compression will help reduce post-D&C bleeding. Once you are fully awake and able to eat, drink, and walk on your own, you will be discharged. Because the effects of anesthetic medication can alter alertness, hand-eye coordination, and reflexes, you should not drive for twelve hours following the procedure. You will thus need to arrange to have someone drive you home.

Before you leave the hospital (or office), you will be given discharge instructions. You will be told to "take it easy" for the next three or four days: no heavy lifting, exercising, or other hard physical work. You will be asked to refrain from sexual intercourse and not to use tampons or to douche for one week. You can resume your normal diet as soon as you are able to take food and fluids by mouth.

After the Miscarriage

Once your miscarriage is over—your pregnancy tissue has passed spontaneously or been removed by a D&C—several other issues arise.

Warning Signs to Watch For

- Bleeding that intensifies rather than diminishes
- The appearance of a foul-smelling discharge
- Fever—temperature of 99.5 degrees or higher
- Abdominal or pelvic discomfort or pain
- Persistent nausea or vomiting

If these or any other unusual symptoms occur, you need to get back in touch with your doctor to rule out the possibility of having complications from the miscarriage or the D&C procedure.

When Will the Bleeding Stop?

If the pregnancy tissue has passed on its own, your bleeding may last from five to ten days after the miscarriage. During this time, any remaining pregnancy tissue inside your uterus liquefies and comes out as a mixture of blood and clots. The amount of blood passed should decrease each day, the flow gradually turning from red to pink to white.

If you underwent a D&C, most of the tissue will have been removed from the uterus during the procedure. Thus there will be little tissue remaining inside the uterus from which to bleed. The bleeding will generally stop within three to five days after the procedure.

Resumption of Normal Periods

Whether a D&C is or is not performed, the level of HCG in your blood will fall rapidly after the miscarriage. This decrease in HCG prompts your body's hormonal system to resume the production of the hormones involved in the cyclic pattern of the ovulation cycle. You will generally have your first ovulation two to four weeks after the miscarriage. A normal

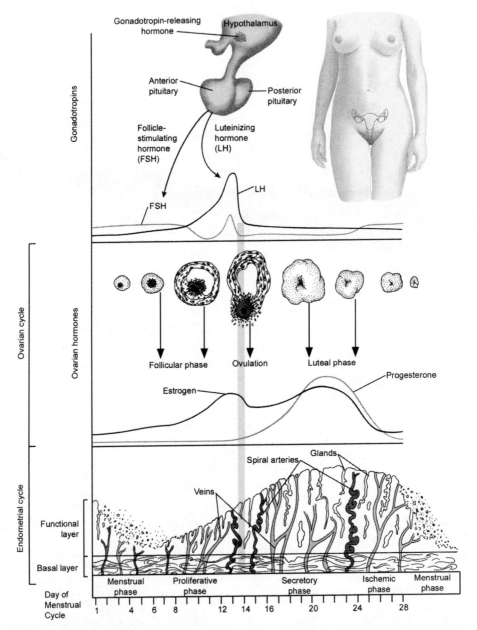

FIGURE 1.3   Time Course of Hormones in Menstrual Cycle, HCG, Endometrial Thickness, and Corpus Luteum

menstrual period will follow this ovulation approximately two weeks later. Thus, you can generally expect to have a period anywhere from four to six weeks after your miscarriage.

Resuming Normal Activities

Many women whose work is not intensely physical find that they are able to go back to their jobs the day after their miscarriage. On the other hand, there is certainly nothing wrong with staying at home for a day or two after a miscarriage, either to rest or to take time to deal with the many intense and complex emotions having a miscarriage can produce.

The same advice applies to exercise. Many women find that in the day or two following a miscarriage, even if they had a D&C, they feel well enough to participate in vigorous physical activity. This, of course, presupposes that their bleeding is light or has stopped and that they are not experiencing significant pelvic pain or cramping.

The situation is different with intercourse. During a miscarriage, and certainly during a D&C, the cervix has opened, allowing blood and tissue to pass through. An open cervix, however, is a potential gateway for bacteria to enter the uterus. It is therefore safer not to put *anything* into the vagina (tampons, having sex) until the cervix has closed and the normal mucus plug, which is a partial barrier to infection, has re-formed. This usually takes about a week, after which it is safe to resume normal sexual activity and to use tampons.

Your Follow-Up Doctor's Visit

You will probably be asked to schedule a follow-up visit with your doctor one or two weeks after your miscarriage. The purpose of this visit is to make certain that you are recovering well both physically and emotionally.

First, your physician will ask you how you are feeling. He or she will want to know whether you are still bleeding and whether you have pelvic pain.

Next, he or she will examine your uterus to make sure that it has returned to its normal size and shape, to look for evidence of infection, and to be certain that no tissue remains inside.

Your doctor may ask you to have a blood sample drawn to confirm that your HCG level is falling appropriately. As I mentioned earlier, there can be other causes for what appears to be a miscarriage, such as a slowly developing normal pregnancy, a tubal pregnancy, or a molar pregnancy. By observing that the HCG level is going down to zero following your miscarriage, your doctor can rule out all these possibilities.

This follow-up visit is also a good time for you to let your doctor know how you are feeling emotionally. Feel free to ask questions about the miscarriage. It is okay to repeat questions that you may have asked before. Sometimes it is difficult to take in the answers to questions while the miscarriage is occurring.

This visit also provides an excellent opportunity to begin planning for your next pregnancy. Your doctor can share with you and your partner the information gleaned from laboratory tests or studies done at the time of the miscarriage. He or she may have suggestions for you and your partner about diet, lifestyle, and pregnancy-related health issues. For example, it is important that women have adequate dietary sources of folic acid when conceiving and during pregnancy. Folic acid decreases the risk of having a baby with spina bifida, a condition in which a baby is born with a spinal cord that has not developed properly. Because it is not always certain that a woman has sufficient folic acid in her diet, it is recommended that all women trying to conceive take a daily multivitamin, almost all of which contain the necessary 400 mcg daily dose of this important nutrient.

Also, the time just after a miscarriage—a time when you know for certain that you are not pregnant—provides an ideal opportunity to catch up on inoculations for diseases to which you are not already immune, such as German measles (rubella) and chickenpox. Protecting yourself from these diseases *before* you become pregnant again eliminates the possibility of contracting them during your next pregnancy and putting that pregnancy at risk. If you are not certain whether you are immune to these diseases, ask your doctor to do a blood test to check for evidence of immunity to them.

Questions That You May Wish to Ask Your Doctor At Your Follow-Up Visit

- What can you tell me about the cause of my miscarriage?

- Should I undergo further testing to determine why the miscarriage happened?
- Was testing done on the fetal material from the miscarriage?
- Can you recommend any counselors who have expertise at helping couples who have experienced a miscarriage?
- Are there any support groups in this area for couples who have had a miscarriage?
- How soon can we try to conceive again?

I will discuss all these questions at length in the chapters to come.

Chapter Summary

Although the process of having a miscarriage can be frightening, painful, and tremendously disappointing for a couple, I have found over the years that it is in the days and weeks *after* the miscarriage that women and their partners experience the most profound emotional distress. If you have just had a miscarriage, you may be upset and confused about what you have just been through. You may feel that something you did brought on your miscarriage. And you may be fearful that you will never have a baby—or another baby, if you already have children.

But by learning more about the phenomenon of miscarriage—which you are doing by reading this book—you are taking the first and most important step toward successfully dealing with your loss.

The first thing you will find is that you are not alone: Millions of couples have experienced the same pain that you are going through. Yet you will learn that most of these same millions of couples have gone on to have as many healthy children as they wished. You will see that rather than a miscarriage being an unusual event, the majority of couples who have two or more children have experienced a miscarriage along the way.

Still, it is totally normal and appropriate for you and others who have suffered a miscarriage to ask the questions that arise after any tragedy: "Why?" and "Why did this happen to *me?*" It has been my purpose in writing *Miscarriage* to answer these questions and the questions that follow naturally from them:

"Why do miscarriages occur?"

"Did I do anything to cause the miscarriage?"

And the ultimate question:

"Will I have another miscarriage with my next pregnancy?"

In the coming chapters, I will discuss the answers to these questions in detail. You will learn what doctors and medical researchers currently know about the answers to them. Most important, I will show you how *you* can use this information to best prepare yourself for having a successful pregnancy in the future.

CHAPTER 2

The Chromosomal Causes of Miscarriage

CHROMOSOMAL MISCOMBINATION IS THE MOST COMMON CAUSE of miscarriage.

This simple statement has profound implications for anyone concerned about miscarriages: couples who have had one, physicians working with these couples, and researchers seeking to learn more about miscarriages so that their frequency can be decreased.

But why do chromosomal miscombinations occur? Why is it that the supposedly "natural" event of pregnancy goes wrong more than 20% of the time?

It is because the biology of reproduction is so extraordinarily complex.

For a baby to be conceived, an egg and a sperm have to combine. The egg—a minute single cell from an adult woman—has to meet and fuse with a sperm—an even smaller one-celled structure from an adult male—to form a brand new entity: an embryo. The genetic material carried in each egg and sperm must be a precise copy of the genetic material of the parents. It has to combine perfectly so that the newly created joint cell, the embryo, will contain all the information it needs for the healthy growth and development of the baby it will become. If this process does not proceed as it should, if any of the literally thousands of steps along the pathway of this development do not occur correctly, then the embryo's genetic material won't be complete. At some point, the embryo will not be able to continue its development. It will die and a miscarriage will occur.

What is the percentage of miscarriages caused by chromosomal misalignment?

At first glance this would seem to be a straightforward question. However, as with many issues concerning reproduction, this is not so. To answer this question we must ask another question: What do we mean by "miscarriage"? Do we mean only pregnancy losses that we know about, that is, miscarriages that occur when a woman is aware that she's pregnant? Or do we mean *all* miscarriages, including those that occur even before a woman knows that she has conceived?

How we define the term *miscarriage* will greatly affect our answer to the question about the percentage of miscarriages caused by chromosomal miscombination. This is because twice as many pregnancy losses occur between fertilization and when a woman learns she is pregnant than occur after she becomes aware that she is. Moreover, the causes of pregnancy losses during these two time periods differ.

Now, if we consider only those pregnancy losses that women know about as miscarriages—the common, everyday definition of the word—then most experts agree the percentage of miscarriages due to chromosomal miscombination is between 50 and 60%. The remainder of "known" miscarriages are caused by other factors: infection, structural abnormalities of the uterus, environmental influences, or—the largest category after chromosomal—unknown.

Answering the Question, "How Do Genetic and Chromosomal Factors Cause Miscarriages?"

When I sit with couples after telling them that they are having a miscarriage, I try to explain to them as clearly and sympathetically as I can why their miscarriage is occurring. Most of my patients have heard about chromosomes and know how important they are for human development. So when I tell them that it is most likely a "chromosomal miscombination" that is causing their miscarriage, they seem to understand.

But in the days and weeks that follow, I often get phone calls from these same patients who ask questions that indicate that it is *not* totally clear to them why a chromosomal miscombination has caused their pregnancy to miscarry.

These questions stem from the ongoing anguish that couples who have just gone through a miscarriage experience. They reflect the urge such couples feel to understand more fully what has happened to them and the pregnancy they had already cherished so much. But answering these questions in anything other than the most superficial way requires that the biology of conception and reproduction be understood in greater detail than is generally the case. So as part of the process of answering these questions for them—and now for you—I have to go over some basic biology.

Genes and Chromosomes

The subject of chromosomes and genetics can seem extremely confusing and complicated. But it does not have to be. To understand why chromosomal miscombinations cause miscarriages, we need know only three things:

1. What are genes?
2. What are chromosomes?
3. How do cells divide?

James Watson and Frances Crick, scientists working in Cambridge, England, in the early 1950s, determined that the basic chemical making up genes and chromosomes is deoxyribonucleic acid (DNA). For this breakthrough, they received the Nobel Prize. A tremendous amount of work over the fifty years since Watson and Crick's discovery has given scientists an in-depth understanding of how DNA determines hereditary features in humans—as well as in animals and plants. In simplest terms, it is the sequence of information coded on the chemical chains of DNA that controls such physical features as eye color—whether it be brown, blue, or green—or hair color—black, brown, or blond. This coding system is responsible for every aspect of human growth and development. Every anatomic and physiologic characteristic we possess, from the shape of our toenails to the amount of blood our hearts pump per minute, is determined by the information in our DNA.

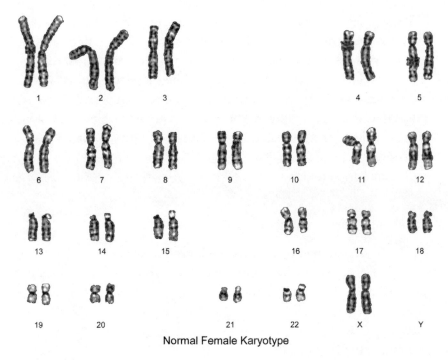

Normal Female Karyotype

FIGURE 2.1 Chromosomes, DNA

Chemically, deoxyribonucleic acid is made up of two components: nucleic acids, of which there are four kinds, and a long molecule in the sugar family called *deoxyribose,* to which the nucleic acids are attached. DNA exists in the form of two paired strands that are joined together and twisted, not unlike a long, narrow piece of tape that has been curled into a spiral. Each DNA molecule is made up of segments, and each segment codes for a specific physical or functional feature. These segments are called *genes.*

The purpose of the sequences found in nucleic acids—what the sequences "code for"—is to determine what sorts of proteins will be produced. If DNA and the genes they contain are thought of as the blueprints for the development of the human body, proteins are the structural materials of which the body is composed. It is the genes that determine what structural materials—proteins—get made and, just as importantly, how they will be put together.

Thus:

Sequences of nucleic acids on DNA are grouped into genes that code for the production of proteins and regulate how proteins are assembled. Proteins form tissues, blood, hormones, and all the other structures of the body.

How many genes are there?

It is estimated that somewhere between 30,000 and 50,000 genes make up what is called the "human genome," the entire sequence of genetic information that humans possess. Amazingly, each cell in the body contains all these genes. This means that every cell in the body contains all the genetic material needed to create any other cell or structure in the body. In fact, every cell in the body contains all the genetic material that would be needed to create an entirely new individual. This is what makes cloning possible.

How Many Chromosomes Do Humans Have?

Chromosomes are strands of DNA. Each species of animal and plant has a specific number of chromosomes that is characteristic for that species. For instance, dogs have 76 chromosomes per cell and tomato plants have 24. Each *human* cell has 46 chromosomes, arranged in 23 pairs.

In each of the 23 pairs of chromosomes, one chromosome is derived from the mother and one from the father. Each pair of chromosomes determines the characteristics of—codes for—specific aspects of fetal structure or function. The two chromosomes of each chromosomal pair both code for the same features—but they may contain different versions of these features, depending on the information inherited from the mother or father. For example, in a certain chromosome pair, one chromosome may have a gene for dark complexion inherited from the mother while the other chromosome in the pair, the one derived from the father, may have the same gene in the light complexion version.

Forty-four of the chromosomes—22 of the pairs—code for bodily structures and functions. The last pair, the 23rd, makes up the "sex chromosomes." This pair determines whether an embryo will develop into a boy or a girl. It also regulates many aspects of sexual function and development, both during the growth of the embryo and in later life. The 23rd pair also controls certain nonsexual functions. If, for instance, a section of genetic material is lacking or incorrect on one of the sex chromosomes, diseases such as hemophilia or Duchenne's muscular dystrophy might develop.

What Portion of a Chromosome's Genetic Material Is Used?

The information on DNA is "translated" by cells and used to form the proteins that go on to make up the various structures of the body. But of the 40,000 or so genes in a person's chromosomes, how is it determined which of them will be activated to direct protein manufacture at any given time? And does each cell, whether in heart, muscle, or brain, manufacture proteins for all of the other parts of the body? Or do the cells of particular organs produce only the proteins that will grow, repair, or replace their own structures?

Although all cells contain all 46 chromosomes, and therefore all cells contain the genetic information for the entire body, usually any given cell makes only proteins that are necessary for that cell's particular function. For instance, cells in the eye will only make proteins that go into eye structures, and cells in the muscles will use only the part of its genetic material that codes for muscle growth, development and function, and so on for each organ. This is true for all structures *except* sex cells— those that will go on to become eggs and sperm. Obviously, the sex cells need to be able to form all the structures required by the new embryos and the fetuses they will become.

Even this briefest of overviews showing the relationship between genetics and bodily growth allows us to begin to understand how marvelously intricate the process of reproduction is. We can also begin to see why, because of this complexity, the process of reproduction might not always work out perfectly.

New Cell Formation and Division

We have seen how the genes on the chromosomes in cells code for the proteins that the cells will produce. But how do cells themselves reproduce? We also have noted that each and every cell of the body contains all of the genetic material of that body. How does this genetic material get passed from cell to cell as new cells grow?

To understand cell growth and multiplication, we must be aware of one key fact: There are two different types of cell division.

The Division of "Body" Cells

The first kind of cell division, the kind that occurs in 99.9% of all the cells in the body, consists simply of cells dividing themselves in half. The other kind of cell division occurs in a small fraction of the body's cells, those cells that go on to become egg and sperm.

There is an obvious and important reason why different kinds of cell division are necessary. When cells of the different parts of the body duplicate, each new cell must contain all the genetic material that the old cell had if it, in turn, is to grow and reproduce itself at some later date. That is, since all cells of muscle or bone or blood contain all 46 chromosomes, when any of these cells divide, both of the cells arising from this division must also have 46 chromosomes.

How do they do this?

Just before a cell divides, each of the 46 individual strands of chromosomes replicates itself, that is, makes a new strand of DNA identical to itself. Thus, just before cell division, there are 46 *double-stranded* chromosomes. As the cell divides, the double-stranded chromosomes split apart, one strand going into one new cell, the other strand going into the other new cell. Each new cell thus winds up with 46 pairs of *single-stranded* chromosomes. When the time comes for each of these new cells to replicate, the process begins all over again.

From the one-cell embryo stage onward, this splitting eventually results in the billions of cells that make up the human body. Yet cells do not stop dividing at maturity. Even in the adult human, when growth and development have been completed, new cells are always being produced in almost every organ to replace older cells that are dying or have become damaged.

This process of simple cell division, with chromosomes doubling and splitting, is called *mitosis*.

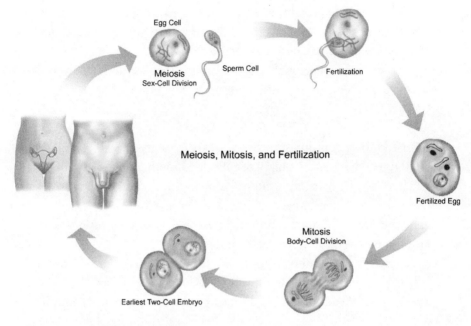

FIGURE 2.2   Cell Division: Mitosis and Meiosis

Sex Cells

With eggs and sperm the process is entirely different. It has to be because in order for pregnancy to occur, a one-cell egg must combine with a one-cell sperm to produce a new one-cell embryo. But if each egg and sperm contained a full set of 46 chromosomes apiece, the new embryo would have 92 chromosomes. This would be incompatible with life. For this not to happen, nature has devised an ingenious system of egg and sperm replication. It is called *meiosis*.

As I mentioned previously, the 46 chromosomes in each human cell are arranged in 23 pairs. In meiosis, no initial chromosome strand replication occurs. Instead, each of the 23 chromosome pairs splits up, one chromosome in each pair going to each of the two new cells. Thus, each new cell—whether egg or sperm—is left with 23 chromosomes apiece instead of the 46 chromosomes that were present in the parent cell. Subsequently, when a 23-chromosome-containing egg merges with a sperm bearing 23 chromosomes, the embryo that results has the normal number of human chromosomes: 46.

Meiosis helps explain many aspects of heredity. For instance, take a pair of chromosomes that code for eye color in an egg or sperm precursor cell. One chromosome of the pair could contain the gene for blue eyes while the other contains the gene for brown eyes. When the precursor cell divides, each new cell takes one of the two chromosomes in the pair. It is random chance which cell will get the gene for blue eyes or the gene for brown eyes. This random selection occurs for every feature coded for by genes—which is every feature a human being possesses. Therefore, although all the chromosomes in an individual come from either the mother or the father, which *combination* of chromosomes an individual inherits from each is determined by the random chance of (1) how the chromosome pairs split and (2) which chromosomes go to which new egg or sperm cell.

Egg and Sperm Development

One of the most fascinating things about the development of eggs and sperm is that they both start out as the same kind of cell. At the very earliest stages of embryonic development, there are no eggs or sperm. There are only very primitive "sex cells" that have the capacity until approximately the sixth week of gestation to develop in either a male or female direction. Which path they take is determined by hormones produced in the young embryo according to the chromosomal structure of its sex chromosomes, pair 23. If a Y chromosome is present on pair 23, male hormonal factors will be produced that will cause testicles to be formed and the sex cells in these testicles to become sperm precursors. If, on the other hand, there is no Y chromosome, the same tissue that in a male would become testicles will develop instead into ovaries. The primitive germ cells in these ovaries, not exposed to male hormones, will develop into eggs.

Eggs

At its peak, during mid-fetal development, the number of egg precursors in a female fetus is approximately 20 million. By birth, however, nine-tenths of these will have spontaneously dissolved, leaving approximately 1 to 2 million. During the growth and development of the girl into a young woman, many more of these egg precursors will disappear.

During a woman's reproductive life, if she is not pregnant and does not suppress ovulation with the birth control pill, she will produce approximately four hundred mature eggs. That is, she will ovulate approximately four hundred times.

As a woman approaches the menopause, she begins to run out of eggs. Since the eggs and the cells around them are responsible for estrogen production, this running out of eggs leads to decreased hormone levels. So in addition to her no longer being fertile—not producing eggs each month—a menopausal woman's estrogen levels fall, she stops having periods, and she may develop hot flashes.

Although at birth a woman will have all the eggs she will ever have, these eggs are not completely developed. Rather, they stop growing and dividing before birth. They do so right in the middle of their first chromosomal split. This arrested process of chromosomal division does not restart again until years later at sexual maturity when ovulation begins. It is only with the onset of ovulation that this first step of egg precursor division completes itself.

The second step, the one that leads to the production of a fully mature and fertilizable egg, does not occur until the actual moment of penetration by a sperm. Only then does the egg finally complete its cell division. Only then can the chromosomes of the egg combine with those of the sperm to form the earliest one-celled embryo.

Sperm

Sperm develop differently. New sperm are made throughout a man's life as long as his testicles are intact and as long as he continues to produce the male hormone testosterone. Like the egg, sperm precursors undergo two consecutive cell divisions. The first results in the number of chromosomes in each cell going from 46 to 23. In the second, two 23-chromosome cells derived from the initial male sex cell make exact copies of their chromosomes before themselves splitting in half. This results in 4 sperm from a single sperm precursor.

The process of sperm production differs from the formation of eggs in two ways: It is not cyclic and sperm maturity does not depend upon fertilization. Also, unlike egg production, sperm production occurs continuously once adolescence is reached. There is no fixed number of sperm at birth as there is with eggs.

The length of time it takes from the development of the initial sperm precursor cell until sperm are mature and capable of fertilizing an egg is approximately seventy days. This prolonged maturation of sperm has important health implications. If a man is exposed to noxious environmental influences or even has a high fever that could affect the health of his sperm, the abnormal sperm so produced may not be ejaculated until as long as two months later. Therefore, when a man and woman conceive a child, the harmful influences to which the man was exposed in the two months before conception could affect the health of the sperm that went into forming the child.

When Egg Meets Sperm

The ovaries are located on either side of the uterus and are adjacent to the ends of the fallopian tubes. Therefore, when an egg emerges from the surface of an ovary at ovulation, it usually finds its way into the fallopian tube next to which it lies. The ends of the fallopian tubes are composed of soft pink fronds of tissue that help guide the egg from the surface of the ovary into the tubes.

At the time of ovulation, cervical mucus is optimally primed to allow sperm to penetrate it. At other times in the menstrual cycle, the cervical mucus is thick and does not readily allow passage of the sperm. Given favorable cervical mucus, sperm enter the uterine cavity and swim up into the openings of the fallopian tubes. They next swim—and are pushed along by fine hairs inside the tube—toward the tube's end.

If all goes well, egg and sperm will meet in the middle or outer part of a fallopian tube. Usually, scores of sperm reach the egg at approximately the same time, each vying to be the one to fertilize the waiting egg. Through a complex biochemical process, one of the sperm surrounding the egg penetrates its mucinous outer layer. This process occurs successfully once every four ovulations. That is, when an egg is exposed to sperm under ideal conditions, a recognizable pregnancy will occur approximately 25% of the time.

Once inside the egg, the wall of the sperm cell dissolves, exposing its contents, including its chromosomes, to the inner environment of the egg. At this point, the final chromosomal division of the egg occurs. The egg splits into two units: One contains the sperm cell and its genetic material, the other becomes a mere cellular remnant that plays no further role in reproduction.

This new cell containing the contents of both the egg and the sperm becomes the new embryo. It has inherited two sets of chromosomes, the one from the father's sperm and the other from the mother's egg. These two sets of 23 chromosomes link up to form 23 pairs of chromosomes in the new embryo. Depending on whether the sperm that enters the egg has an X or a Y sex chromosome, the embryo will become either a female or a male fetus.

The Early Embryo

The newly fertilized egg is the earliest identifiable entity of what will grow up to be an adult woman or man. From its location in the fallopian tube, the early embryo now reverses the upstream trip the sperm had recently made. It floats down the fallopian tube back toward the uterus. Approximately seven days after fertilization, it will implant in the thick, secretion-rich lining of the uterus called the *endometrium*. This lining tissue has been hormonally prepared just for this purpose—implantation of the embryo by the hormones produced during the first three-quarters of a woman's menstrual cycle. When fertilization and implantation do not take place in any given cycle, this thickened endometrium is shed in the form of a menstrual period.

As soon as the embryo reaches the endometrium, it begins to grow into it. As it does so, it sends out special cells that are called—intimidatingly—*syncytiotrophoblasts*. These cells begin to absorb life-sustaining materials from the nutrient-rich endometrial lining and to pass them back to the embryo. The syncytiotrophoblast cells proliferate and further penetrate into the wall of the uterus. These cells will eventually develop into the placenta. As the placenta continues to develop, grow, and deepen its root system, it is able to supply the embryo with oxygen, fluid, and nutrients.

In the days that follow, as the cells of the embryo divide and divide again, they begin to take on specialized functions. This process is called *cellular differentiation*.

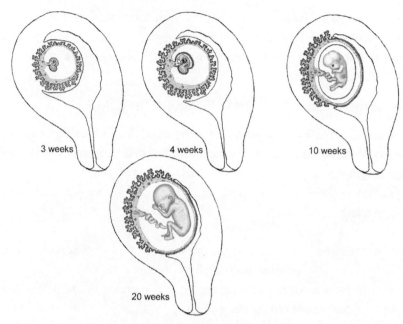

3 weeks
4 weeks
10 weeks
20 weeks

Fetus at Various Stages of Development

FIGURE 2.3 Normal Early Embryos in the Uterus

It must be remembered that each of the embryo's cells contain all the genetic material necessary to direct the growth and development of the new person the embryo will become. For much of a cell's life, most of this genetic material is not used. During cell differentiation, however, certain parts of the genetic information each cell carries are "turned on." The remainder stays inactive. The parts of the chromosomes that are turned on in any given cell cause those cells to develop in certain directions: into blood cells, bone cells, placental cells, and so forth. In this way, the cells of the embryo are able to differentiate themselves into the different organs and structures that will make up the fetal body.

One of the very earliest things a fertilized egg does is to produce the hormone *human chorionic gonadotropin* (HCG), as discussed in Chapter 1. Although at first HCG is produced at very low levels, the amount of it made each day rises rapidly as the number of embryonic and placental cells increases. This rise is so dramatic that in the first several weeks of pregnancy the level of HCG in a woman's blood doubles every forty-eight hours. By following the rate of rise of blood levels of HCG in the earliest pregnancies, it is possible to get a sense of whether a pregnancy is proceeding normally even before a fetus is visible on ultrasound.

Why Chromosomes Misalign As Often As They Do

Armed with what we now know about reproduction, we can go back to answer the question posed at the beginning of this chapter: How do genetic and chromosomal factors cause miscarriages?

The answer involves every step of the complex process described in the previous pages:

1. The copying, splitting, and recombination of chromosomes as egg and sperm develop from their earliest precursor cells
2. The intricacies of fertilization as egg and sperm combine to form a new, independent entity, the embryo
3. The process of embryo implantation into the uterus
4. Early cell division and differentiation into specific types of tissue in the embryo

Abnormalities of Chromosome Number

As we have seen, each time an egg and sperm are made, a sex cell precursor containing 46 chromosomes must go through two divisions to wind up with either an almost-mature egg or four totally mature sperm, each containing 23 chromosomes. For this to happen successfully, chromosomes in the original precursor cell had to pair up with their correct mates, had to split apart at the correct moment, and had to copy themselves accurately. All these steps had to proceed perfectly if the newly derived egg and sperm were to wind up becoming competent reproductive cells containing all the necessary chromosomal material—and none extra.

For instance, a pair of chromosomes from an egg or sperm precursor cell might not separate cleanly, the result being an unequal division of chromosomal material. Should this happen, one of the chromosomes of the pair would have more than half the original DNA while the other one would have less than half. Therefore, as these chromosomal strands

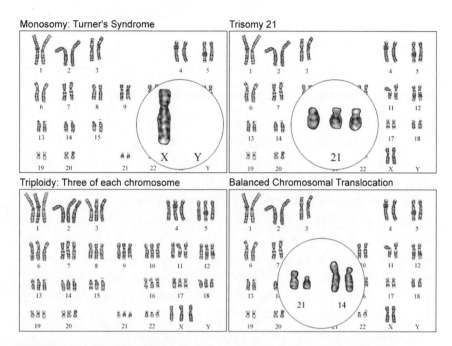

FIGURE 2.4   Abnormal Chromosome Karyotypes: Monosomy, Trisomy, Triploidy, and Translocation

moved into the cells they were going to become a part of, one cell would have an excess of genetic material while another cell would be missing some. Both of these situations are usually incompatible with an egg or sperm's successful participation in fertilization. Even if fertilization did occur, normal fetal growth and development would be unlikely.

It must also be remembered that the development of the oocyte—the egg precursor—was interrupted in the middle of its first division at or near birth. The cellular division of this oocyte does not resume until ovulation takes place, which might be from twelve to forty-five years afterward. This means that the chromosomes contained in the oocyte will have been suspended in mid-splitting position for all those years. During that time, they may well have been exposed to damaging environmental influences, cosmic rays, and other potentially mutating factors. Is it any wonder that when the chromosome-splitting process finally does restart, it sometimes does not go perfectly? The malfunctioning of older chromosomes is one of the major causes of chromosomal abnormalities. That is why Down syndrome and other chromosomal abnormalities are more commonly seen in the fetuses of older women.

Abnormal Chromosomal Splitting: Nondysjunction

All these abnormalities of chromosomal reproduction—not pairing up correctly, not splitting correctly—are called *nondysjunction*. Nondysjunction results in cells having an abnormal number of chromosomes, a situation called *aneuploidy*. Studies have shown that from approximately 3 to 4% of all sperm and from 10 to 20% of all oocytes are aneuploid. If an aneuploid egg is fertilized, or if an aneuploid sperm fertilizes an egg, an aneuploid embryo will result. By definition, an aneuploid egg or sperm either does not have a complete set of chromosomes or has an excess of them. Therefore, an aneuploid embryo will contain either too little or too much genetic information. This situation will lead to the abnormal development of the embryo's structural or physiologic features. Usually, such an embryo will die and the pregnancy will miscarry.

The most common example of aneuploidy seen in living infants is Down syndrome, where each cell in the baby has three copies of chromosome 21. Down syndrome occurs when an egg containing two copies of chromosome 21 is fertilized by a normal sperm, or when a normal egg is fertilized by a sperm containing two copies of this chromosome. The resulting embryo will have a total of three copies of chromosome 21 per cell. This type of chromosomal abnormality is called *chromosomal trisomy*.

Trisomy—the presence of three copies of any of the chromosomes— is the most frequent chromosomal cause of first-trimester miscarriages. It is known to be related to aging ovaries. The chromosomes most often involved in these trisomies are chromosome 16, chromosome 21 (causing Down syndrome), and chromosome 22. Why these chromosomes triple up more often than others is not known. It may be because other chromosomal trisomies are so lethal that they leave egg and sperm incapable of fertilizing one another—thus embryos with these chromosomal structures rarely form. Alternatively, it may be that when other trisomies occur they result in miscarriages at such an early stage that not enough pregnancy material is recovered for their chromosomal makeup to be identified.

But trisomy is only one of several different categories of chromosomal abnormalities.

Monosomy is the opposite of trisomy. It is the condition in which one of the 23 pairs of chromosomes *lacks* a chromosome. Thus in monosomy the total number of chromosomes in each cell is 45. Monosomy accounts for 25% of all miscarriages caused by chromosomes—as opposed to 50% of all chromosomal miscarriages that are caused by trisomies. Interestingly, the only monosomies that ever develop as far as the embryo stage are of the X sex chromosome in pair 23. Fetuses containing cells monosomic for any of the other 22 pairs of chromosomes, or of the Y chromosome in pair 23, have never been observed. Apparently, such a chromosomal arrangement is incompatible with life.

Fetuses with a single X chromosome present in pair 23 and a total of 45 chromosomes per cell occasionally survive until birth. When they do, they have a characteristic set of anatomic features called *Turner's syndrome*. Turner's syndrome girls and women—for with only one X and no Y chromosome all are "female"—are almost always infertile, usually have wide flat chests and thickened, web-like necks, rarely undergo sexual development, and may be mentally retarded. However, more often than with most other chromosomal abnormalities, individuals suffering from Turner's syndrome can go on to become healthy adults and to lead relatively normal lives, reproductive ability excluded.

Triploidy (as opposed to trisomy) is the situation where an embryo has received an entire extra set of 23 chromosomes, giving each cell a total of 69. Each cell thus contains three full sets of chromosomes. This most likely occurs when two sperm fertilize one egg or a sperm fertilizes an egg that has not yet completed its final chromosomal division from 46 to 23. Triploidy causes approximately 20% of all chromosomal miscarriages. Unlike a *trisomy*—Down syndrome, for instance—the occurrence of embryos having three complete sets of chromosomes is not related to the age of the mother or father. When triploidies occur they are always incompatible with survival of the embryo.

Other abnormal combinations of chromosomes also occur. These range from cells with *tetraploidy*—four complete sets of chromosomes in the embryo for a total of 92—to *mosaicism*, where two or more different cell lines, each of which has a different chromosomal composition, develop in the same embryo. Mosaicism is a rare but particularly interesting phenomenon because individuals with it are essentially made up of the cells of two different people. What the final anatomic and physiologic results of a mosaic embryo are is dependent upon the percentage of cells of one or the other kind in that embryo. Although mosaic fetuses can survive to be born and grow into children and adults, such individuals often have significant health problems, including malignancies of the testes or ovaries.

Translocations

Although the great majority of chromosomal abnormalities causing miscarriages are due to mistakes in chromosome splitting during sex cell formation and miscombination during fertilization, the chromosomal content of an embryo can be abnormal for other reasons as well. For instance, one parent might permanently carry an abnormal chromosome that is transmitted to his or her embryo during reproduction. How might this happen?

Certain individuals have chromosomes that are complete in that they contain all the genetic material they are supposed to but have those chromosomes abnormally arranged. For instance, approximately 1 in 1,000 individuals will have part of chromosome 14 attached to chromosome 13, or a piece of chromosome 14 attached to chromosome 21. Such individuals themselves have all the genetic information necessary for their normal growth and development. But when their sex cell precursors divide to form eggs or sperm, the abnormal arrangement of their genetic material causes the eggs or sperm they produce either to be missing genetic material or to have an excess of it. Either way, a situation is created in which many of the eggs or sperm that a parent passes on are defective. These abnormal eggs and sperm will be not be capable of participating successfully in reproduction. The parents are said to have "balanced" *chromosomal translocations*. These parents can conceive children but have a significantly higher rate of infertility, miscarriage, and fetuses with congenital anomalies. That the rate of miscarriages and abnormal infants is not even higher in such chromosome carriers is because the early embryos formed from those abnormal sperm or egg often die before a pregnancy is clinically recognized.

How Chromosome Abnormalities Cause Miscarriage

We've seen that sometimes chromosomes do not replicate and divide correctly during the formation of new cells. We've also looked at why such biologic "mistakes" might occur. But what is it specifically about the abnormal or incomplete chromosomes in cells that prevents the normal development of the embryo?

The mechanism by which biologic structures are made has been discussed above: The nucleic acid sequence in genes on chromosomes determines which proteins a given cell makes. These proteins go to form the various structures of the body.

But it is not only correctly produced proteins that are necessary for the survival of the embryo. As scientists learn more and more about how living organisms develop, it has become clear that the *organization* of development—which building blocks go where, and when—is just as important as the structure and number of the building blocks themselves.

As an example, let's look at one specific physiologic feature of eggs.

At a certain point in an egg's development, the complex mixture of mucus and proteins that forms the membrane surrounding an egg must be penetrable to surrounding sperm. Yet immediately after a single sperm has entered the egg, this same membrane must be capable of changing its structure so that it can prevent any other sperm from entering. Thus not only must the information on the egg's chromosomes direct the production of all of the various components of the egg's membrane, but it also must send signals—usually in the form of chemical messengers—to direct when and how these structures should change over time so that the egg membrane can perform its biologic function correctly. If the genes in the embryo do not properly orchestrate the production of the right structural and messenger proteins at the right time, successful pregnancy will not occur.

Another example is when information stored on chromosomes, transmitted by chemical messengers, causes certain cells of the fertilized egg to form placental cells instead of embryo cells. These placental cells provide for the interchange of oxygen, nutrients, and fluids between the mother and the growing embryo. From the moment of their differentiation, these placental cells take an entirely different pathway of development. They use parts of their chromosomes that the cells of the embryo, which go on to make up the fetus, do not use.

These genetically determined chemical messengers, known as *growth factors*, are what cause the various tissues of the evolving embryo to develop correctly: blood vessel cells in one place, spinal cord tissues in another, and bowel tissues in a third. In addition, these messengers "preprogram" the embryo to begin certain physiologic activities at precise points during its growth. Thus the heart begins to beat, blood begins to circulate, and fetal swallowing of amniotic fluid occurs in an ordered and exacting sequence that is precoded in the embryo's genetic material. These are but a few of the thousands of developmental activities that must occur correctly at the right time and at the right place if an embryo is to grow into a fetus and then a baby.

This, then, is why abnormal chromosomal structures lead to miscarriages: Not only will abnormal chromosomes "miscode" for the development of the building blocks of all tissue, the proteins, but they will likely produce incorrect messenger signals as well. Either sort of biologic mistake—incorrect proteins or incorrect physiologic signaling—can be fatal to a developing embryo.

Your Role in Causing Chromosomal Abnormalities Leading to Miscarriage: None

For many women, the shock and disappointment of having a miscarriage is so great that even if they come to understand that miscarriages are frequent, spontaneous, natural events, they will often still ask the question: "Did I do anything wrong to cause me to lose the pregnancy?"

As far as the chromosomal causes of miscarriage go, the answer is simple: no.

Chromosomal miscombination occurs spontaneously and randomly. We do not know why in the formation of egg or sperm cells a pair of chromosomes might not divide correctly, might become tangled up with each other, or might pull more chromosomal material into one cell than another. What we do know is that specific causes of such chromosomal misalignments have been sought for over fifty years—and none have been clearly identified. We also know, through multiple research studies, that there is no increase in the risk of chromosomal abnormalities—and therefore in miscarriages caused by them—from alcohol, tobacco, exercise, sexual activity, travel, overwork, and a whole host of other factors that women often imagine might have caused their miscarriages to occur.

For many years there had been reports that certain "recreational drugs" caused chromosomal abnormalities. The most frequently accused agent was LSD, although at times it was also rumored that marijuana could alter chromosomal structure. Most research, however, does not substantiate these claims. Some studies have shown that cells in artificial laboratory preparations of LSD do develop abnormal chromosomes, but this appears to be solely a laboratory effect. Among the millions of young people who used LSD in the 1960s, 1970s, and later, no increases have been found in miscarriages or in birth defects in their children.

We know of two factors that *can* increase the risk of chromosomal abnormalities: the age of the mother and radiation—either therapeutic, industrial, or military. But we have no control over how old we are, and certainly we do not choose to undergo nonmedical radiation exposure. More to the point, maternal age and radiation exposure cause only a small proportion of the chromosomal abnormalities that lead to miscarriage. *Most chromosomally caused miscarriages occur randomly and spontaneously to women of all ages for no known reason.*

Given All That Can Go Wrong, It Is Amazing How Often Things Go Right

The summary given above of the biology of reproduction in humans barely scratches the surface of the complexities involved. For every small aspect of the process I have discussed, there are shelves of textbooks and libraries full of journal articles. And the amount of knowledge we possess about this process expands exponentially each decade.

Given all the intricacies involved, it is nothing short of miraculous that the vast majority of the time women produce healthy eggs and men healthy sperm. That an egg and sperm combine to form a fetus one out of four times they are exposed to each other is even more astounding. That the single-celled embryo that results from this union will grow into a multibillion-celled human being with organs all in the right places, and all functioning more or less normally most of the time, is awe-inspiring indeed.

Given all this biologic success in the face of almost unbelievable complexity, miscarriages take on a new perspective. Although they are personal tragedies for those to whom they've occurred, from a biologic point of view miscarriages can be seen as nature's way of imposing quality control. If an organism does not have an intact "control center," if its blueprints for development are incorrect, or are incomplete, or contain duplications, then the organism will not survive. How could it? A functioning adult human being is such an enormously complex entity that the vast majority of the structures and functions that allow it to exist must be perfectly developed. A miscarriage, therefore, is the only logical outcome when the necessary chromosomal information required for growth and cellular differentiation is imperfect.

What happens if a fetus survives a chromosomal abnormality it has inherited? In some fortunate cases the body has built-in redundancies that allow a baby to be born and to survive even when some systems are missing or inadequate. Examples are certain blood abnormalities such as thalassemia or sickle cell anemia. Most of the time, however, the result of inadequate or incorrect chromosomal information in a live-born baby is one or more major birth defects. Some of these may be obvious, such as in hereditary dwarfism, Down syndrome, or cystic fibrosis. Others may be subtle and may be discovered only through complex biochemical testing. Occasionally, babies are born with such severe defects or diseases that one could only wish a miscarriage had occurred.

To Save or Not to Save a Threatened Pregnancy?

This is an extremely sensitive and controversial issue not only among women who are pregnant and are experiencing difficulties with their pregnancies but also for reproductive specialists. If you have had a miscarriage in the past, or have had difficulty becoming pregnant, the sight of bleeding in early pregnancy will probably be frightening to you. It will likely make you want to do anything possible to "save the pregnancy." Several therapies are frequently proposed to help women who are experiencing such symptoms. You may be urged to go to bed rest, not to exercise, not to have sex, and generally to change your lifestyle until the bleeding has stopped. Often the suggestion will be made, either by you or your doctor, that you be given "hormones" to "support" your pregnancy in an attempt to prevent miscarriage. It is thought that in some pregnancies the mother's own hormone production from her placenta and ovaries is inadequate to sustain the pregnancy and that a miscarriage will thus result. To prevent this, it is suggested that supplemental hormone therapy be given. Most commonly, the hormone recommended is progesterone. Progesterone is considered *the* pregnancy hormone and is generally found in high levels in all pregnant women.

But this treatment has never seemed to me to make sense—and many other obstetricians feel the same way. In the first place, despite the theory of inadequate progesterone having been around now for more than twenty years, no medical study has conclusively shown that giving women progesterone in early pregnancy decreases their chances of miscarrying. Given the hundreds of thousands of women over the years whose pregnancies have been supplemented with progesterone with this aim in mind, it is remarkable that if the therapy is valid no one has yet conclusively demonstrated it to be so.

Even more relevant, in my opinion, is the following: If your embryo, placenta, and ovaries are not producing adequate amounts of progesterone, instead of just treating the problem, I'd want to know the reason for it. A healthy pregnancy should produce all the hormones it needs for its own survival. If it does not, it might well be that the chromosomal makeup of this pregnancy does not contain all the genetic information necessary for the development of a healthy baby.

For these reasons I am leery about intervening when a pregnancy is threatened. The only exception is in the unusual circumstance when the mother has some specific anatomic problem that could cause her to miscarry. One such situation is cervical incompetence. This is when a woman's cervix is not strong enough to hold in a growing pregnancy. The cervix dilates prematurely, allowing the fetus to fall out of the uterus—but more about this in the next chapter. As for hormonal intervention, I'd recommend waiting until there is some reliable information proving that supplemental progesterone helps prevent miscarriages before taking the chance of intervening inappropriately—and perhaps contributing to the continuation of an abnormal pregnancy.

Predicting Whether or Not the Chromosomes in Any Given Newly Fertilized Egg Are Normal

Until very recently, trying to determine the chromosomal status of an early fetus was impossible. However within the last ten years reproductive technologies associated with in vitro fertilization (IVF) have made possible *preimplantation genetic diagnosis (PGD)*. PGD enables infertility specialists to check chromosomes in an embryo both for specific genetic conditions and for chromosomal structural abnormalities.

In PGD, cells from an early IVF embryo are removed and the chromosomes they contain undergo genetic analysis before the embryo is implanted into the uterus. If the analysis of the chromosomes shows evidence of the presence of genetic disease or structural abnormality, then the embryo from which the cells came would not be used for implantation. If, on the other hand, the chromosomes of the tested cell are free of abnormality or disease, then implantation of that embryo can proceed with confidence that the resulting baby will not be affected by any of the conditions for which testing was done. While some centers are doing PGD only for couples who have specific genetic diseases in their families that they do not wish to see reproduced, other IVF centers are doing PGD routinely in all their IVF patients.

This sort of analysis also permits the sex of an embryo to be determined. This can be extremely important because many chromosomally inherited diseases occur only in one sex or the other, usually in males. The reason is this: As discussed previously, the 23rd pair of chromosomes, the sex chromosomes, differs in men and women. In men, this pair consists of an X chromosome and a Y chromosome. The sex chromosomes in women are made up of two copies of the X chromosome. Thus the male sex chromosomes form the only pair of chromosomes in the body for which there are not two similar chromosomes containing genes for the same characteristics. Because of this there is no biological fallback position in case one of the genes on a male's X chromosome is abnormal.

If there were a gene error on any of the other chromosomes in a cell, the other copy of the gene on the chromosome's pair-mate would step in and make all or most of the necessary proteins, hormones, messengers, and so forth, to compensate for the abnormal gene. But in male sex chromosomes, there is no redundancy. If an abnormality occurs on the male's single X chromosome—such as happens in hemophilia and muscular dystrophy—there is no second X chromosome containing another correct copy of the missing genetic information to compensate for it.

The knowledge of whether an embryo is male or female, therefore, can be used to guide decisions to prevent the occurrence of hereditary diseases that are due to abnormalities of chromosome 23, the sex chromosome. For example, a family undergoing IVF may have a genetic history of the sex-linked disease hemophilia. By determining which of several available fertilized eggs are male or female, embryonic chromosomal analysis could help the family pick a female embryo to implant. In this way they can avoid the chance of having a boy who might go on to develop hemophilia with all the attendant medical problems that child would suffer.

In the very near future even this sort of prenatal diagnostic testing will be supplanted. Some centers are now identifying specific markers for hemophilia with PGD. Thus it will no longer be necessary to refrain from implanting male embryos in couples with a history of hemophilia. Cells from a specific embryo—male or female—will be examined to see if they contain the gene markers for hemophilia and decisions about implantation can be made accordingly.

Such chromosome testing of embryos is wonderful and exciting new technology. But will it help most women avoid having miscarriages?

Unfortunately I have to say that I doubt it, at least in the near future. The reason I say this is simple: All of the marvels of PGD are currently available when you have an embryo *outside* the body—as in IVF—or when pregnancy tissue is available through amniocentesis or chorionic villous sampling (CVS). Of course, most pregnancies are conceived naturally, not through IVF, and the miscarriages that occur in these natural pregnancies usually do so before it is safely possible to perform amniocentesis or CVS. Thus in order to utilize PGD to "prevent" miscarriages, cells would somehow have to be removed from a minute embryo inside a woman's uterus in the earliest weeks of pregnancy. Such testing would be tremendously invasive and would have the potential of damaging other cells of the embryo or interfering with the delicate early placenta. Perhaps someday when fetal cells can be obtained by safer means—picked up in the vagina after having been shed through the cervix, floating free in the mother's blood—PGD will be more applicable to the majority of pregnant women. As Vivian Lewis, a world-renowned reproductive scientist, said:

> Until there is a better understanding of the cellular events which are involved in meiosis and fertilization, little can be offered therapeutically. For many patients, the knowledge that chromosomal problems are usually *random events* is important in offering them hope that the next pregnancy will be normal.

Hope—and more. For if you have had a miscarriage, knowing how the reproductive process works will allow you to come to understand—and to fully believe—that the miscarriage was not your fault. It enables you to know which aspects of reproduction you do control and which you do not. Such knowledge arms you with a factual, scientific basis for confidence in your reproductive future.

CHAPTER 3

Age, Anatomy, and Hormones

EACH MONTH IN MY OFFICE I ENCOUNTER PATIENTS WITH THE following kinds of problems:

A forty-one-year-old woman who has decided that now is the right time in her life to get pregnant. She has heard that pregnancy may be more difficult at her age, and she wants to know what her chances are of ever having a baby.

A woman who had a miscarriage last year and was told at the time that her uterus had two compartments instead of one. Her doctor said that this probably caused her miscarriage. She wants to know if she will ever be able to carry a pregnancy to term or if her uterine abnormality will forever prevent her from having a baby?

A thirty-four-year-old woman with a long history of irregular periods who has had several recent miscarriages. Her menstrual cycles vary between twenty-two and forty-five days. She knows that this has something to do with her not producing eggs on a regular basis due to an irregularity of her female hormones. She wonders whether she will ever be able to get pregnant. She also is afraid that her "hormone imbalance" may make it impossible for her to sustain a pregnancy even if she does conceive.

All three of these women share common concerns about their ability to have a baby. These concerns involve issues of age, anatomic abnor-

malities, and hormonal function. In this chapter I will discuss these issues—age, anatomy, and hormones—to see exactly how they might affect your ability to become pregnant and stay pregnant—that is, not to
miscarry. I will also discuss in detail what you can do to maximize your
chances of having a successful pregnancy should any of these problems
apply to you.

Age

From a medical and biologic point of view, the ideal age for a woman to
have a baby is somewhere between eighteen and thirty-two. Between
these ages, a woman is physiologically in the best shape for carrying a
pregnancy and delivering a healthy child. Additionally, her eggs will
have had less time than an older woman's to be injured by exposure to
potentially damaging environmental factors.

For men, the best age to father a child varies. This is because of the
difference, as discussed in Chapter 2, in how men and women make their
reproductive cells. Women possess all the eggs they are going to have by
the time they are born. Men continue to make new sperm throughout
their lives. Therefore, a man should be able to inseminate a woman with
new, healthy sperm well into old age. This is in fact what usually happens unless some factor connected with age—cancer, diabetes, hypertension—diminishes a man's ability to produce sperm or to get them where
they need to be.

If we take all this into account, we realize that as men and women age
it *does* become more difficult for them to conceive. Older couples also
have a higher miscarriage rate than younger couples. Why is this? Let us
take a look at the various factors that link advancing age, infertility, and
miscarriage.

Too Young

Surprisingly, girls aged seventeen and below do not seem to suffer an
increased risk of miscarriage. This does not mean that it is good for
such young women to become pregnant because such pregnancies are
often social catastrophes for them. Moreover, an adolescent who becomes pregnant does so at a time when her pelvis is not fully grown.

She may not have her full adult stature, fat stores, and the physical strength she will have when she is a more mature woman. Also, she is at significantly increased risk of experiencing pregnancy complications. Such conditions as toxemia—high blood pressure caused by pregnancy—and preterm labor are much more common in very young pregnant women than in women who become pregnant when they are eighteen or older.

Only slightly older women—women between the ages of eighteen and twenty-four—have the best pregnancy outcomes. Their fertility is the highest, their miscarriage rate is the lowest, and their pregnancy complication rate is minimal.

There is no evidence of an increased risk of miscarriage in pregnancies fathered by young men. Young men have high sperm counts and a high proportion of healthy sperm. Just as is true for very young women, fatherhood at an age before one is socially and financially ready to become a parent can be disastrous. But biologically there do not seem to be any impediments to young fatherhood.

Too Old

For older women, the situation is entirely different. The odds that a forty-year-old woman will have a miscarriage are from 25 to 50% higher than for younger women, and the miscarriage rate rises with each passing year.

For men, as already mentioned, the issue is solely that of sperm numbers and sperm health. As long as a man produces enough viable sperm to get a woman pregnant, whether a miscarriage occurs because of age is largely determined by the female partner.

Let's look at the effects of age on eggs and sperm in more detail.

Women and Their Eggs

There are several physiologic reasons why older women are more likely to have difficulty getting pregnant and more likely to miscarry than are younger women:

1. As women grow older they run out of eggs. The fixed number of eggs with which they were born diminishes with time. It is thought that

the "healthiest" eggs ovulated early in a woman's menstrual life. These eggs were also the most robust, made the most hormones, and were most likely to produce a successful pregnancy.

2. The longer eggs are in a woman's body before they ovulate the more they are exposed to the possibility of damage. Such damage may come from several sources:

   —cosmic rays from outer space—a form of radiation—that are always bombarding the earth and to which a woman's eggs are constantly exposed

   —toxins in the environment and food supply

   —the spontaneous breakdown over time of the physical structure of the egg and the genetic material it contains

3. An older woman is less likely to be able to provide adequate hormonal support for her pregnancy. The hormone-producing cells in her ovaries are not as potent as they once were. One or both ovaries may have been damaged in the past by infection, ovarian cyst formation, or surgery. The central cyclic hormonal mechanisms controlled by glands in the brain—the hypothalamus and pituitary glands (more on this later in the chapter)—may no longer function as smoothly and competently as they did when the woman was younger.

4. The intrauterine environment—the physical conditions inside the uterus in which the embryo must grow—may not be optimal. This condition may occur for a variety of reasons that will be discussed in the next section.

5. Finally, as all men and women grow older they may develop various medical problems. These problems can either decrease fertility or decrease the chances that an early pregnancy will survive, thus increasing the chances of a miscarriage occurring. Examples of such conditions are thyroid disease, lupus, and diabetes.

Two common gynecologic disorders that many women worry may increase their risk of miscarriage—but which fortunately do not—are scarring of the fallopian tubes and pelvic endometriosis.

Scarring of the fallopian tubes can result from surgery on abdominal or pelvic organs, pelvic infection, or adhesions after ovarian cyst rupture. Although blockage of fallopian tubes can make it difficult to *become* pregnant, it has no effect on a pregnancy once that pregnancy is established.

Endometriosis is a condition in which cells from the tissue lining the uterus—the endometrium—migrate through the fallopian tubes and implant inside the pelvis. Each month, these cells are stimulated by the estrogen produced during a woman's menstrual cycle. As these cells grow, they can damage a woman's fallopian tubes and ovaries. As with tubal scarring, endometriosis can be a major cause of *infertility*. However, it does not seem to cause *miscarriages*.

Ovulation Timing

Long-term chromosomal damage to a specific egg is not the only way in which egg factors can cause miscarriage; the timing of conception can be a factor as well. Pregnancies in which conception occurs two to three days after ovulation are more susceptible to miscarriage and birth defects than are those that occur either right at ovulation or just before. This is especially relevant because women are often told that they can determine the sex of a baby by timing intercourse either earlier or later in their cycles. (This, by the way, is not true.) Fortunately, such increased risk is minimal. What risk exists is likely related to deterioration in various components of the egg during the days after its release.

The Father

Age is less a factor for men than for women as far as miscarriages go. The major problem encountered by men who are trying to father a baby is infertility. Still, there are some age-related factors for men that may contribute to miscarriage:

1. As with women, the longer a man lives, the more likely it is that he will be exposed to radiation, toxic chemicals, and other deleterious environmental factors. These can seriously damage the sperm he produces during the seventy days it takes sperm to grow and mature.
2. Sperm precursor cells—the cells from which sperm arise—may be injured by these same environmental factors. If this happens, all subsequent sperm derived from them will be abnormal.

Yet injuries to sperm precursor cells or to sperm themselves do not result in miscarriage as often as does egg damage in women. This has to do with numbers: Each month only one egg is produced, carrying with it whatever burden of previous damage it has suffered. But with each ejaculation, millions of sperm are released. Tremendous competition ensues among these sperm to be the first one to penetrate an egg. Thus, even if some damaged sperm are produced each month, it is extremely unlikely that they would be able to beat out healthy undamaged sperm in the race to fertilize an egg. The chances, therefore, are scant that a less-than-perfect sperm would give its chromosomes to a new embryo.

Anatomy

I'll never forget one young girl I saw early in my career. Her mother brought her in because she had experienced excruciating pain during each of the four periods she had had since starting to menstruate. The mother told me that her daughter's cramps were so severe that she had to stay home from school and miss sports. Once she even had to go to an emergency room.

Now, painful periods in a young woman are not unusual. The uterine muscle, which is thick and strong, expels menstrual blood and tissue by squeezing it out. This, and hormones produced by the uterus called prostaglandins, can cause severe period cramping. However, this young girl's menstrual pain was far in excess of what is normally seen.

On her physical examination things initially seemed normal. But during the internal part of the examination I noticed an unusual bulge in the upper right wall of this girl's vagina that felt as if there was a collection of fluid behind the vaginal tissue. Although fluid-filled cysts in the vagina are not rare, I had not seen one before in a girl this young.

So that I could more accurately evaluate what was going on, I recommended to the mother that she bring her daughter back during one of her periods when the pain was at its worst. I would repeat the examination at that time. The mother agreed.

When I next saw the young woman, she was bent over in agony. She told me that she had been having terrible pain and cramping since the previous night. She said that the pain was as bad as it had ever been.

I examined her. She had a normal amount of menstrual flow in her vagina. But on internal exam, I felt a much greater amount of bulging at the upper right wall of her vagina than I had felt previously. I then realized what the problem was. I ordered an ultrasound. The results confirmed my suspicion: This young woman suffered from *uterine duplication syndrome*. That is, she had a double set of reproductive organs—two uteruses, two cervixes, and two vaginas. However, one of her two vaginas, the right one, did not have an opening to the outside. While menstrual flow from her left uterus and vagina was normal, menstrual blood from the right uterus was being trapped in the pocket formed by the closed-off second vagina. It was the stretching of this pocket of tissue and the pressure it produced in her pelvis that caused this girl the excruciating pain she was experiencing.

Once the anatomic cause of this young woman's pain had been determined, it was a relatively simple matter for me to surgically remove the wall separating her two vaginas. This left her with a single joint vagina that allowed normal menstrual flow from both uteruses. There being no more trapped blood, the young woman's menstrual pain disappeared. Fortunately, the kind of problem she has—double uterus and cervix— should not interfere with her becoming pregnant and only slightly increases her risk for miscarriage and preterm labor.

Though this case might sound extreme, anatomic problems of the reproductive organs are not rare. They are of two general types. One kind is *congenital*, defects that a woman is born with. The other kind is *acquired* and develops during a woman's life either through spontaneous abnormal growth, damage from accidents or childbearing, or surgery. Both congenital and acquired abnormalities can cause major difficulties for a woman in becoming pregnant and staying pregnant.

Congenital Anomalies

To understand how abnormalities of the female reproductive organs occur, you must know a little bit about the development of these organs in the embryo.

It turns out that most of the internal sex organs of both males and females are derived from tissues that make up the urinary tract structures of the early embryo. These structures develop into reproductive organs under the influence of hormonal messages controlled by the fetus's sex chromosomes, either XX or XY. If a fetus has XY for its sex chromosomes, the hormones the fetus produces will cause its urinary tract structures to develop into male reproductive organs. If the fetus's sex chromosomes are XX, the same early anatomic structures will grow into female reproductive organs.

In the female fetus, the lower ends of the urinary tract tubes join together to form the uterus, cervix, and vagina as development proceeds. The middle portions of these urinary tubes do not fuse. Instead, they develop into the fallopian tubes, one on each side of the uterus.

The ovaries are not derived from these early urologic tube tissues but rather from the special sex cell precursors discussed earlier. By a process different from that followed by the early urinary tract structures, each of the ovaries winds up next to the uppermost portion of the fallopian tube on its side of the pelvis.

Many things need to proceed correctly if reproductive organs are to develop properly from their urologic and sex cell precursors. If even one step in this developmental process goes awry, abnormalities will result. Either the urologic tubes might not fuse as they are supposed to or one or both ovaries might be missing, underdeveloped, or in the wrong place in the pelvis.

Defects of the Uterus, Cervix, and Vagina

There are many different kinds of uterine, cervical, and vaginal defects. Which defects are present in any given individual are determined by how much of the natural fusion of the early urologic tubes does or does not take place. Thus there can be

- an entire double set of uterus, cervix, and vagina;
- a double uterus with a single cervix and vagina;
- a single uterine cavity with a *septum*—a thick piece of fibrous tissue that divides the uterus almost in half—that did not dissolve when the urologic tubes merged to form the uterus.

Another kind of "anomaly" I see every day in my office is called a *tipped uterus*. A tipped uterus, medically described as a *retroflexed uterus*,

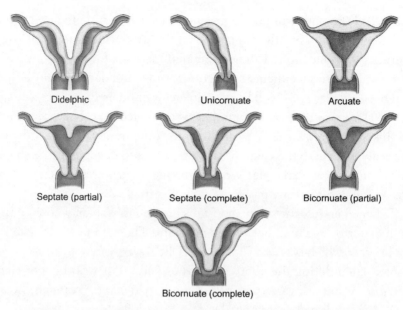

Didelphic   Unicornuate   Arcuate

Septate (partial)   Septate (complete)   Bicornuate (partial)

Bicornuate (complete)

FIGURE 3.1   Congenital Anomalies of Female Pelvic Organs

is a uterus that, instead of leaning forward in the pelvis, leans backward. It occurs in approximately 15 to 20% of all women. It is not so much an anomaly as a variation of normal anatomy. It has no effect upon fertility, miscarriage, menstruation, or sexuality. Often, however, when a physician tells a patient that she has a retroflexed uterus, he or she forgets to reassure the patient that this is a common benign condition, that it will have no effect on her fertility, and that nothing need be done about it.

Why Defects Occur

Embryologists think that the majority of congenital anatomic defects of reproductive structures are merely random instances of maldevelopment with no particular identifiable cause. Such defects are present in from 1 in 500 to 1 in 2,000 female fetuses. Thus, though certainly not common, they are by no means rare. Almost every gynecologist who has been in practice for a while will have seen several cases in his or her career.

Some reproductive organ abnormalities are known to be caused by chromosomal malfunction. For normal development to occur, fetal tissues have to be stimulated by the correct hormones at exactly the right moment. However, if a fetus's sex chromosomes do not function correctly, the right hormones will not be produced, or if they are produced, they will be produced too early, too late, or in the wrong amounts. Tissues requiring the stimulation of these hormonal messages for proper development will not receive them at the correct times and development either will not take place or it will be incomplete or disordered.

We also know the cause of another type of defect: the *T-shaped uterus*. In this abnormality, the ends of the embryonic urologic tubes fuse abnormally and cause the cavity inside the uterus to develop in the shape of a T instead of a triangle. Women having such uteruses have an increased rate of infertility problems and miscarriages.

T-shaped uteruses are seen almost exclusively in women whose mothers took estrogenic hormones when pregnant. These hormones, the most common of which was *diethylstilbestrol* (DES), were often given to pregnant women during the 1950s and 1960s because it was thought that doing so would decrease their risk of miscarrying. Later research, however, showed that this was not so.

Tragically, there is more to the story. It turned out that many of those girls and women exposed to DES when their mothers were pregnant with them developed serious medical problems. They sometimes developed a rare form of cancer in the cervix and vagina called adenocarcinoma. Many cases of this formerly rare kind of cancer were seen in the 1970s and early 1980s. Many of these "DES daughters" also had abnormally shaped cervixes that predisposed them to preterm delivery. Finally, these women frequently had the T-shaped uteruses mentioned above. Boys and men exposed in the same way to DES had a high incidence of penile abnormalities and fertility problems.

Another rare abnormality of reproductive organs can occur when a fetus is exposed to both male and female hormones during development. When this happens, genital organs and sex cells of both sexes can form in one person. Such individuals are called *hermaphrodites*. They are considered "true" hermaphrodites if they have both ovarian and testicular tissue. They are said to have "false" hermaphrodism if their external or internal sexual organs and structures do not match their chromosomal sex, that is, XX or XY. Thus, a chromosomal female can have clitoral enlargement caused by excessive male hormone effect during embryonic development that makes her look as if she has a penis. Similarly, under certain circumstances (inherited cellular insensitivity to testosterone) a chromosomal male (XY) can lack visible penis and scrotum and at puberty have marked breast development, giving the external appearance of a female. Individuals with "false" or "pseudo" hermaphrodism can undergo surgical correction of their external genitalia to match their chromosomal or hormonal sex. They are sometimes able to have children. Individuals with true hermaphrodism are almost always infertile.

Anatomic Defects and Miscarriage

When a fertilized egg descends from the fallopian tube into the uterus it must find a safe, appropriate place to implant itself. In some uterine defects, the lining tissue of the uterus is intact and there is no barrier to implantation. This is the case with double uteruses. A pregnancy can implant in either uterus and proceed normally.

On the other hand, when the uterus contains a septum—the thick, fibrous dividing structure discussed above—it is not covered by the normal embryo-friendly uterine lining tissue, the endometrium. Therefore, if a fertilized egg attempted to implant on a septum, most likely it would be unable to obtain a good foothold. A miscarriage would then occur. Even if implantation were achieved, the fibrous nature of the septum would not allow the digging in of placental tissue and the growth of the maternal blood vessels necessary to support an early pregnancy. At some early point in that pregnancy, embryonic development could no longer be sustained and a miscarriage would result.

In other instances it is thought that the shape of a uterus with an anomaly may limit the normal growth of a fetus. A certain amount of space is necessary for a fetus, the placenta, and the bag of waters to develop. Usually, a uterus of normal size and shape will expand to whatever volume is necessary. But when certain uterine abnormalities are present, the uterus grows to a particular size but can stretch no further. Miscarriage or preterm labor may result.

Diagnosing Anatomic Defects

There are several means by which your doctor can tell whether you have an anatomic abnormality. The simplest is by doing a physical examination.

During the pelvic part of the examination, a double vagina, a double cervix, or an abnormally shaped uterus can often be determined either visually or by the doctor feeling them with his or her hands.

Often reproductive abnormalities are diagnosed coincidentally while you are having some other procedure or study. For instance, you may need to have a laparoscopy for a condition unrelated to infertility or miscarriage such as pelvic pain or an ovarian cyst. A laparoscopy is a procedure where, under anesthesia, a long telescope-like tube is inserted through a small incision under your navel. The internal contents of your abdomen and pelvis can be seen through this scope. Congenital abnormalities of the uterus are often identified in this way.

Similarly, hysteroscopy is a procedure during which the inside of your uterus is examined through a telescope-like device inserted through your vagina and cervix. Should you undergo a hysteroscopy, perhaps to determine the cause of heavy menstrual bleeding, any uterine abnormalities present can be seen.

Sometimes when a woman is being evaluated for infertility a test called a *hysterosalpingogram* (HSG) (or *tubogram*) will be ordered. The

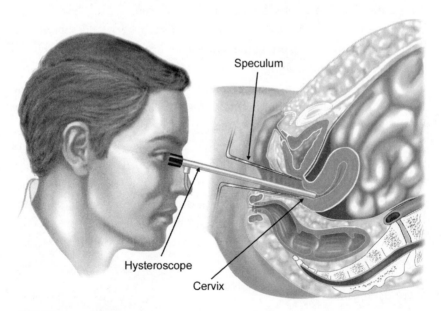

FIGURE 3.2   Hysteroscopy

purpose of this test is to outline the inner shape of the uterus and fallopian tubes. The test is performed by inserting a special catheter into the cervix and uterus and slowly injecting through it an opaque liquid solution that x-rays cannot pass through. When this solution fills up the internal structures of the cervix, uterus, and fallopian tubes, an x-ray is taken. By evaluating the x-ray outline of these dye-filled organs, anatomic abnormalities can readily be diagnosed.

Finally, an ultrasound examination of your pelvis might detect structural abnormalities in one or more of your reproductive organs.

Treating Congenital Anomalies

There are two ways to correct congenital abnormalities of the uterus, cervix, or vagina.

The original method, now rarely used, involves open abdominal surgery to reconstruct the abnormal pelvic organs. The operation consists of surgically entering the uterus and excising abnormal tissues, such as a septum. The uterus is then sutured back together into more-or-less normal shape.

The second, newer, method is via hysteroscopy. As mentioned above, when a hysteroscopy is performed, a telescope-like device is placed through the cervix and into the uterus. Various instruments can be placed through the hysteroscope to cut, burn, or remove abnormal tissue. The hysteroscope allows many uterine abnormalities to be repaired without major abdominal surgery. Not only is no abdominal incision needed with this technique but also less blood is lost and there is less chance that scar tissue will form. Scar tissue in the pelvis and on fallopian tubes could itself impede fertility.

To Treat or Not to Treat

As is true of many things in medicine, the question of whether to treat uterine anomalies is not as straightforward as it might seem. There are three reasons for this:

1. It is not always clear that uterine anomalies have to be repaired to prevent pregnancy loss. As discussed above, only certain anomalies

interfere with pregnancy. And even with these anomalies—*uterine septii*, for example—most pregnancies proceed normally. For other kinds of defects, such as double uterus, the miscarriage rate is not that much higher than it is for women who have normal uteruses. One would operate on a uterine anomaly only if there was a substantial chance of decreasing the risk of a miscarriage.

2. Both means of surgical correction of uterine abnormalities—open surgery or hysteroscopic surgery—carry the possibility of complications. Whether approached intra-abdominally or through the vagina, surgery on congenital uterine defects can sometimes result in heavy bleeding, infection, or damage to other pelvic structures. Sometimes the surgery itself is so difficult that a hysterectomy becomes necessary. Thus, whether to operate on uterine anomalies is a classic example of the medical dictum "first do no harm."

3. The third factor that must be taken into account is a patient's reproductive history. If a woman is first discovered to have a uterine anomaly after she has had two or three successful pregnancies, obviously nothing should be done. As the saying goes, "If it ain't broke, don't fix it." On the other hand, if a woman has already had one or more miscarriages and has a uterine anomaly, the decision to operate is clearer.

The most difficult situation is when there is a known significant uterine anomaly, for instance, a uterine septum, in a woman who has not yet been pregnant. On the one hand, pregnancies in women with such a defect often do poorly. On the other hand, if the woman has never been pregnant before, she may be one of the 30 to 40% of women with this kind of defect who will have a normal pregnancy. Whether to operate preventively—given the risks mentioned above—or whether to wait until a woman has already lost a pregnancy—is an area of controversy about which obstetrical experts themselves disagree.

An additional item must be considered when a decision is made about whether to operate on an abnormal uterus. Many of the procedures to fix these problems will so weaken the uterus that a cesarean section will be necessary for safe delivery of the baby at the end of a pregnancy. Now, for many women who have had miscarriages, how the baby comes out is unimportant as long as they have a healthy baby to bring home. However, for women who very much desire a vaginal delivery, this potential weakening of the uterus might be the deciding point in determining whether they wish to undergo uterine surgery for an anomaly.

Acquired Anatomic Abnormalities: Incompetent Cervix

It's one of the more terrible things I see in obstetrics. A woman with a much-wanted pregnancy calls up when she is in her fifth month saying that something is coming out of her vagina. There is usually panic in her voice, especially if she has had difficulty becoming pregnant or has had miscarriages before. I ask her to come into the office and I examine her. What I see is heartrending: The cervix has changed from its normal long, thick, and closed configuration and is now open to a diameter of two to three inches. Usually either the bag of waters or a fetal limb is hanging out.

In such situations a woman usually has not had labor pains. These cervical changes are therefore called silent dilatation as opposed to the normal cervical dilation that is caused by the force of the painful contractions of labor. The cause of such silent dilatation is almost always a condition known as *cervical incompetence*.

Cervical incompetence happens when the fibrous tissue making up the cervix has become stretched, torn, or otherwise weakened. Although the condition can arise as a congenital anomaly, it is most often the result of surgical or pregnancy trauma. It is of paramount importance to differentiate cervical incompetence from preterm labor because their causes and treatment are entirely different.

Cervical Incompetence and Miscarriage

The cervix acts like a cork in a bottle. It is physiologically designed to be strong enough to withstand the pressure of a growing pregnancy for forty weeks, yet malleable enough to stretch and open up during labor. If, however, the fibrous tissue that makes up the cervix is torn or weakened, it will not be able to withstand this pressure. It may begin to open up months before it should. Once it has stretched past a certain point— usually two to three inches—the force of gravity and the pressure of the uterus itself will cause the bag of waters to bulge out or to rupture. When this happens, the process is almost impossible to reverse. The usual result is a miscarriage or a very preterm delivery well before a baby can survive.

Diagnosing Cervical Incompetence

The major problem with cervical incompetence is that it often causes a miscarriage before its presence is suspected. The diagnosis is made by medical history, physical examination, and ultrasound.

The typical medical history of a patient with cervical incompetence is that of a woman who has experienced a previous late miscarriage without having had any labor-type contractions. There was either a sudden gush of fluid as the bag of waters broke or the unexpected feeling of intense pelvic pressure as the fetus descended into the vagina.

It is difficult to diagnose cervical incompetence before pregnancy. Many methods have been suggested over the years to accomplish this but none have proven accurate.

During pregnancy, cervical incompetence can be diagnosed either by physical examination or by ultrasound. Patients who are at high risk for cervical incompetence because of their medical or obstetrical histories are examined frequently to see if there is any thinning out or dilation of the cervix. Traditionally this has been done by a doctor feeling the length of the cervix with his or her fingers. More recently, however, ultrasound examination of cervical length has proven to be a more accurate predictor of those cervixes that will dilate prematurely.

In early pregnancy the length of the cervix is usually 4–5 cm. If at any point ultrasound measurement shows the cervix to be shorter than 2.5 cm, odds are that cervical weakness is present and that the cervix will open up if not prevented from doing so. If such cervical thinning or shortening is noted in the absence of uterine contractions, the diagnosis of cervical incompetence is confirmed, hopefully in time to successfully correct the problem.

Causes of Cervical Incompetence

Several things can cause cervical incompetence, some of which I have discussed already. A weakened cervix can be present from birth—congenital—or it can be acquired, that is, caused by some condition arising during a woman's life.

Congenital

Some women are born with a cervix that contains less than an adequate amount of strong connective tissue. When put to the test of pregnancy, the cervix proves unable to withstand the stresses placed upon it. This may lead to premature cervical dilatation.

Another cause of congenital cervical incompetence is DES exposure. The cervixes of female infants born to women who took DES in pregnancy in hope of avoiding miscarriage often are shorter than normal, abnormally shaped, and weak. These DES daughters are thus predisposed to cervical incompetence and premature delivery. Fortunately, not all female fetuses exposed to DES have such abnormalities. Also, as these are anatomic and not chromosomal changes, they are not hereditary. DES effects will not be passed on to future generations.

Acquired

The above describes forms of cervical incompetence with which a woman might be born. Most cases of incompetent cervix, however, are acquired. Trauma to the cervix is the leading cause, and it can occur in several ways.

1. When a woman's cervix is seen on Pap smear to contain abnormal cells, various diagnostic and treatment methods are employed to resolve the problem. These tests and treatments can sometimes lead to a weakening of the cervix. A diagnostic biopsy or surgical excision may interrupt the normal rings of fibrous tissue in the cervix, thus impeding its ability to remain shut under the weight of a pregnancy. If too many such procedures are performed on a cervix, the cumulative damage it suffers puts it at high risk for incompetence.
2. A second cause of cervical weakening is the trauma of recurrent stretching. Whenever a woman has a D&C, miscarriage, or therapeutic abortion, her cervix is mechanically dilated so that access can

be gained to the uterine cavity. The recurrent stretching of a cervix before it is naturally ready to be stretched—which is at the end of a pregnancy—can result in the permanent tearing of multiple strands of cervical fibrous tissue. This tearing weakens the cervix and predisposes it to premature dilation.

3. The extreme cervical stretching that occurs during childbirth can sometimes damage a cervix, leading to cervical incompetence in subsequent pregnancies. This is especially so if the babies delivered are large or if instruments such as forceps were required to assist in delivery.

Treating Cervical Incompetence

It has been said that experience is a bad teacher—it is always late coming to work. In no condition in obstetrics is this truer than with cervical incompetence. This is because usually the first inkling an obstetrician has that a woman has an incompetent cervix is when she comes into the office about to lose her pregnancy. By then, of course, it is too late. It is possible to be suspicious that a given woman is at increased risk for cervical incompetence. This might be so in someone who has undergone multiple procedures to her cervix or who has suffered several late miscarriages. But even in women with such histories, most won't develop incompetent cervix. It is therefore necessary to perform frequent cervical checks on many women who might have cervical incompetence in hope of finding the occasional woman who does. If found early enough, it is possible that treatment can be administered to prevent the cervical weakness identified from leading to the loss of the pregnancy.

Another difficult problem with incompetent cervix is that treatment is almost always for the next pregnancy. Too often, cervical incompetence has resulted in a lost pregnancy before a diagnosis could be made or therapy implemented.

That said, if the diagnosis of cervical incompetence has been made, the recurrence of miscarriage due to it can be prevented by various means. Some of these preventative measures are things you can do yourself. First, discuss with your doctor the possibility of going to full or partial bed rest at some point early in your pregnancy. We know that the cause of miscarriage in cervical incompetence is the force of gravity pushing the fetus, placenta, and bag of waters against a weakened cervix. Decreasing the effect of gravity on the cervix can thus help prevent the kind of pressure that can lead to miscarriage. This can be accomplished to some degree by your spending several hours a day lying down. When you stand or sit, the weight of your pregnancy is directly over your cervix. When you are lying down, gravity does not push your pregnant uterus down against your cervix nearly as much. For this reason, some degree of bed rest is often a component of therapy for the treatment of incompetent cervix.

Second, forewarned is forearmed. Knowing that you have cervical incompetence, your doctor can watch you carefully for signs of cervical change. This is done through frequent office visits, frequent pelvic examinations, and frequent ultrasounds. In this way, it is hoped that any changes in your cervix can be detected early and can be treated immediately before dilatation has progressed too far to be stopped.

The definitive treatment for cervical incompetence is a procedure called *cervical cerclage*. This involves placing several strong sutures around your cervix at the point where it joins the uterus. These sutures literally tie the cervix shut. The procedure is performed in the operating room as outpatient surgery. You will usually be given either general or spinal anesthesia.

Cervical cerclage has a high success rate—60% or more in preventing miscarriage or preterm birth. But it is not without its failures. There is also some degree of risk involved in the procedure. Placing the suture into and around the cervix can cause rupture of the membranes or extremely preterm labor, both of which usually lead to miscarriage.

If cervical cerclage sutures are successfully placed, they stay in the cervix for the duration of the pregnancy. They are usually removed three to four weeks before a woman's due date. In almost all women thus treated the subsequent labor proceeds normally. Should labor begin before the cerclage sutures have been removed, they would have to be taken out immediately. If left in place, the force of the uterus contracting against a tied-up cervix could cause tearing open of the cervix or even uterine rupture.

Whether to place cerclage sutures in a woman who has lost a prior pregnancy because of cervical incompetence is a relatively easy decision to make. The benefits clearly outweigh the risks. However, when a woman has risk factors for cervical incompetence but has not yet lost a pregnancy, the decision to treat is not so easily made. On the one hand, it is hard to tell a woman who is suspected of having cervical incompetence but has not yet lost a pregnancy that she cannot be treated until she proves she has the condition—by losing a pregnancy! On the other hand, it would be a tragedy if, while putting in the cerclage, a woman's bag of waters ruptured and a miscarriage resulted when the diagnosis of incompetent cervix had not yet definitively been determined.

If you have been diagnosed as having cervical weakness or have had a miscarriage that might have been caused by an incompetent cervix, understanding what cervical incompetence is and how it can affect your pregnancies will allow you to participate more knowledgeably in the discussions you have with your doctor about your condition.

Fibroids

Roughly one in every four women has fibroids. Fibroids are benign tumors of the uterus made up of smooth muscle and fibrous tissue. Most of the time they are small, from one-half to two inches across. However, they can grow extremely large, reaching the size of melons. They can be present without causing symptoms or they can cause heavy menstrual bleeding, severe distortion and enlargement of the uterus, and intense intra-abdominal pressure. Because they are sensitive to hormonal stimulation, they tend to grow during a woman's reproductive life and shrink to the point of disappearing after a woman reaches the menopause. During pregnancy, because of the high level of hormones produced, fibroids often grow rapidly. The enlarged fibroids present in pregnancy can cause preterm labor, pressure on the fetus, and severe pelvic pain.

Fibroids and Miscarriage

Uterine fibroids generally do not cause miscarriage. Many women have remarkably large multiple fibroids and still conceive, carry a pregnancy to term, and deliver normally. But because fibroids occur as commonly as they do—in 25% of all women—even a small increase in the rate of miscarriages caused by fibroids results in a large number of miscarriages.

The main way fibroids cause miscarriages is by preventing the implantation and growth of an early embryo and placenta. A fibroid, as its name suggests, is composed mainly of fibrous tissue, the same kind of tissue that

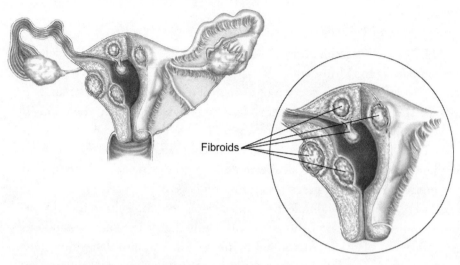

FIGURE 3.3   Fibroids in a Uterus

grows in a uterine septum, discussed previously. This kind of tissue does not have the same blood supply or receptivity to penetration by the placenta as does the normal lining tissue of the uterus. Should a fertilized egg implant over the site of a fibroid, the ability of its placenta to put down roots would be significantly limited. Thus the placenta's growth would be inadequate to provide nourishment for the growing embryo and a miscarriage would likely occur.

The fibroids most likely to lead to miscarriage are those just under the surface of the inner uterine wall. These are called *submucosal fibroids*. Fibroids in the middle of the wall or on the uterus's external surface may cause other problems in pregnancy, such as preterm labor or pelvic pain. But since fibroids in these locations do not interfere with placental implantation, they are not likely to cause a miscarriage.

No one knows for sure what causes fibroid tumors. We do know that fibroids run in families and that certain racial groups such as African Americans develop fibroids more frequently than others. We know that fibroids begin as small "seeds" of fibrous tissue that can enlarge under the hormonal stimulation of the menstrual cycle. They can be solitary or multiple. Sometimes when operating to remove fibroids, I will find as many as twenty to thirty of them. Some of these may be from eight to ten inches across; others may have a diameter as small as half an inch.

Diagnosing Fibroids

The two most common methods of diagnosing fibroids are physical examination and ultrasound.

During the pelvic portion of a physical examination, a physician feels the size and shape of the uterus. In a nonpregnant woman, the uterus is generally the size and shape of a pear. If fibroids are present, the uterus will feel larger than that and will often feel irregular. However, it may be impossible during a physical examination to distinguish a large fibroid uterus from either a pregnant uterus or a large ovarian cyst.

The other common means of diagnosing fibroids is ultrasound. Ultrasound examination of the pelvis can easily detect irregularities and enlargement of the uterus caused by fibroids. It can also determine their number, size, and shape. Ultrasound is especially useful in distinguishing between a uterus enlarged by fibroids and the other possible causes of a pelvic mass mentioned above—a pregnancy or ovarian cyst or tumor. There is also a newer technique, a specialized form of ultrasound called hysterosonography, that can help diagnose fibroids. In hysterosonography, fluid is used to distend the uterine cavity while an ultrasound examination is performed. Submucosal fibroids—fibroids just under the lining tissue inside the uterus—can then be clearly identified.

If still more information is needed, perhaps in preparation for the surgical removal of fibroids, two minor operative procedures can be helpful. The first is laparoscopy, which I described earlier. With the use of the laparoscope the entire pelvis, including uterus, tubes, and ovaries, can be seen and evaluated. Photographs can be taken for later reference and review.

The second procedure is hysteroscopy, the procedure in which a small scope is placed directly into the uterine cavity. Hysteroscopy is the best technique for diagnosing fibroids on the inside of the uterus, those most likely to cause miscarriages.

Treating Fibroids

Before addressing the issue of how fibroids are treated, a more pertinent question must first be answered: *Should* fibroids be treated? Perhaps to your frustration, the answer is a definite "It depends."

I told you before that roughly 25% of all women have fibroids. Many women who have fibroids do not even know that they do. Most of the time fibroids are small and do not cause problems. Thus, most of the time they do not need to be treated.

However, if a woman has had several miscarriages and is known to have fibroids in her uterus, it would be reasonable to treat them because they may have caused or contributed to the miscarriages. In addition, fibroids can cause other sorts of gynecologic problems—or might do so in the future. They can cause excessive menstrual bleeding, bleeding between periods, or pelvic pain. Fibroids can also grow so large that they put intense pressure on other pelvic structures such as the rectum, bladder, or ureters (tubes leading from the kidneys to the bladder).

Fibroids can be treated in three ways.

One is hormonal. Since the growth of fibroids is stimulated by estrogen, depriving a woman of estrogen can keep her fibroids from enlarging and even cause them to shrink. Certain medicines can turn off a woman's production of estrogen by inducing a temporary, artificial menopause. Over several months, a lack of estrogen can cause the fibroids to decrease in size by 50 to 75%. However, the imposition of such artificial menopause comes at a cost: Severe menopause-like symptoms such as hot flashes, night sweats, vaginal dryness, and insomnia are common. Significant bone loss can also result. Most discouraging, upon discontinuation of hormonal treatment, fibroids will generally grow back to their pretreatment size.

The second method of treatment for fibroids is to remove them surgically, a procedure called *myomectomy*. This, as is true of surgery for uterine anomalies, can be accomplished either through open abdominal surgery, through the laparoscope, or by use of the hysteroscope. By removing all or most of the fibroids, the uterus can be restored back to its normal size and shape. These operations, however, are not without risk. Bleeding can be severe, and so much fibroid material may have to be removed that almost no uterus is left for the surgeon to put back together. In such cases a hysterectomy may be necessary. Other possible complications of myeomectomy are the formation of intra-abdominal scar tissue and a weakening of the uterine walls. As with surgery on a uterine anomaly, the uterus may be so damaged by fibroid surgery that a future delivery would have to occur via cesarean section or else risk rupture of the uterus during labor.

If you have fibroids and have had a miscarriage, your first thought might be to ask your doctor to remove the fibroids. But it is important for you to keep in mind what I have discussed in Chapters 1 and 2: The vast majority of miscarriages are *not* caused by a physical factor but are the result of chromosomal misalignments during fertilization. You also now know that in a subsequent pregnancy your odds for *not* miscarrying are approximately 80%. Therefore, you must weigh the possibility that the surgical removal of your fibroids might be helpful for you against the larger probability that your next pregnancy would be successful anyway. You must also understand that the surgical removal of your fibroids could cause more problems than it solves because of the possible formation of scar tissue, weakened uterine walls, and the potential need for a hysterectomy. Again, this is a decision you will need to make after discussing your specific circumstances with your doctor.

A new third technique for treating fibroids has been developed over the last decade: *uterine artery embolization*. Specially trained physicians called interventional radiologists are able to thread catheters through blood vessels in the groin and up to the arteries that feed the uterus. When these catheters are in place, balls of an inert foam-like material are injected into the arteries, thus blocking or significantly reducing blood flow through them. This procedure "starves" the fibroids of the oxygen, nutrients, and hormones they need to support themselves and to grow. The fibroids shrink or even disappear. Uterine artery embolization being a newer technique, however, there is not yet much data to show how successful women are at becoming pregnant and bringing a baby to term after having had their fibroids treated in this way.

Asherman Syndrome

Occasionally a patient will tell me the following story: All her life she has had regular periods until recently when she had a D&C for a miscarriage. Since then, although she experiences breast tenderness and PMS regularly every month, she has not menstruated once. On questioning her, I may learn that she has had more than one D&C in the past. Also, it may be that when she had her last D&C, her doctors had a difficult time removing all the tissue from inside her uterus. They may have had to scrape the uterine walls vigorously for a long time.

There are many reasons why a woman might stop having her periods. However, when this occurs in close proximity to her having had a D&C, one diagnosis comes instantly to mind: *Asherman syndrome*. Asherman syndrome is scarring of the lining of the uterus caused by damage to the uterine wall. Such damage might be caused by repeated D&Cs or a D&C performed while a uterus is infected. The normal uterine lining tissue is replaced by scar tissue. This scar tissue is unresponsive to hormonal stimulation and does not produce a monthly menstrual flow. For that reason, despite generating normal hormones every month, a woman with Asherman syndrome has no endometrial tissue to thicken and shed each month in the form of a period.

Asherman syndrome can cause miscarriages. With absent or extremely thinned-out and scarred uterine lining tissue, a fertilized egg will experience difficulty in implanting. Alternatively, an early embryo that does implant may not be able to establish an adequate blood supply to support its continued growth. A miscarriage would thus result.

Diagnosing Asherman Syndrome

The main clue in diagnosing Asherman syndrome is a woman's medical history: The association of the sudden cessation of periods with her having had a recent D&C for a miscarriage or any other reason. The diagnosis of Asherman syndrome is then confirmed either by hysterosalpingogram, hysterosonogram, or standard hysteroscopy. In a hysterosalpingogram, one would see an irregular pattern of dye inside the uterus indicating an interruption of the normal smooth uterine lining tissue by strands of fibrous scar tissue between the front and back walls of the uterus. With hysterosonogram or hysteroscopy, the scar tissue in the uterus can be seen directly.

Treating Asherman Syndrome

If you are diagnosed as having Asherman syndrome, your treatment will initially involve cutting the fibrous tissue adhesions that bind the front and back walls of your uterus. This cutting is done with special miniature surgical scissors on the end of a hysteroscope. After the adhesions have been cut, it is important to prevent their reformation. Thus, after lysis of the adhesions you would likely have an intrauterine device (IUD)—usually used as a form of birth control—placed into your uterus. The IUD physically separates the front and back walls of the uterus and thus helps prevent scar tissue from reforming. After the procedure, you will be treated with oral hormonal therapy, usually in the form of moderately high doses of estrogen, to help stimulate the growth of whatever normal uterine lining tissue still remains. After several months of tissue regrowth, your doctor will tell you that you can stop the hormonal treatment and attempt to conceive if you wish (after the IUD has been removed).

Hormones

The most uncomfortable situation I encounter in working with women who have miscarried occurs when I am presented with the following type of request:

"Doctor, one of my friends had a miscarriage recently. Her physician recommended that she take hormones the next time she got pregnant to guard against having another one. When she got pregnant again she took the hormones and her pregnancy went perfectly. She now has a beautiful, healthy baby. Shouldn't you give me hormones the next time I get pregnant?"

The reason for my discomfort is that the temptation and pressure to prescribe this sort of treatment is great. But whether hormones are effective in preventing miscarriage—or are even safe to take in pregnancy—is still uncertain. This is the most controversial area in the field of miscarriage research. Although many practitioners provide hormones to patients who have miscarried, there is no compelling evidence to show that these hormones do any good. It is of great concern to me—and to many other physicians—that such therapy is so commonly employed without any true evidence for its usefulness. In addition to the administration of hormones not being a rational, scientific way to practice medicine, there is always the possibility that the treatment may lead to future problems with babies similar to those seen after the administration of DES years ago. I briefly touched on the subject of hormone supplementation to support pregnancy in the last chapter. Let's now take a look in greater detail.

What Are Hormones?

Hormones are complex chemical structures that are produced by various organs such as the adrenal glands, the pituitary gland, and the pancreas. They can be of different chemical types and they have multiple and varied functions. For example, insulin controls blood sugar levels, estrogen in women and testosterone in men control sexual function, and thyroid hormone helps control metabolism.

Hormones, once produced, are distributed via the bloodstream to the entire body. They work by acting at the level of individual cells to cause specific biochemical changes.

The way the body regulates its hormone levels is intriguing. It does so by the use of *feedback loops*. Insulin produced by the pancreas is a good example of this.

Each gland that produces hormones has a means of measuring either the blood level of that hormone or the effect the hormone has on the body. Insulin lowers blood sugar. The pancreas, which makes insulin, senses the level of blood sugar in the body at any given moment and adjusts its production of insulin accordingly. If the blood sugar level is high, more insulin is produced. If it is low, less is made.

All hormones work this way. By so doing, the glands of the body appropriately regulate their hormone production. This self-regulation is called *homeostasis*.

The sex hormones, of which estrogen and testosterone are the best known, are slightly different from other hormones. First, they are the only hormones whose production depends on the sex chromosome makeup of the individual. If two "X" chromosomes are present as the sex chromosomes, ovaries develop and estrogen is made. If the sex chromosomes are "XY," testes develop and testosterone is made.

Second, there is a complicated and not yet entirely understood time sequence controlling the production of sex hormones. Sex hormones are present only in low levels during infancy and childhood. Just before the onset of puberty, a complex signaling process involving chemical messengers made in the base of the brain causes the levels of sex hormones to rise precipitously. They reach adult levels during the teenage years and remain there. In men, testosterone remains at adult levels well into old age. In women, the production of estrogen begins to fall around age forty-five and generally stops three to eight years thereafter.

What Role Do Sex Hormones Play in Supporting a Normal Pregnancy?

Let's at this point briefly review what has to happen hormonally for a woman to ovulate, conceive, and begin a pregnancy (see Figure 1.3 on page 18).

Specific groups of cells in the base of a woman's brain cyclically produce hormones that stimulate the hypothalamus, a structure that sits just above the pituitary gland at the bottom of the skull. Once so stimulated, the hypothalamus produces other hormones that activate the next link of the chain, the pituitary gland.

The pituitary gland then makes two hormones that stimulate the ovaries: follicle stimulating hormone (FSH) and luteinizing hormone (LH). These travel in the bloodstream, reach the ovary, and start the sequence of events involved in early egg development. Once stimulated, the cells surrounding the early egg begin to produce estrogen and progesterone. Approximately fourteen days after this multistep hormonal cycle begins, an egg is fully mature and ready for ovulation. It is released from the small cyst in the ovary in which it was growing and finds its way to the end of the adjacent fallopian tube.

The area on the ovary from which the egg emerged becomes the site of intensive hormone production. It is called the *corpus luteum*. Over the next two weeks, the corpus luteum produces large amounts of progesterone in anticipation of the fertilized egg that might implant in the uterus. If this implantation occurs, the corpus luteum continues to produce progesterone for approximately eight more weeks until the placenta takes over this vital function. If, however, no egg is fertilized and no embryo implants, the corpus luteum lives out its normal lifespan of fourteen days and begins to disintegrate. As it does so, its progesterone production drops precipitously. With progesterone no longer being produced, the lining tissue of the uterus, which had grown lush under the stimulation of estrogen and progesterone, can no longer support itself. It begins to break up and emerges from the uterus as menstrual flow.

Progesterone is a remarkable hormone. It has many vital functions. Its first role is to support the growth of early pregnancy. A pregnant woman produces huge amounts of progesterone compared to the amount she normally makes. This progesterone not only prepares the lining tissue of her uterus for implantation but also is vitally necessary for her pregnancy's survival. It is well known, for example, that if a woman in early pregnancy requires surgery and the progesterone-producing corpus luteum is damaged or accidentally removed, her pregnancy will miscarry.

But progesterone does more than keep the early embryo alive. It is also required for later embryonic growth and development. It facilitates placental blood vessel penetration into the uterine wall, allowing for nutrient and fluid transfer between the mother and fetus. It also alters the mother's immune system so that it will not reject the fetus even though 50% of the fetus' chromosomes are foreign to her.

Corpus Luteum Deficiency

Corpus luteum deficiency happens when the corpus luteum formed after a woman ovulates does not produce sufficient progesterone to allow a pregnancy to develop normally. Some physicians believe that corpus luteum deficiency can result in a miscarriage.

However there is much controversy among reproductive experts as to whether this condition—corpus luteum deficiency—actually exists, and if so, what its consequences are.

Those who are skeptical about the supposed role of corpus luteum deficiency in causing miscarriage argue that (1) the association of lower blood progesterone levels and miscarriage in early pregnancy has never been adequately established, and (2) "fixing" the problem—elevating a woman's blood levels of progesterone by giving her supplemental progesterone—has never been proved to change the outcomes of pregnancies.

So what does all this have to do with miscarriage?

A lot. For there are several ways that an inadequate amount of progesterone can negatively affect a pregnancy and thus lead to miscarriage.

First, if there is inadequate progesterone production, the lining tissue of the uterus may not be sufficiently thick and richly supplied with blood vessels to allow a fertilized egg to implant and to participate in its early development into an embryo.

Second, without adequate levels of progesterone, the fertilized egg and early embryo simply will not grow. Development will cease in its earliest stages and an early miscarriage will result.

Third, as has been discussed, progesterone is necessary to prevent the maternal immune system from rejecting the foreign antibodies in embryonic and placental tissue.

In addition, new research shows that progesterone has effects on later pregnancy that had not been previously suspected. It turns out that the initial process of blood vessel growth into the placenta—controlled in large part by progesterone—has a tremendous amount to do with how well the placenta functions later on in pregnancy. If, during their early growth, these blood vessels do not receive adequate hormonal support, it can lead in later pregnancy to the deterioration of the membranes between the mother's placental blood vessels and those of her fetus. Such deterioration makes the exchange of oxygen and nutrients between the mother and the fetus more difficult and may result in an inadequate supply to the fetus. Inadequate placental function in late pregnancy can also lead to toxemia of pregnancy, a dangerous condition marked by elevated blood pressure in the mother and lack of proper oxygenation of the fetus.

Diagnosing Corpus Luteum Deficiency

The three most commonly employed tests to diagnose corpus luteum deficiency are basal body temperature charting, endometrial biopsy, and the direct measurement of blood levels of progesterone.

Basal body temperature charting involves taking your temperature every morning before getting out of bed and marking that temperature on a graph. It turns out that your temperature rises by approximately one-half to one degree after you ovulate. Thus a rise in your basal body temperature is a relatively accurate means of determining when in the month you make an egg and hence can become pregnant.

It is just following ovulation that your body begins to produce progesterone. Therefore following your basal body temperature during the course of your menstrual cycle will allow you and your doctor to know how long after ovulation you continue to produce high levels of progesterone—and will indicate deficiencies of production that could indicate corpus luteum deficiency.

Endometrial biopsy is more involved. During the menstrual cycle, the lining tissue of your uterus, the endometrium, undergoes specific structural changes every day. These changes are caused by the type and amount of hormonal stimulation—estrogen and progesterone—the lining tissue receives. In the second half of your cycle, endometrial development is particularly dependent upon your progesterone level. Thus, in the second half of your menstrual cycle, if your endometrium is not appropriately developed you and your doctor know that you have not been making adequate amounts of progesterone. To evaluate the stage of development of your endometrial lining tissue, your doctor will perform an endometrial biopsy.

To do this, he or she will place an instrument into your uterus and scrape off a piece of the lining tissue. A pathologist will then make microscopic slides of this tissue and evaluate them. If the development of the tissue is judged to be inadequate for where you are in your cycle, you will be diagnosed as having corpus luteum deficiency.

A final diagnostic option is for your doctor to measure your blood level of progesterone at specific points in your cycle. Although this is the most accurate way of knowing how much progesterone you are producing, there are problems with this technique. First, the amount of progesterone made by your corpus luteum may fluctuate from hour to hour, making a sample taken at any one time not necessarily representative of your average progesterone blood level. Second, the level of progesterone necessary for adequate early pregnancy function is not known. That is, women with normally developing pregnancies have been found to have a wide range of progesterone levels. Therefore it has been hard to define a level of progesterone that can be clearly described as "inadequate."

Treating Corpus Luteum Deficiency

There are two main ways proposed to treat corpus luteum deficiency.

The first is to supplement your progesterone blood level directly by giving you progesterone medication in the form of pills, shots, or vaginal inserts. The progesterone so administered is absorbed by your body and added to whatever amount of progesterone you have made yourself.

The second method is to boost your own production of progesterone. This can be done by manipulating the ovulation process. Fertility specialists have known for many years that certain medications enhance a woman's ability to ovulate. By inducing ovulation with these medicines, often more robust eggs will develop, that is, eggs accompanied by cells that produce copious amounts of progesterone and other hormones.

Should Corpus Luteum Deficiency Be Treated?

As has been mentioned, this is a controversial question, even among reproductive specialists. The key here is this: Does corpus luteum deficiency even exist, much less need to be treated? Scores of articles have appeared in the medical literature seeking to prove or refute the notion of corpus luteum deficiency. Yet despite all this research, no definitive conclusions have yet been reached. One would think that if such an entity as corpus luteum deficiency exists or that it plays a major role in causing miscarriages, definite proof of it would have been seen by now.

On the other hand, those who do treat suspected corpus luteum deficiency say the following:

1. We know progesterone is necessary for successful pregnancy. Therefore, if a woman with a history of miscarriages has even the possibility of inadequate progesterone production, supplementation should be given to insure that she has adequate progesterone levels to support her pregnancy.
2. As far as is known, administering progesterone has no downside. There have been no reports of an increase in birth defects when progesterone supplementation has been given.
3. There are many instances where, after a woman has had several miscarriages, a subsequent pregnancy treated with progesterone has succeeded.

But the arguments *against* treating women with progesterone supplementation are to me more compelling:

1. Because pregnancies treated with progesterone have been successful when previous pregnancies miscarried does not prove that the addition of progesterone made a difference. For as we have seen, 80% of *all* pregnancies following a miscarriage proceed normally even when no therapy is employed. Thus far, there have been no good studies showing that administering progesterone to women who have had one or more previous miscarriages decreases the risk of miscarriage in a subsequent pregnancy.

2. We do *not* know for certain that there is no "downside" to progesterone administration in early pregnancy. Some thirty years ago, physicians thought DES would be helpful in preventing miscarriages and posed no risk. It was only years later that female fetuses of mothers who took this hormone were seen to have high rates of vaginal and cervical cancer, infertility, and preterm labor. Therefore, before giving *any* medications to pregnant women, we need to be absolutely certain from long-term data that there will be no deleterious consequences to their use.

3. Perhaps the most compelling argument against supplementing with progesterone is the following: If a pregnancy resulting from a given ovulation is not able to produce enough progesterone to sustain itself, might there not be other things wrong with it? Are we certain that we wish to artificially sustain this pregnancy by hormonal intervention?

Suffice it to say, currently it is not known with certainty whether progesterone supplementation to prevent miscarriage really works. However, an answer to this question may soon be forthcoming. Several large studies are now underway in which newly pregnant women whose previous pregnancies ended in miscarriage have been divided into two groups. One of these groups was treated with progesterone supplementation; the other group, similar in all other respects, was not. Soon we will know whether the treated group did have a lower rate of repeat miscarriage than the nontreated group. The answer to this question will provide important practical information for all women who have suffered a miscarriage and for all those who work in the field of pregnancy loss.

Thyroid Disorders

A patient I saw early in my career made a profound impression on me. She had been trying to conceive for over two years. Before this, she had experienced two miscarriages. She had seen many gynecologists and infertility experts and had undergone multiple diagnostic tests and therapies. Despite this, no specific factor could be found for her not becoming pregnant and not being able to maintain a pregnancy. She was still childless.

She had come to see me for a routine gynecologic exam. I went through my normal history taking and physical examination. I was surprised to find that when I examined her neck, her thyroid gland seemed enlarged. The remainder of her examination was entirely normal. Although she was not suffering symptoms consistent with an excess or deficiency of thyroid hormone, I nevertheless ordered thyroid blood tests. I wanted to see whether her thyroid enlargement was accompanied by over- or underproduction of thyroid hormone.

To my surprise, two days later I got a report indicating that this woman was profoundly hypothyroid. This means that her thyroid gland was not making adequate amounts of thyroid hormone. I referred her to an endocrinologist—a hormone specialist—who confirmed my findings and went on to treat her. Within three months, the patient conceived and later that year delivered a healthy baby.

This is by no means to say that thyroid problems are an explanation for anything but a small minority of infertility or miscarriage problems. It does show, however, how dependent reproduction is on many functions and organs of the body entirely outside the reproductive system. It also demonstrates how important it is that an evaluation of the potential causes of miscarriage be comprehensive. This subject will be discussed in detail in Chapter 9.

What Is the Thyroid Gland and What Does Thyroid Hormone Do?

The thyroid gland sits in the front of the neck just below the larynx (voice box). It is made up of two lobes, one on each side of the midline. Most of the time, the thyroid gland cannot be felt. However, when it is enlarged or contains cysts or nodules, it is readily detectable on physical examination.

The thyroid gland produces the hormone thyroxine. Thyroxine has many functions, the major one being to regulate metabolism. That is why people who have too much thyroid hormone are often thin, overly warm, and anxious, and why people with low levels of thyroid hormone often move slowly, have slow reflexes, and are overweight.

Thyroid hormone is important in reproduction—even though specifically *how* it affects conception and pregnancy is not known. What is known is that normal amounts of thyroid hormone are necessary for successful ovulation, fertilization, and pregnancy development. Women who have hypothyroidism or hyperthyroidism often experience difficulty in becoming pregnant and do have higher miscarriage rates than women with normal thyroid function.

Treating Thyroid Abnormalities

If your thyroid blood level is found to be abnormal, the first thing your doctor will do is to try to get it back to normal. If the level is low, your own production of thyroxine must be supplemented with thyroid medication. This is usually in the form of pills that you take once a day. Your thyroid blood level will then be retested repeatedly to make sure that your blood levels become and remain appropriate. If this does not happen, the dose of your medication will be adjusted until a normal blood level of thyroxine is attained.

If you have an excess of thyroid hormone, you will be given medication to suppress your thyroid gland's overproduction of it. If your thyroid gland repeatedly resists such medical suppression, at some point you may have to have your thyroid gland partially or totally inactivated. This is done either by radiation therapy or by surgical removal. If your hyperthyroidism—overactive thyroid—makes it necessary to resort to such extreme measures, you may well have to take thyroid replacement medication for the rest of your life.

Your doctor's second goal will be to treat the specific *cause* for your under- or overproduction of thyroid hormone. If an inflammatory or immune condition is causing the problem, you will likely be treated with aspirin or other anti-inflammatory medications. If your diet is lacking the minerals necessary for the production of thyroid hormone, such as io-dine, you will be given either medication or dietary instruction to correct this deficit. If tumors or cysts are interfering with your thyroid function, they will be removed or drained.

Conclusion

Thus far in our effort to learn why miscarriages occur, I have discussed several of their most common causes. You have seen why chromosomal abnormalities, the largest cause of miscarriage, result in pregnancy loss. You have now also seen the role that age, anatomic abnormalities, and hormones play in determining whether a miscarriage will occur. I hope it is becoming clearer to you exactly which causes of miscarriage are be-yond your control—chromosomal abnormalities and age—and which ones can potentially be fixed—anatomy and perhaps hormones.

Next, I will explore how infections can lead to miscarriage, how often this happens, and what can be done about it.

CHAPTER 4

Infection and Miscarriage

IN THE SPRING, IT'S CHICKENPOX. IN THE SUMMER, LYME disease. In the winter it's colds, various forms of flu, and sinus infections. No matter what the season, I can be certain that each week I will get at least several calls from my pregnant patients asking whether the infection they have just contracted will cause them to miscarry or will otherwise affect their pregnancies.

Odds are that you will experience some sort of infection during your pregnancy. We are all exposed every day to infectious viruses and bacteria. The risk of infection is heightened if you work, as many women do, in the fields of teaching, childcare, and health care, where you frequently come into contact with individuals having various illnesses. Whether it is a routine cold or an earache, a bowel bug or a urinary tract infection, infections make us feel lousy. Occasionally, they can make us seriously ill. Therefore, it is a simple and logical step for you to wonder whether the infection that made you sick might also make your fetus sick.

Numerous questions follow from this: How will this tiny fetus respond to an infection that can lay low a full-grown adult? Will the infection interfere with fetal growth and development? And finally, might the infection overwhelm the fetus, causing its death and leading to a miscarriage?

The good news is that most infections have no effect on pregnancy. The bad news is that this is not universally so. *Infectious diseases can and do cause pregnancy loss and birth defects.* This is true for conditions ranging from common childhood illnesses to sexually transmitted diseases and from infections acquired from contact with animals to those acquired by eating contaminated food products. In addition, vaccination—

which is designed to prevent people from acquiring infections—can it-self occasionally cause miscarriage and birth defects.

Because infections in pregnancy occur as commonly as they do, it is important for us to know what relationship there is, if any, between these infections and miscarriage. In the pages that follow, we will take a look at the most common infections pregnant women get and discuss what the consequences of these infections are for their pregnancies. We will also discuss how the body protects itself against infecting viruses and bacteria. Last, we will look at an ingenious technique devised over two hundred years ago for protecting us from some of these infections: vaccination.

What Is Infection?

An infection occurs when some sort of "germ"—a bacteria, a virus, or any of multiple other kinds of organisms—invades a "host"—either a person, an animal, or another kind of living creature—and causes damage to that host. We humans have many kinds of viruses and bacteria that live in our body routinely that do not cause infection. In fact, many of them are vital to our continued good health. Therefore, we usually limit the term *infection* to organisms that are not supposed to be there and are harmful to us.

Inside a host such as a healthy human being, organisms find a perfect place to set up housekeeping. Our bodies provide warm temperatures, ample supplies of food, and transportation in the form of the blood stream. Under these optimal conditions, the number of invading organisms can increase explosively.

This increasing mass of organisms competes with its host—us—for nutrients. These organisms also secrete various waste products, known as toxins. Toxins can cause effects ranging from fever and aches and pains to organ destruction and heart failure. The toxins can also cause leaki-ness in tissue membranes such as those of the nose, bowel, and bronchial tubes. This leakiness produces nasal secretions, diarrhea, or the accumu-lation of fluid in the lungs—pneumonia.

Those are some of the reasons infections make us ill. But what we want to know is how infections cause miscarriage.

They do so in four basic ways:

First, infections of the cervix or uterus can cause a hostile environment for the implantation and growth of an early embryo. This is due to the way the body responds to any infection. When exposed to foreign microorganisms, the body tries to destroy them. It has two means for doing this: (1) It produces white blood cells that actually eat up the invading bacteria or viruses. (2) It makes its own defensive chemical warfare agents—antibodies and cell-destroying biochemicals—that it directs toward the invaders. This process of producing antibodies and biochemical agents designed to fight infection is called the *inflammatory response*. This is what makes a sore throat red and why pus, which is a collection of white cells and dead bacteria, accumulates in a dirty wound.

The inflammatory response, however, can be excessive. It can operate so vigorously that it creates a hostile environment for normal bodily functions. Concerning pregnancy and miscarriage, the same cells and toxic chemicals that can kill invading bacteria can also prevent the implantation of an embryo or cause the death of an early fetus. In either situation, the result will be a miscarriage.

Second, an inflammatory response in the placenta provoked by infection can impair the placenta's ability to function properly and thus lead to miscarriage. The placenta can become infected in two ways: (1) Bacteria spreading upwards from the vagina to the uterus or (2) bacteria entering the placenta through the mother's bloodstream. Whatever the cause, infection of the placenta results in an inflammatory response of white blood cells and antibodies of the sort described above. This can have several consequences.

The inflammatory reaction can decrease the placenta's ability to exchange nutrients and waste products with the fetus. It can interrupt the placenta's attachment to the uterine wall. It can weaken the membranes surrounding the fetus, causing them to rupture. It can cause either massive swelling or structural deterioration of the placenta to the extent that the placenta can no longer support the pregnancy. All of these will eventually lead to miscarriage.

Third, infectious organisms can pass from the mother through the placenta to the fetus, resulting in fetal infection and death. A classic example is German measles. The virus that causes German measles, the rubella virus, can travel from the mother's blood stream through the placenta and into the fetal blood stream, where it can continue to proliferate. As it does so, it can damage a variety of fetal tissues. This damage can result in fetal blindness, deafness, mental retardation, and miscarriage.

Fourth, an infection in a pregnant woman may cause her to have symptoms and side effects that themselves lead to miscarriage, birth defects, or, in later pregnancy, fetal death.

One example is fever. It has long been known that if a woman has a sustained temperature elevation while pregnant, her pregnancy is at increased risk of miscarriage and her fetus is at increased risk of having birth defects. Experiments performed on chicks and other animals have confirmed this. These experiments show that high temperatures during embryonic life interfere with the growth of fetal cells and with the way these cells develop into normal anatomic structures. This can lead to major birth defects or, if too severe, to fetal death.

Additionally, a pregnant woman can become so sick from her infection that the internal environment she provides for her fetus is compromised. Her blood may become poisonously acidic, her own blood oxygen level may fall, or she may become so dehydrated that the blood flow to her fetus significantly diminishes. If severe enough, any of these problems can result in miscarriage.

Organisms That Cause Infection

There are many organisms that cause infection. You are probably familiar with most of them.

Viruses

The smallest known living creatures, viruses are found everywhere in the animal kingdom. They cause diseases ranging from trivial illnesses such as colds and sore throats to life-threatening conditions such as AIDS and equine encephalitis. An interesting feature of viruses is that they cannot reproduce themselves. To procreate, they must merge with and hijack the reproductive structures of other cells. Yet, despite their small size and reproductive limitations, they are incredibly hardy. When present in epidemic form, they cause some of the worst scourges known to humankind—yellow fever, influenza, smallpox, and the like.

Bacteria

Bacteria are more complex organisms. They are single-celled creatures that are capable of their own reproduction. We live in harmony with many of them. They inhabit our mouths, our intestines, and our skin. Bacteria play a tremendously important role in the world around us: They cause grapes to ferment into wine and milk curds to turn into cheese. They cause the leaves that fall each autumn to decompose into the new topsoil that nourishes the following year's plants.

Other bacteria, however, can be deadly. They cause such common illnesses as food poisoning, wound infections, and strep throat. They are also responsible for such disastrous diseases as meningitis, pneumonia, and gangrene. They can infect every tissue of the body. Even the "friendly" bacteria in our mouths, gut, and skin can be harmful if present in excessively high numbers or in parts of the body where they don't belong.

Other sorts of microorganisms can also infect humans and result in miscarriage or other disease. Some are slightly more primitive than bacteria but share many of their characteristics and behaviors. Others are parasites that need humans and other animals as hosts in their complex egg-larval-adult reproductive cycle. Examples are the bacteria-like chlamydia, the corkscrew shaped spirochetes of syphilis, and the parasitic trophoblasts of toxoplasmosis.

My purpose in telling you about these various organisms is not to turn you into a microbiologist. Rather it is to help clarify for you the various kinds of infectious organisms that exist and to explain to you what effects they can have on you and your pregnancy. I hope that by the end of this chapter, the role of infection in causing miscarriage will be clearer to you and therefore be less frightening.

Common Infections and Their Connection to Miscarriage

There are very many kinds of infections to which pregnant women are subject—but only some of them cause miscarriage. Therefore, as I discuss with you the effects of various infections on your pregnancy, I want you to keep in mind that most of the time these infections will not be harmful to your fetus and will not cause you to miscarry.

Everyday Illnesses

Most pregnant women will experience one or another of the following conditions during their nine months of pregnancy.

Colds, Coughs, and the Flu

The common cold and variants of it such as sore throats, bowel bugs, and the flu are all caused by viruses. Even though viruses cannot reproduce themselves and must use another cell's reproductive equipment to multiply, they are very efficient at this. That is why there are so many kinds of viruses and why they cause so many sorts of common illnesses.

The viruses that cause cold-like illnesses invade the respiratory system and its appendages, such as the ear canals and sinuses. Their presence in sufficient numbers provokes the body to mount an inflammatory response. This inflammatory response of white cells, antibodies, and potent germ-destroying chemicals causes leakiness of the tissues of the nose and throat. The fluid produced by this leakiness results in mucus production, postnasal drip, and cough. Cold viruses sometimes enter the bloodstream and affect the entire body by causing chills, fever, and muscle aches. Fortunately, the viruses that cause colds, coughs, and flu almost never cause miscarriage.

Since pregnancy lasts for nine full months, you have a good chance of getting a cold, a sore throat, or the flu at some time during this period. We must assume that your fetus is exposed to these cold viruses when you become sick since we know that many other kinds of virus particles can travel through the placenta and into a fetus. However, studies have repeatedly shown that women who get colds and cold-like illnesses during pregnancy do not have a higher miscarriage rate than women who do not. The viruses that cause these conditions are probably not as potent as viruses that cause other sorts of disease that *can* lead to miscarriage.

My patients often ask me whether their fetuses "catch cold" when they do. No one knows. We just know that when pregnant women get a cold—which they do as often as anyone else—we do not detect any fetal consequences from it: miscarriage, birth defects, or preterm labor.

The Centers for Disease Control recommends that women in their second and third trimester of pregnancy get flu shots during flu season, which is late fall and winter. They make this recommendation not to prevent miscarriages but rather in an attempt to spare pregnant women the severe illness that flu causes.

What you need to know: Cold, coughs, and flus do not cause miscarriage.

Vaginal Infections

The two major kinds of vaginal infections are yeast and bacterial. Yeast infections are characterized by vaginal itchiness and burning and are often accompanied by thick white cottage-cheese-like discharge. Bacterial infections of the vagina cause burning at the vaginal opening and produce a yellow, gray, or green discharge that sometimes has a fishy odor. Since the vagina is a warm, moist, dark place, it is a perfect environment for the growth of yeast and many kinds of bacteria. That is why yeast and bacterial infections are so common in women, pregnant or not.

During pregnancy, the vagina becomes an even more hospitable spot for the growth of these microorganisms. The glucose (sugar) content of vaginal cells is elevated during pregnancy and provides an excellent growth medium for infectious organisms. Moreover, during pregnancy, a woman undergoes subtle immunologic changes, perhaps related to the fact that she does not reject the 50% of genes in her embryo that are foreign to her. These changes alter her ability to respond to various infections. Such factors make vaginal infections even more common in pregnancy than they are for nonpregnant women. They generate innumerable questions to me from my patients about the effect they might have on their pregnancies. Until very recently, I have always been able to respond that neither yeast nor bacterial vaginal infections cause miscarriage. I say "until recently" because new information has emerged about the effect of bacterial vaginal infections on pregnancy.

With yeast infections, the answer that they do not cause miscarriages still holds. Yeast infections are limited to the vagina and the vulva—the skin outside the vagina and immediately adjacent to it. They do not spread into the cervix and uterus, where they could infect the embryo, or into the membranes surrounding the embryo.

The latest news concerns bacterial infections. It has been known for some time that bacterial infections of the vagina can interfere with the process of *becoming* pregnant by causing damage to sperm. It has also been known that bacterial vaginal infections can cause preterm labor. But over the last three years, several studies have been published that demonstrate a direct link between bacterial vaginal infections and miscarriage. This relationship is thought to be due both to the toxins produced by the bacteria and to the inflammatory response generated in the cervix to these infections. Both of these interfere with the implantation of the early embryo and with the ability of the placenta to exchange nutrients between the fetus and the mother.

Thus, if you are pregnant or are thinking about becoming pregnant, it is important that you notify your doctor if you have any of the symptoms of a vaginal bacterial infection: vaginal irritation, a heavier-than-normal gray, yellow, or green vaginal discharge, or a foul-smelling discharge. You can then be treated—several oral and vaginal medications for this condition are safe to take in pregnancy—and thus eliminate one possible cause of miscarriage.

What you need to know: Vaginal yeast infections do not cause miscarriage; bacterial vaginal infections may do so. Be sure to contact your doctor if you suspect you have either one so that a precise diagnosis can be made and appropriate treatment begun if necessary.

Urinary Tract Infections

The bladder and the urine it contains are normally sterile. However, because of the nearness of the rectum and vagina to the urethra—the fleshy tube out of which we urinate—bacteria are almost always present in this area. It is not unusual for some of this bacteria to back up into the urethra, especially the relatively short one-and-a-half-inch urethra of a woman, and then ascend up into the bladder. Once in the bladder, these bacteria can multiply rapidly, causing infection.

Urinary tract infections (UTIs) are common in women for three reasons: (1) their relatively short urethras; (2) continual moistness in the vaginal-urethral area caused by vaginal discharge; and (3) the combination of heavy secretions and mild trauma to the vaginal and urethral area during sexual activity.

UTIs cause burning, pain on urination, and the sensation that the bladder is not empty after voiding. If severe, blood can be present in the urine. Fortunately, UTIs are almost always easily treated with oral antibiotics.

Urinary tract infections do not cause miscarriage. They are almost always limited to the bladder and never reach the uterus. Only when urinary tract infections become severe and extend up to the kidneys can pregnant women become so sick with high fever and shaking chills that the pregnancy can be put in jeopardy. Fortunately, this seldom occurs. Urinary tract infections, just like bacterial vaginal infections, can cause preterm labor in the second and third trimesters of pregnancy. But unlike bacterial vaginal infections, they are not a cause of miscarriage.

Infections You Can Get from Kids

Pregnant women come into contact with children frequently. Thus they are frequently exposed to childhood illnesses. Consequently, one of the questions I am most commonly asked by my pregnant patients is whether such childhood illnesses—chickenpox, mumps, fifth disease, and so forth—will cause them to miscarry or will otherwise harm their pregnancies.

In addition to frequent exposures, there is another reason that pregnant women are at risk from common childhood infections. Many conditions that cause only mild illnesses in children can cause devastating illnesses in adults. The chickenpox that will make a child sick for several days can cause severe, life-threatening pneumonia in an adult, especially one who is pregnant.

Let us take a look, therefore, at some of these childhood infections to see what effects they can have on you when you are pregnant.

Chickenpox

Chickenpox, technically known as varicella, is caused by the herpeszoster virus. It is a common childhood illness that is seen most often in springtime. As with most common childhood illnesses, the incubation period is between fourteen and twenty-one days. It is spread by respiratory secretions.

Children with chickenpox first experience cold-like symptoms, then develop a red rash that evolves into small blisters—"vesicles"—all over the body. These can be extremely itchy, and they last for seven to fourteen days. Although complications do sometimes occur with chickenpox in children—high fevers, meningitis, infections of the brain—they are rare. Once infected, an individual is immune for life.

The diagnosis of chickenpox is suspected by knowing that an individual has been exposed to someone with chickenpox and is confirmed by the characteristic rash and vesicles. Blood antibody tests positive for chickenpox antibodies verify the diagnosis. Fortunately, through childhood exposure, 95% of American women are immune.

Over the last several years, the first-ever chickenpox vaccine has been developed and released. Although it is not currently recommended for routine administration, things are moving in that direction. Certainly, if you are contemplating pregnancy and are not immune to chickenpox, you should be vaccinated. If you do not know your immune status, you should find out by having your doctor perform a blood test for chickenpox antibodies. After vaccination, it is recommended that you avoid becoming pregnant for three months to minimize the chance that the vaccine itself could harm your pregnancy.

Chickenpox can have three effects on a pregnancy:

1. It can make the mother extremely ill.
2. It can cause birth defects in the baby. These include smaller-than-normal head size, the abnormal growth of limbs, skin scars, and mental retardation.
3. It is also suspected of causing first-trimester miscarriages.

"Suspected?" Surprisingly, it is not conclusively known whether chickenpox definitely increases the risk of miscarriage. One would think, given the frequency with which both chickenpox and miscarriages occur, that this question would have been answered by now. However, because so many adult women are immune to chickenpox, no one hospital or doctor's practice sees that many cases of pregnant women with this disease. Therefore, no one has yet been able to collect sufficient data to answer this question definitively.

Of the studies that have been done—all of which have involved relatively few patients—no clear answer has emerged. Some of the studies have reported no increase in the risk of miscarriage with chickenpox in pregnancy, while others have shown a clear-cut increase in risk. In two studies, tissue collected from women who had chickenpox in pregnancy and who subsequently miscarried was examined. Many of the tissue samples tested were found to be infected with the chickenpox virus, supporting the view that chickenpox can cause miscarriage.

Thus there is evidence on both sides of the debate. This means that despite knowing the other problems chickenpox may cause in pregnancy—maternal illness, birth defects, newborn babies infected with severe cases of chickenpox—we still do not know for certain whether chickenpox in pregnancy specifically increases the risk of miscarriage. As noted above, a definitive answer to this question must await the accumulation of data on a sufficient number of women who have had chickenpox in the first trimester of their pregnancies.

How worried should you be, therefore, if you are not immune to chickenpox and you are exposed to it or get it while pregnant? If you have been exposed (i.e., spent time with someone who has chickenpox or who develops it within fourteen days of your contact with him or her) your physician will want to watch you closely and do blood tests to determine whether you have actually become infected with the chickenpox virus. If you have been, it will be extremely important that you be monitored to make sure you do not develop complications—such as pneumonia—from your infection. Your doctor will probably recommend that you receive a varicella-zoster immunoglobin (VZIG) shot. VZIG is made from antibodies collected from people who have had chickenpox. Although VZIG may not be able to prevent you from becoming ill from chickenpox, it can help make your case of it milder and may decrease possible harmful effects on your pregnancy.

If you do contract chickenpox during pregnancy, you will likely have one or more extra ultrasound examinations to make sure that the fetus appears to be developing normally and to look for fetal abnormalities. Given the kind and severity of birth defects a fetus exposed to chickenpox can develop, you may be offered the option of pregnancy termination.

What you need to know: It is not known with certainty whether chickenpox in early pregnancy increases the risk of miscarriage. It *is* known that chickenpox in pregnancy can cause other major problems for both the fetus and mother. Certainly the best policy is to be certain that you are immune to chickenpox or, if you are not, to get immunized before you become pregnant.

Fifth Disease

Fifth disease, known to pediatricians as *erythema infectiosum,* has been around for a long time. It is only recently, however, that it has come to the attention of the general public. It is another of the childhood viral illnesses like chickenpox, measles, German measles, and mumps. It got its name by being the fifth such infection identified. It is caused by the *parvovirus,* a virus usually seen in elementary school children and people who are in contact with them.

Fifth disease occurs most frequently in winter and spring. Like other childhood illnesses, it is spread by respiratory secretions. In children, the symptoms are usually trivial: A rash resembling a slapped cheek appears on the face, there is a generalized red lacy rash over the body, and a child will experience fatigue and headache. Adults who contract fifth disease are more likely to have joint pains, which may or may not be accompanied by a diffuse red rash. Although adults sometimes suffer significant complications from fifth disease—hepatitis for example— adults infected with parvovirus usually experience no symptoms. The only way they will ever know that they have had fifth disease is if their blood is tested and found to be positive for parvovirus antibodies. If a *pregnant* woman acquires fifth disease, however, the consequences can be disastrous: miscarriage, fetal death, or severe illness in the newborn after birth. Fortunately, approximately 50% of women come into pregnancy immune from fifth disease even though they are unaware they ever have had it.

More is known about fifth disease in the second half of pregnancy than about its effects in the first trimester. When a woman is infected with fifth disease in the second or third trimester of pregnancy, approximately 20% of the time the virus will travel from the mother through the placenta and into the fetus. There, for reasons not yet completely understood, the virus may destroy the baby's red blood cells. This creates fetal anemia, decreased oxygen supply to fetal tissues, and eventually heart failure. Babies so affected can become massively swollen and eventually die. Curiously, although fetal deaths from heart failure are seen, no increase in the incidence of other sorts of birth defects or health problems seem to occur with babies from these infected pregnancies.

Although we don't know as much about parvovirus infections in the first trimester of pregnancy, we do know that they increase the rate of miscarriage over normal by about 20%. Whether these miscarriages result from the same phenomenon experienced by older fetuses—fetal anemia leading to heart failure—or whether they are caused by some other mechanism is as yet undetermined. The good news is that the majority of fifth disease infections during the first trimester of pregnancy do *not* result in miscarriage.

If you are exposed to fifth disease while pregnant, your doctor will do antibody tests to check your immunity status. If you have evidence of antibodies acquired in the past, you are immune to fifth disease and will not get it again. If you are not immune, you will be checked for evidence of "new" antibodies. The presence of such antibodies would indicate that you have recently been infected with fifth disease. If you have, your doctor will likely order serial ultrasounds to check the health of your fetus and to look for signs of its developing heart failure. If such signs are detected, there are various therapies available that can improve the performance of the baby's heart. Such therapies, however, are not always successful.

Most fetal effects of parvovirus occur within eight weeks of infection if they are going to occur at all. Therefore, if all is going well with a fetus two months after its mother was infected with fifth disease, there is little likelihood that miscarriage, heart failure, or fetal death will occur.

What you need to know: Fifth disease can cause miscarriage, but usually does not. You should do your best to avoid becoming exposed to it. However, given the number of pregnant women who come into contact with potentially infected children at home or at work, total avoidance is often not feasible.

German Measles (Rubella)

German measles is the classic example of a childhood illness that is trivial in children but that can have disastrous effects on the fetus of an infected pregnant woman. Caused by the rubella virus, German measles is similar to other childhood infectious illnesses in that it is also spread by respiratory secretions and has a fourteen-to-twenty-one-day incubation period. Its major symptoms are fever, chills, swollen nodes, rash, and joint ache. Once a person has had German measles, he or she will have lifelong immunity from it. Standard German measles inoculations given routinely to children provide immunity for decades—but the protective effect may have worn off by the time that child grows into a woman and has her own babies.

Although a mild disease for children, German measles in pregnancy can result in grave injury to a fetus. It frequently causes miscarriage, fetal death, and congenital rubella syndrome, a condition marked by deafness, blindness, heart damage, mental retardation, or any combination of these.

The highest priority in dealing with the risk of German measles in pregnancy is to prevent it. All women of childbearing age should know their rubella immunity status and, if not immune, should be vaccinated. Most women who work with children or work in health care institutions are routinely tested for such immunity. Many women are tested as part of their premarital blood work. If you do not know your rubella immunity status, it would be a good idea for you to ask your doctor to test you.

Unfortunately, there is no treatment for rubella. Nor is there any way currently known to prevent miscarriage or birth defects if you contract German measles during pregnancy. Because of the potentially devastating effects congenital rubella syndrome can have on a baby, women who do get German measles during pregnancy are usually offered the option of pregnancy termination.

What you need to know: German measles can cause miscarriage and severe birth defects. The best—and only—treatment is prevention. Make sure you are immune before you become pregnant.

Measles and Mumps

Because of almost universal vaccination in the United States, measles and mumps are rarely seen in pregnancy. Certainly in the past, these two illnesses were relatively common, and in other parts of the world today they continue to be so. Measles causes a severe upper respiratory tract infection and a diffuse rash. Mumps causes a flu-like illness, but is most noted for its association with painful, swollen glands, especially under the jaw and behind the ears. On rare occasions, it can affect the pancreas, testicles, and ovaries. In the most extreme adult cases, mumps infection of the ovaries or testicles can cause severe swelling and pain and can destroy the ability of these structures to make eggs or sperm.

Measles and mumps both cause a small but definite increase in the rate of miscarriage. The rate of birth defects seen in fetuses whose mothers have been infected with measles and mumps is also increased, but only slightly.

Fortunately, most people are immune to measles and mumps from routine immunization in childhood. But for those women who are not immune, the risk and danger of these diseases is real, even in the United States. Given the many potentially nonvaccinated individuals in urban and even suburban communities—immigrants, those who were never inoculated as children—it is not at all unlikely that a pregnant woman might be exposed to one of these infections while working, shopping, or performing routine activities out of the house.

What you need to know: Measles and mumps both increase the risk of miscarriage and birth defects. They can cause a pregnant woman to become seriously ill. Make sure you are immunized to both of them.

Coxsackievirus: Hand, Foot, and Mouth Disease

The coxsackievirus is the cause of the common childhood rash called hand, foot, and mouth syndrome—not to be confused with the livestock condition hoof and mouth disease. This summertime childhood illness is common wherever young children get together. It is marked by flu-like illness, red rash, and painful blisters on the hands, feet, lips, and gums. It is generally a mild illness and complications are rare. Once introduced into a household, it can spread rapidly to other family members.

Fortunately, there does not seem to be an increased risk to pregnancy from coxsackievirus infection. Although the virus is known to pass through the placenta to the fetus, there is no evidence that it causes either an increase in miscarriages or birth defects.

What you need to know: Relax—there is no evidence of increased risk of miscarriage with coxsackievirus. The blisters will go away in four to seven days.

Cytomegalovirus

Cytomegalovirus (CMV) is the most common infectious cause of birth defects. It occurs in from 1 to 2% of all pregnancies. Depending on the population tested, somewhere between 35 and 90% of all adult women will have been infected with CMV at some point in their lives. It is especially common in teachers, preschool workers, and nurses who work with babies and children.

Once acquired, CMV can continue to infect individuals for years. These individuals may also "shed" the virus, that is, be a source of infection, for long periods. Most adults who get CMV do not even know they have it because they have no symptoms. Only approximately 15% will experience the mononucleosis-like complaints of fatigue, fever, sore throat, swelling of the lymph nodes, and enlargement of the liver and spleen. CMV is spread via body fluids: airborne respiratory particles, saliva, urine, feces, blood, and sexual secretions.

If a woman acquires CMV during pregnancy or has an ongoing infection with it, the virus can cross the placenta and severely injure her fetus. Common effects seen in infected fetuses are:

- swelling of the liver and spleen,
- jaundice,
- decrease in the clotting factors in the blood,
- infection of the eyes and ears causing blindness and deafness,
- calcifications in the brain resulting in mental retardation.

Unfortunately, there is no treatment for CMV and no means to prevent it. Currently, all that can be done is to diagnose it when it occurs and evaluate infants born from infected pregnancies. Moreover, individuals who get CMV do not develop the sort of protective immunity to it that occurs with other diseases. A mother who has had CMV in the past can become infected with CMV again. If she is pregnant when this happens, her fetus is still at risk for CMV complications. Although antiviral drugs and a CMV vaccine are being developed, they are not currently available for general use. Despite all this, there is some good news about CMV: Your chances of having a baby damaged from a CMV infection is less than one-tenth of one percent.

Although CMV has great potential to harm an older fetus, it is not yet known for certain whether it causes an increased risk of miscarriage. Just as with chickenpox, we must await the results of large studies involving hundreds of pregnant women infected with CMV to obtain a definitive answer to this question. Several such studies are currently underway. But given the severe effects CMV has on second- and third-trimester fetuses, it is likely that infections with CMV in early pregnancy also injure fetuses and increase the risk of miscarriage.

What you need to know: CMV can cause severe damage to infants born after an infected pregnancy, but the risk of this happening to any pregnant woman is less than one-tenth of one percent. CMV probably increases the risk of miscarriage, but this is still not known with certainty.

Diseases You Can Get from Sexual Partners and Their Associated Risks for Miscarriage

So much has been written about sexually transmitted diseases that they are often a source of concern for pregnant women. We will now explore the effects such infections can have on pregnancy and, specifically, look to see if they increase the risk of miscarriage.

Herpes

Of all the infections that can affect pregnancy, herpes is the one that causes my patients the most anguish. It's not so much that they are afraid of what the infection might do to the pregnancy, although that's part of it. Mostly it is the feeling so many people with herpes have that they have done something wrong and their herpes infection is punishment for their past behavior. That millions of other people also have genital herpes provides them no consolation. These feelings of guilt are only magnified when women who have herpes, now grown-up, married, and pregnant, learn that this condition may put their pregnancy at risk.

Let's take a closer look at this condition, so common yet so filled with negative associations.

Genital herpes is a sexually transmitted infection caused by the herpes simplex virus, the same kind of virus that causes cold sores. With the advent of greater sexual freedom from the 1960s and on, herpes vulvar infections have become the most frequently occurring sexually transmitted disease. The virus is spread by contact with an infected individual who has active lesions.

The initial episode involves painful sores in the genital area and swollen groin lymph nodes. It is often accompanied by a flu-like illness. During this initial episode, the sores last from ten to fourteen days.

Herpes infections can recur, sometimes as frequently as once a month, sometimes as rarely as once a year or less. The occurrences are almost always of shorter duration and are less painful than the initial attack. Although medication can decrease the frequency and severity of herpes recurrences, there is currently no real cure for the infection.

There are two strains of the herpes simplex virus. Type 1 classically involves infection of the inside and outside of the mouth. Type 2 usually involves the sexual organs. But either type can be found in either location.

The major issue concerning herpes in pregnancy is when the lesions appear in relation to the onset of labor.

Any primary—first-time—attack of herpes will result in the herpes virus being carried throughout the body in the blood stream. This is what causes the flu-like symptoms of herpes infections. In pregnancy, fortunately, the blood-borne herpes virus only rarely penetrates the placenta to infect the fetus. Thus the risk of fetal injury from primary herpetic attacks in pregnancy is minimal. However, the risk of miscarriage is considerable. Although the percentage of early pregnancy loss said to be caused by first-time attacks of herpes in a pregnant woman varies from report to report, the range is from 5 to 40%. Whether such losses are due to some viral effect on the uterus or placenta or whether they are caused by the fever and other symptoms the mother experiences is not clear.

With recurrent episodes of herpes during pregnancy—but prior to the onset of labor—there appears to be no harmful consequences to the fetus. This is because with recurrent lesions the herpes virus is present only where the specific herpetic lesions recur—the vulva, the vagina, and the cervix. The herpes virus does not get into the blood stream.

Herpetic attacks during labor are another matter. When herpes sores are present during labor—either from primary or recurrent attacks—a fetus passing through the birth canal is at risk of acquiring severe, life-threatening infection. The incidence of getting such an infection is 50% if the sores are from a primary herpetic attack and from 1 to 2% if the sores are from recurrent lesions. Such infections involve every organ of the fetus. The mortality rate for infected infants approaches 60%. Those who do not die may suffer mental retardation and other permanent neurologic damage. This is why if a woman going into labor has herpes lesions present, she is usually delivered via cesarean section.

What you need to know: First-time herpes infections during pregnancy increase the rate of miscarriage. Recurrent herpes episodes do not. Fetal contact with a mother's herpetic sores during labor and delivery can cause a life-threatening fetal infection.

Genital Warts and Human Papilloma Virus (HPV)

Genital warts, also called condyloma, are small, irregular outcroppings of tissue that occur in the vaginal and rectal area. They resemble any other kind of wart. They are caused by the human papilloma virus (HPV) and are generally acquired from contact with an infected sexual partner. They can also be "autoinnoculated"—spread by a person himself or herself—from one part of the body to another. Although they may become large and uncomfortable during pregnancy, they do not increase the risk of miscarriage. They may, however, serve as a warning sign that other potentially harmful sexually transmitted diseases may be present and should be checked for.

Human papilloma virus in the vaginal canal can also cause precancerous cellular changes in the cervix. These, if untreated for several years, can develop into a full-blown cervical cancer. Pap smears usually detect such lesions at an early stage. If caught early, the abnormal cells constituting such lesions can be eradicated and cervical cancer prevented. Fortunately, the HPV virus has no effects on early pregnancy and does not increase the risk of miscarriage.

What you need to know: The human papilloma virus, either in the form of genital warts or cervical abnormalities, does not cause miscarriage.

Mycoplasma, Chlamydia, Ureaplasma, and Gonorrhea

These are all sexually transmitted microorganisms that can cause infection in a woman's reproductive organs. The infections so generated often result in infertility because of scarring of the fallopian tubes. These organisms also pose the risk that an infant passing through an infected birth canal during delivery may become infected.

Whether infections with mycoplasma, chlamydia, or ureaplasma increase the risk of miscarriage is controversial. Many experts on infection in pregnancy think that these three microorganisms are part of the normal bacterial content of the vagina and cervix. They point to several studies showing that perfectly healthy women who have had successful pregnancies will often test positive for one or more of these organisms.

But other studies show that mycoplasma, chlamydia, and ureaplasma are found more often in women who have had early miscarriages than in women who have not.

Even though it is not certain that the presence of these organisms increases the risk of miscarriage, it still makes sense to be tested for them if there is any chance you have ever been infected with them. Even if it turns out that these organisms do not cause miscarriage, the infections they generate can cause other problems in pregnancy such as preterm labor or serious fetal infection. If you do test positive for one or more of these organisms, you and your sexual partner should be treated with the appropriate antibiotics. Fortunately, there are effective medications for these infections that are safe to take in pregnancy. After treatment, both of you should be recultured to make certain that the infection is gone.

Gonorrhea presents no ambiguity. It is known for certain that the implantation of an embryo in a uterus infected with gonorrhea can result in a potentially dangerous worsening of the mother's infection. Such severe infection would result in miscarriage.

What you need to know: Gonorrhea causes miscarriage. The jury is still out on mycoplasma, chlamydia, and ureaplasma. In any event, you should be tested for all these infections at your first prenatal visit if there is any chance whatsoever that you have been exposed to one of them.

Syphilis

Syphilis is a highly contagious sexually transmitted disease that can cause devastating illness to those who acquire it. It is caused by a corkscrew-like organism—the spirochete—called *treponema pallidum*. Although syphilis still affects millions of people around the world, it is, fortunately, uncommon in the United States.

The multitude of symptoms and wide range of complications resulting from syphilis are notorious. It can cause anything from mild sores of the genital organs to life-threatening neurologic disease. It can result in pregnant women miscarrying or their babies having severe congenital anomalies. Because of the profound dangers syphilis poses in pregnancy, it is the only disease for which testing is mandatory (in most states) before a marriage license is issued.

Syphilis can cause both miscarriage and stillbirth. In the past, it was one of the most common causes of fetal death. Even though it is not seen frequently today in the United States, it is such a dangerous disease that it should certainly be screened for in anyone contemplating pregnancy.

What you need to know: Syphilis causes miscarriages and has other devastating effects on pregnancy. Although the disease is rare, you should be tested for it. Fortunately, this test is routinely performed as part of the blood work done at your first prenatal visit.

AIDS and HIV Infection

AIDS is, of course, a devastating disease. It is caused by the human immunodeficiency virus (HIV). It can produce infection in every part of the body and cause profound weakness, organ dysfunction, and death. It can also make a man or woman susceptible to a great variety of other illnesses and infections. It is no surprise, therefore, that recent studies have shown an increase in the risk of miscarriage in women infected with the HIV virus.

There are several reasons why this is so:

1. Anyone with AIDS will be debilitated by the disease. Thus, a pregnant woman with AIDS is under even more physiologic strain than her pregnancy would normally impose. At some point, her body's ability to support the needs of the pregnancy may become exhausted.
2. The alterations in a pregnant woman's immune status, which is at the heart of HIV disease, will make her susceptible to other diseases and infections. Not only will these complicate her HIV infection but they may also result in miscarriage or fetal death.
3. It may be that the immune system alteration caused by HIV infection will interfere with the implantation of the early embryo. A pregnant woman's immunologic system has to function sufficiently well for her to be able to accept her fetus's half-foreign genetic content yet reject all

other foreign antigens. The presence of the human immunodeficiency virus may alter the ability of the woman's immune system to do this.

Although not specifically related to miscarriage, one other profoundly serious complication is associated with AIDS in pregnancy: the risk that the baby will be born infected with AIDS. Until 2000, the rate of this occurring was approximately from 20 to 30%. The vast majority of such babies died within one to two years of birth. Fortunately, there are continuous improvements in the medicines available to treat pregnant women with AIDS in order to decrease their risk of giving birth to infected babies. Currently, under the most up-to-date medical protocols, the rate of fetal infection from an HIV positive mother has decreased to 10 to 15%.

What you need to know: AIDS, in addition to all the other medical problems it causes, significantly increases the risk of miscarriage.

Things You Contract from Animals or Food

Many of the bacteria, viruses, and other microscopic organisms that infect animals and food can also infect humans. Several of these infections can cause miscarriage. Let us examine which ones these are and see how they are acquired.

Toxoplasmosis

With the exception of the question, "Could I be carrying twins?" toxoplasmosis is the pregnancy condition that I'm asked about most often. Every week I must see two or three newly pregnant patients who come in to the office panic stricken because they have a cat and have heard something about the possibility of a cat-transmitted infection threatening their pregnancy.

Toxoplasmosis is a parasite that humans can acquire from eating uncooked meat or by contact with cat feces. Only first-time infections with toxoplasmosis can harm a pregnancy. Fortunately, these occur rarely: Only 1 in 1,000 pregnant women will ever get toxoplasmosis. Women who have had toxoplasmosis in the past are not at risk. Unfortunately, toxoplasmosis is not one of the diseases for which immune status is routinely tested, even for cat owners. So if you own a cat or eat raw or nearly raw meat, ask your doctor to do a blood test to evaluate your infection and immune status to toxoplasmosis. As with fifth disease, there is a movement among obstetricians to include testing for toxoplasmosis routinely at the initial prenatal visit.

When toxoplasmosis does occur during pregnancy, it can have serious consequences. It frequently causes miscarriages. Severe birth defects can occur in those fetuses that survive. This is especially true in first-trimester exposure to toxoplasmosis.

An infected adult usually has only mild symptoms such as fatigue, swollen glands, and sometimes a mild upper respiratory infection. Often there are no symptoms at all and a woman may not know that she has been infected. Infants who become infected with toxoplasmosis during pregnancy, however, can experience a host of serious disorders: infection of the eyes causing blindness, swelling of the liver and spleen, anemia, jaundice, hydrocephalus (water on the brain), microcephaly (smaller than normal heads), neurologic damage, or mental retardation.

The business about cats, by the way, only applies to cats that are allowed outdoors where they can hunt. Certain forms of toxoplasmosis are carried by rodents and are spread to cats who catch and eat them. Most cat owners have either acquired toxoplasmosis long ago or have cats that are not infected and are not likely to become so. So for a pregnant woman to reduce her risk of becoming infected with toxoplasmosis, she needs to avoid eating raw meat and fish—yes, sushi, too—and avoid coming into contact with cat litter. Pregnant women who do not have cats should think twice about getting one for the first time during pregnancy and, of course, should also avoid eating raw meat and fish.

Interestingly, despite the widespread publicity toxoplasmosis receives, I have seen only one baby affected by it my twenty-two years of practice.

What you need to know: Toxoplasmosis can cause miscarriage but is a relatively rare condition. Try to avoid acquiring it by limiting your exposure to cat feces and avoiding raw meat or fish while pregnant. You do not have to get rid of your cat—just let your partner change the litter.

Parrot Fever (Psittacosis)

This is a rare disease almost always limited to birds or grazing animals such as goats or sheep. It has long been known as a peril to livestock because it causes miscarriages in animals raised for commercial production. It can, however, infect humans. Should you become infected with this bacteria-like organism for the first time during pregnancy, you could suffer a miscarriage.

In those unusual cases in which humans do become infected with psittacosis, there is almost always a history of close contact with animals. In fact, in the one case I have ever seen of parrot fever in pregnancy, a newly pregnant woman mentioned to me while I took her medical history that her pet parrot had recently died. About ten days later, she experienced a miscarriage. Analysis of her miscarriage tissue showed it to be infected with psittacosis.

What you need to know: Don't worry about this one unless you own pet birds or live on a farm that raises livestock. If so, ask your vet whether there is any chance your pets or farm animals could be infected with psittacosis.

Listeriosis

There have been several reports in the news recently about cases of listeriosis. Listeriosis is a bacterial infection generally acquired from food and food products such as infected eggs, undercooked meats, and soft cheeses made from nonpasteurized milk. The symptoms are similar to those of many other infections: fever, back and muscle aches, and joint pain. Listeriosis can cross the placenta and infect the fetus. It can cause miscarriage and, in later pregnancy, stillbirth.

What can you do about it? Even though infection with listeriosis is rare, it is best to be safe and avoid raw eggs, undercooked meats, and cheeses or other dairy products made from unpasturized milk during pregnancy. Since listeriosis bacteria remain dormant longer than other kinds of bacteria, it is especially important that you wash all fruits and vegetables thoroughly before eating.

What you need to know: Listeriosis does cause miscarriages. Especially when pregnant, take precautions with at-risk foods.

Campylobacter

Campylobacter is a bacterial infection that not many people outside of medicine know about. It comes from animal sources such as meat—usually chicken—or milk. It is found in homes and in commercial kitchens. Although usually present in food, the bacteria can also be found on cutting boards and other implements used to prepare fowl, fish, or meat. Humans infected with campylobacter generally suffer fever, abdominal pain, and severe diarrhea. It has long been known to cause miscarriages in animals. It has also been found to cause miscarriages in humans.

How can you protect yourself from acquiring campylobacter infection? As with other meat-borne infections, the best means of prevention is to make sure that all chicken, meat, and fish that you eat is well cooked and that the plates, cutting boards, and utensils that you use to prepare and eat such foods are carefully cleaned.

What you need to know: Campylobacter does cause miscarriages. Proper food and utensil hygiene is the best defense.

Lyme Disease

Although this condition has undoubtedly been around in the past, it is only over the last fifteen years that it has become widespread. Lyme disease is acquired from the bite of a deer tick, usually while walking in woods or fields where there is tall grass. It is most commonly seen in the northeastern and midwestern parts of the United States. It is thought that the increase in the deer population over the last several decades in these areas is responsible for the increased incidence of the disease.

Lyme disease can be a very serious condition. The first symptoms are usually fever, headache, joint pain, and an expanding round red rash on the limbs, often initially appearing like a bull's eye. If untreated, severe and permanent arthritis, meningitis, heart disease, and neurologic injury can result.

Whether Lyme disease causes miscarriage is another situation in which doctors have to say, "We don't know yet." Cases of miscarriages and stillbirths have been reported with women who have acquired Lyme disease during pregnancy. But whether these events occurred more often than they would have otherwise has not yet been determined.

What you need to know: We do not yet know for certain whether Lyme disease causes miscarriage. Because it has so many other devastating consequences, it is vital that you get checked if you think you have been bitten by a tick or if you develop symptoms of the disease after being outdoors in at-risk areas. As always, prevention is better than treatment: Be sure to wear protective clothing while walking in infected areas to avoid being exposed to the disease in the first place.

o   o   o

Until now I have discussed the various sorts of infections that pregnant women can get and how they may or may not contribute to causing a miscarriage. I have briefly discussed treatment for these infections and have mentioned the terms *immunity* and *risk of recurrence*, but have not defined them in detail. I now want to take a look at the body's own mechanism for dealing with infections: the immune system.

How Your Body Fights Back

Clearly, humans are vulnerable to many infections. But the body doesn't just sit back and take it all without a fight. Indeed, it has a complex, aggressive, and effective system of responding to potential infecting organisms. As I discussed at the beginning of this chapter, this protective function is largely performed by specialized blood cells.

Among the various components of the blood—oxygen-carrying red cells, platelets for clotting, fluid to move things around—are cells specifically designed to recognize and destroy invading organisms. These are the white blood cells. They do their job of destroying infectious cells in two ways.

The first is that some white cells make specific chemicals that latch onto the invaders. These chemicals are called antibodies. They are amazingly specific. They will recognize only the precise kind of invading cells against which they were produced, and no others. Once released by white cells into the blood stream, these antibodies find and bind to their targets. They then initiate a cascade of other cellular events that set the invading cells up for destruction.

The destruction of the invading cells is consummated by another variety of white cells called—believe it or not—"killer lymphocytes." These "killer" cells attach themselves to the antibody-primed bacteria or viruses and set to work by surrounding them, gobbling them up, and digesting them.

In general, these mechanisms are very effective. We are all exposed every day to millions of potentially infectious viruses and bacteria. Yet most of the time we are not sick. It is a tribute to the efficiency of our body's defense mechanisms—antibody production and cellular destruction of invading cells—that we remain as free from infectious diseases as we do.

Then why do we sometimes get sick? Maybe the invading organisms we are exposed to one particular day are so virulent that they temporarily overwhelm our body's capacity to destroy them. At other times, the numbers of invading organisms may be so great that the body cannot muster a sufficient antibody and cellular immune response in time to prevent being overwhelmed by them. There may also be times when our immune system is just not functioning at peak performance. This can happen because of fatigue, emotional stress, malnutrition, or other disease processes such as AIDS.

Unfortunately, sometimes the body's immunologic system can be overprotective. Some diseases, such as strep throat, cause the body to go overboard in making protective antibodies. For example, the specific kind of antibodies the body makes against the streptococcus bacteria—the cause of strep throat—can also cause damage to other parts of the body, most specifically to the heart. This can result in rheumatic fever and its most feared complication, rheumatic heart disease. Before the era of antibiotics, rheumatic heart disease was one of the leading causes of heart damage. Today, as soon as strep throat is diagnosed it is treated with penicillin and the bacteria are destroyed. Thus, the body never starts making antibodies against it and no inadvertent damage to the body's own tissues ever takes place.

Antibodies and Immunity

Physicians use the body's capacity to make very specific antibodies as a means of diagnosing whether someone is immune to a certain kind of infection or has recently acquired it. This is done by measuring the types and levels of antibodies in a person's blood.

It turns out that we all have five kinds of antibodies. Antibodies in the M and G families are the ones that fight bacteria, viruses, and other microorganisms that invade the body. Those in the A and E families are responsible for dealing with allergies, fighting skin infections, and controlling or eliminating parasites. The functions of antibodies in the D family are not well understood.

Although there are major biochemical differences between the M and G antibodies—the ones that fight bacteria and viruses—their most important distinction is that they are produced at different lengths of time from exposure to the organism. This difference in timing is used to help in the diagnosis of many diseases and as an aid in evaluating a person's immunity status.

M class antibodies—called "IgMs"—are the ones first made against infecting organisms. They begin to be produced within days of the body's exposure, reaching their peak level in the blood stream four to six weeks after initial contact. After approximately two months, the IgM antibodies are broken down and rapidly disappear.

G class antibodies—"IgGs"—are not produced until six to eight weeks after initial exposure to an infection. Once production begins, IgGs are made in large quantities and remain present in the blood stream for life.

IgM antibodies are thus the first to fight invading organisms. IgG antibodies appear later to finish the job. Furthermore, IgG antibodies remain on patrol in the blood for life in case similar organisms attempt to invade the body again. If such infectious organisms did try to reinvade, they would be immediately overwhelmed by these preexisting IgG antibodies.

By testing you for IgM and IgG antibodies, your doctor can tell whether you are immune to a certain kind of infection. Your doctor can also tell whether the exposure that resulted in your immunity was recent or happened in the past. For instance, the presence in your blood of IgG antibodies for a given disease indicates that you were infected or inoculated at least two months before your blood test because it takes that long for IgG antibodies to be produced. Conversely, if IgM antibodies against a certain organism are found in your blood, we know that your contact with the organism was within the last two months. This means that if a pregnant woman is found to have IgM antibodies to any infectious organism, it is almost certain that she has been infected with this organism recently, very likely while pregnant. Her fetus, therefore, is at risk for whatever complications are known to be associated with that organism.

If you have no IgM or IgG antibodies in your blood to a certain type of infection, you have never been exposed to the organism that causes it.

You are then at risk of becoming infected. If you are in this situation and you are contemplating pregnancy, you should get yourself vaccinated and wait three months before trying to conceive.

Vaccination

In the eighteenth century, Edward Jenner, an English physician, noticed that when a smallpox infection devastated a community, milkmaids often were not infected. He also had observed, as had many physicians at the time, that if a person survived an infectious illness he or she rarely, if ever, experienced that illness again. Finally, Dr. Jenner knew that cows are susceptible to a condition similar to but milder than smallpox called cowpox.

Putting all this together, Dr. Jenner surmised that the reason these milkmaids did not get smallpox was that they had in the past acquired the milder cowpox from the animals they tended. He reasoned that if exposure to this milder disease could protect these girls from smallpox, perhaps exposing all people to mild versions of various diseases could provide a general means of protection from infectious illnesses. Thus began the process of vaccination, which over the last two hundred years has probably saved more lives than anything else except soap.

There are two basic kinds of vaccines. One kind is produced by using only parts of the bacterial or viral particle for which the vaccine is being made. This is often sufficient to induce our bodies to produce antibodies against these organisms. The other kind of vaccine employs weakened but live forms of the entire virus or bacteria. This technique produces a mild but easily controlled infection against which our bodies make antibodies. The antibodies thus produced ward off future attacks of the disease for which we are inoculated. Vaccines of this latter type are called "live vaccines."

Both kinds of vaccines work well and pose no risk for most people at most times of their lives. However, in a pregnant woman, even the mild infection caused by live vaccines can result in miscarriage, birth defects, or fetal death. This is why live vaccines are not used during pregnancy. Thus, even if you were found at your first new obstetrical appointment not to be immune to German measles or chickenpox, you would not be vaccinated against them. You unfortunately would have no option but to try your best not to be exposed to these diseases for the remainder of your pregnancy. Within days of giving birth, you would be inoculated to protect you against infection from them in future pregnancies.

Conclusion

From our discussion above about pregnancy and infection, there are a few points in particular that I think it important for you to remember:

1. Many common infections in pregnancy cause miscarriage, others do not, and still others we do not know enough about to say with certainty. Each kind of infection has distinct consequences and must be evaluated accordingly.
2. Many infections pregnant women acquire are amenable to treatment. Others are not—they just have to run their course. As with any infection or illness, prevention is always better than cure. Therefore, if you are thinking about becoming pregnant, you should make certain that you are immunized against German measles, chickenpox, measles, and mumps. Additionally, you should make sure that you are immune—or else get immunized to—any other immunizable diseases to which your lifestyle, job, or geographic location might make you particularly subject.
3. The antibody component of the body's immune system has both rapid-acting and delayed-acting components. The delayed-acting component—IgG antibodies—usually provides protection for life from recurrence of the disease against which the antibody was made. By evaluating the presence and type of antibodies in a person's blood, it is possible to tell whether someone has immunity to or has recently acquired a given disease.

Until this point, I have examined the role of biological forces in causing miscarriage: chromosomes, anatomy, hormones, and infection. In Chapter 5, I will shift the focus to the nonbiologic as we look to see how environment and lifestyle can affect the fate of early pregnancy.

The Role of Lifestyle and Environment in Causing Miscarriage

FORTY YEARS AGO, MOST OF THE PATIENTS AN OBSTETRICIAN saw were housewives. If these women worked outside the home, they likely held jobs in the traditional fields of teaching, nursing, or food service. There were, of course, female doctors, lawyers, and business executives then—but such women were unusual. No matter where they worked, women were rarely exposed to advanced technology. The most high-tech tools that women—or men for that matter—generally dealt with were automobiles, televisions, and telephones. In addition, sports for women were mainly limited to tennis, golf, and swimming.

Today, of course, the world is different. Women now do every sort of work, from engineering to the military, from carrying mail to researching the human genome. In addition to telephones, televisions, and cars, we now have computers, microwave ovens, and cell phones. Moreover, nowadays there is no physical activity or sport in which women do not participate.

There is one thing, however, that has not changed: It is still women who get pregnant. And this is not likely to change anytime soon.

In our discussion of miscarriage, therefore, it is important for us to ask what effect these tremendous changes in women's work, leisure activities, and technological environment might have on the risk of pregnancy loss. Certainly my patients are aware of these changes and worry about them. I am constantly asked whether the various things they do or are exposed to will increase their risk of miscarriage. This is even more so for those of my patients who have already had a miscarriage. They wonder whether sitting in front of their computers all day at the office, having run a 10K race, or living down the road from a chemical plant might have caused their pregnancy loss.

Our task in this chapter will be to look at the relationship between lifestyle, environment, and miscarriage. By the conclusion of the chapter, I hope that you will have a better understanding of what factors at home, work, and in your leisure time activities might affect the health and safety of your early pregnancy. I will tell you this up front: The information presented here will in general be reassuring. As you will see, only a small percentage of miscarriages are caused by lifestyle and environmental factors. The physiologic process of human pregnancy is tremendously resilient. It can absorb many bumps and blows, yet remain unscathed. But certainly some exposures can harm an early pregnancy and cause either miscarriage or birth defects. Let us look, therefore, at specific lifestyle and environmental issues to determine where danger does and does not lie.

Mechanisms: How Lifestyle and Environmental Issues Can Cause Miscarriage

In previous chapters, I have discussed why miscarriages occur. As you have seen, understanding what causes miscarriages involves understanding the biology of early pregnancy and seeing what can go wrong during each stage of fetal development. Let us therefore use this approach to analyze how various lifestyle and environmental exposures might increase your risk of having a miscarriage.

For you to become pregnant, three crucial things have to happen: You need to make a healthy egg, your partner needs to produce healthy sperm, and your fallopian tubes have to be open so that the egg and sperm can get together. Additionally, four other conditions must be present:

1. Your uterus must be anatomically capable of carrying a pregnancy.
2. You must be free from infections that can injure an early pregnancy.

3. Your hormone levels must be adequate to support your growing pregnancy.
4. The environment of your body, especially your uterus, must be conducive to fetal growth.

If anything you do or come into contact with in your home, work, or leisure life i nterferes with any of the these pregnancy requirements, your risk of having a miscarriage increases. For example, if at work you are exposed to chemicals that are toxic to the cells of your early embryo, your odds of having a miscarriage go up. If your partner works with industrial solvents or agricultural pesticides, his sperm may be damaged, putting the survival of your early embryo at risk even if fertilization does take place. If you consume substances such as alcohol or tobacco that can injure your growing fetus or constrict the placental blood supply nourishing it, your chances of miscarriage increase.

The good news, however, is that such factors are only rarely the cause of miscarriage. Only occasionally does a miscarriage happen because a pregnant woman is exposed to a potentially harmful agent or activity. The cause of the vast majority of miscarriages is the random miscombination of chromosomes at the time of conception. The reality is that if your pregnancy begins with the successful merging of the chromosomes of the egg and sperm, it is extremely unlikely that you will have a miscarriage.

Now on to specifics.

The Home

Our homes turn out to be relatively safe places, at least as far as pregnancy is concerned. There is very little in the average home that will harm your pregnancy or increase your risk of having a miscarriage.

Household Cleaners and Other Chemicals

There is no evidence linking routine household cleaners or chemical products to miscarriage. Items that you might come into contact with, such as detergents, ammonia, drain and toilet cleaners, and so forth, do not cause miscarriage and will not harm your pregnancy.

Painting

It is amazing how often young couples become pregnant while fixing up their old homes or moving into new ones. Thus, one of the more common questions I am asked by my pregnant patients is whether it is all right for them to paint. Fortunately, I am able to give them reassuring news: There is no evidence whatsoever to show that exposure to paints increases the risk of miscarriage. This is true even for women who are professional painters, either housepainters or artists. Although it would seem that the strong odors produced by paint products might be inhaled in sufficient quantity to harm a pregnancy, this has never been shown to be the case. I do recommend, however, that while painting—or while exposed to any strong fumes during pregnancy—you keep windows open or otherwise establish good ventilation.

Construction

Most of the steps involved in construction pose no risk to pregnancy. If you are building a house, making renovations, or adding another bedroom, you need not be concerned that you are putting your pregnancy at risk. The various phases involved in most building projects—framing, plasterboarding, plumbing, electrical work, and so on—have not been shown to increase an exposed pregnant woman's risk of miscarriage.

There are, however, a few areas where you do have to be careful.

During the preparation for construction, existing structures often have to be torn down. These structures may contain lead paint. If so, the dust created by the demolition will be filled with lead particles. If you were to inhale the particles in sufficient quantity, this airborne lead could raise the amount of lead in your blood to toxic levels. Such high maternal blood lead levels have been associated with an increased risk of miscarriage. Dust particles from the demolition of asbestos insulation also pose a problem to a pregnant woman's health—but they are not a cause of miscarriage.

What can you do to decrease your risks in such a situation? Some construction techniques enable an area to be totally closed off and made airtight. If this is not possible at your construction site, you have two options:

1. Test the paint surfaces in the structures to be torn down to see whether they do in fact contain lead paint.
2. Arrange to be away from your house during demolition.

Coating floors with polyurethane is another potential risk related to construction. Although I know of no specific study linking household polyurethane exposure to miscarriage, polyurethane is similar to other complex organic chemical compounds that *are* known to increase the risk of miscarriage. On the other hand, the risk to a pregnant woman of exposure to polyurethane fumes, if there is any, must be small. Hundreds of thousands of pregnant women have lived in homes where floors have been polyurethaned over the last thirty years. If there were an excess of miscarriages or other pregnancy problems in these women or their babies, obstetricians and pediatricians surely would know about it by now. However, just to be safe, I advise my pregnant patients—and my patients with young children—to try to find another place to stay for the first twenty-four hours after polyurethane is used in their homes to allow time for the fumes to dissipate.

Air and Water Quality

Although you would think that the purity of such basic items as air and water would be vital to the health of early pregnancy, there is no research demonstrating that living in areas where air pollution is common or where water quality is not ideal increases the risk of miscarriage. For instance, women living in the often smog-filled environment of Los Angeles do not have a higher miscarriage rate than women living in areas free of air pollution. Furthermore, with the exception of isolated episodes of groundwater contamination, it has never been shown that the general quality of water in any particular state, city, or town has resulted in the women who drink it having more miscarriages than women anywhere else. Also, whether or not a town's water is chlorinated has no effect on the miscarriage rate.

The exceptions mentioned are a few specific instances where there has been actual poisoning of a region's water supply. Two famous occurrences of this over the last fifteen years were in the area of upstate New York near the Love Canal and in Silicon Valley, California. In both these situations, thousands of barrels of toxic chemicals leaked into the ground and polluted the water table. Women living in both these areas did have a higher than normal rate of miscarriage and had multiple other health and pregnancy problems.

Microwave Ovens

Microwave ovens generate heat by the use of high frequency radio waves. Such waves can, of course, be harmful to humans. After all, we are made up of the same kinds of tissues that are in the meat we eat—and we have all seen what happens to meat when we cook or warm it up by microwave.

However, for microwaves to injure us, we would have to be exposed to them directly. We would have to be close enough to the source of the microwaves so that their energy was not dissipated, and we would have to be at that spot in the middle of the microwave oven where the waves are focused.

None of these things happen from routine exposure to kitchen microwave ovens. First, the microwave tube that generates the energy is surrounded by the metal case of the oven. This case, if intact, provides a total barrier to microwave leakage. Thus barring extreme physical damage to the oven itself, microwaves will not escape.

Second, the electromechanical device that produces the microwaves focuses them to the center of the oven. Your abdomen when pregnant—assuming it is not directly inside the oven!—will not be in the path of the focused waves.

Thus, microwave ovens—unless obviously physically damaged—are perfectly safe to use during pregnancy.

Hobbies

People participate in so many kinds of hobbies that it is difficult to make a blanket statement about them. My patients' hobbies have included gardening, photography, furniture making, birding, and many other interesting and varied activities. I have encountered only two hobbies in my years of practice that I feel pose a potential danger to pregnancy. These are scuba diving and the making of stained glass.

In stained glass making, pieces of colored glass are connected with strips of lead. The lead is heated until soft so that it adheres firmly to the glass pieces that are to be connected. However, while the lead is being heated, vapors containing lead in gaseous form are produced. If a pregnant woman inhales too much lead vapor, the level of lead in her blood could become toxic to her fetus. Her risk of miscarriage would increase.

In scuba diving, the issues are water pressure and oxygen. When a pregnant woman dives, the pressure on her body is that of the total weight of water above her. There is the potential that such pressure on her abdomen and uterus could be greater than the pressure of the blood in the vessels feeding the uterus. If so, blood flow to the uterus and the fetus would diminish. Similarly, high pressures under water can alter the percentage of the various gases dissolved in a diver's blood. The amount of oxygen in the blood flowing to a pregnant diver's fetus might diminish to dangerous levels. Her fetus might therefore be deprived of adequate oxygen for some period of time.

Because of these concerns, I make the following recommendation to my pregnant patients: If you engage in any sort of hobby around the house that involves the possibility of inhalation of potentially dangerous gases, either stop that work while pregnant or do it only in an extremely well-ventilated location. As for scuba diving, I recommend that women not pursue this activity while pregnant.

Work

The vast majority of women work outside the home during their first pregnancy. Many women continue such work with subsequent pregnancies. It is important, therefore, that pregnant women know what factors in their work environment might pose dangers to their pregnancies and thus increase their risk of miscarriage.

Air Quality and Chemical Exposures

Despite the strong smells and gaseous fumes present at many work sites, there is surprisingly little evidence that exposure to such conditions contributes to miscarriage. This is remarkable when we consider all the different sorts of workplaces there are: factories making rubber, metals, or organic chemicals; farms where fertilizers and pesticides are used in large quantities; and electronic and computer industries where soldering and chemical etching are going on continuously. Yet, as I read the medical literature, I find few reports of specific work environments that increase the risk of miscarriage.

There are, to be sure, certain chemicals that are associated with an increase in the rate of miscarriage. They generally fall into two categories: the so-called heavy metals—lead, mercury, copper, and so on—and complex hydrocarbon (oil- or coal-derived) products. Excessive contact with any of these may put your pregnancy at risk.

Since heavy metals are used in the manufacture of a wide range of products, exposure to them occurs in many kinds of jobs. You might come into contact with them if you work with or near the following:

- Photographic film production or development (silver compounds)
- The manufacture of products containing heavy metals such as batteries, electrical appliances, and chemical products (lead, copper, and other metals)
- The smelting of mineral-rich ores to produce pure metals

Hydrocarbons are also widely used in manufacturing. They are the raw materials out of which many products, such as plastics, cosmetics, and synthetic fabrics are made. They also serve as cleaning agents, solvents, and fuels. Different hydrocarbons have varying effects on early pregnancy. Some are known to increase the risk of miscarriage, some are known to be safe, and for others we have no data.

The following is a partial list of hydrocarbon compounds, all used frequently in industry, that are known to increase the risk of miscarriage:

- Formaldehyde
- Benzene
- Methylene chloride
- Tetrachloroethylene
- Carbon disulfide
- Polyurethane

Two particular hydrocarbons, toluene and perchloroethylene, are especially dangerous in pregnancy. Toluene is a commonly used solvent in chemical and manufacturing industries. Perchloroethylene is used extensively as a dry-cleaning agent. Multiple studies from the United States, Europe, and Southeast Asia have confirmed that both of these compounds considerably increase the risk of miscarriage.

If you know or suspect that these sorts of chemicals are present in your work environment, you owe it to yourself to do three things. First, check with your employer about exactly what chemicals are being used and ask for safety information about them. Further information about the effects of chemical exposures in pregnancy can be obtained from sources such as the Pregnancy Environmental Hotline (800-322-5014), state and local health departments, and the Occupational Safety and Health Administration (www.osha.gov). Second, be sure that you follow all safety precautions recommended to you by your employer. Third, inquire about the air quality where you work. If your job involves exposure to dust or chemical fumes, ask your employer about the quality of ventilation and the possible need for masks or other breathing devices that might increase the safety of your workplace.

Even medical environments are not totally free from exposures that might increase the risk of miscarriage. For instance, it has long been suspected that women working in operating rooms suffered more miscarriages than women working elsewhere in hospitals due to chronic exposure to the anesthetic gases always present in the air there.

Anesthetic gases are used to put and keep patients asleep and to keep patients free from pain during surgery. They are administered via breathing masks or tubes placed into the throat and are given in large quantities and at high flow rates. It is not uncommon for these gases to leak around the breathing apparatus. In addition, the exhalations of the anesthetized patient release these gases into the operating room atmosphere.

Many studies have been done to determine whether nurse anesthetists, anesthesiologists, nurses, and doctors working in operating rooms actually have an increased rate of miscarriage. In the past, such studies have confirmed that this is indeed so. More recent studies, however, disagree with these findings.

There is a simple explanation for this discrepancy. In older operating rooms scant attention was paid to air-flow management. Whatever gases were in operating rooms dissipated only slowly. Newer operating rooms, however, have "scavenger systems" to extract anesthetic-laden air from them and circulate fresh air in its place. Thus, while studies done *before* the use of gas scavenger systems showed increased rates of miscarriage in operating room personnel, more recent studies performed since these systems have been installed don't show this increased risk. Similar results have been found in other areas where anesthetic gases are used: outpatient surgical clinics, dental offices, and veterinary operating rooms.

Thus, if you work at a job where anesthesia is used on the premises, inquire about the ventilation arrangements. Ask whether the facility undergoes inspection by a health department or other licensing agency. If you need help, call your local or state health department or department of labor. Any of these should have personnel who can either aid you in getting the information you need or assist you in getting appropriate changes made in your work environment.

What Does All This Mean?

All this talk about various exposures and increased risks of miscarriage can be scary. We must, however, put this information into perspective. When I talk about an "increase risk of miscarriage," I am by no means saying that all pregnant women exposed to any of the above-mentioned chemicals will miscarry. The vast majority of pregnant women, even if exposed to potentially harmful materials, will not miscarry and will go on to have healthy babies. What I *am* saying is that certain substances increase the *chances* of miscarriage. The degree of increased risk depends on the specifics of the situation: the type of material to which you are exposed, the intensity and duration of exposure, how far along in the pregnancy you are at the time of exposure, and so forth. Fortunately, most people today work in businesses or industries where air quality, chemical exposure, and other occupational risks are monitored closely. Usually monitoring is mandated by law and supervised by state or federal authorities. So while you should exercise care in any environment you are in while pregnant, you need not be constantly afraid that your pregnancy is at risk. As mentioned above, fetuses with normal chromosomes are hardy creatures. They do not often miscarry. The key point is this: Although some workplace exposures can be harmful, *most women doing most jobs in most environments do not have an increase in the risk of miscarriage.*

Electromagnetic Radiation

The electromagnetic spectrum is the name given to all the kinds of energy that exist in wave form. It is made up of many different phenomenon that we might not ordinarily think of as being similar: light, radio, sound waves, microwave energy, x-rays, cosmic rays, and infrared light. Because we know that certain kinds of radiation, such as x-rays, can be harmful during pregnancy, it is natural to wonder whether other forms of radiant energy might also be dangerous to a pregnant woman.

Fortunately, there is no evidence that any of the most common forms of electromagnetic energy are harmful. This includes radio, television, microwave transmission, radar, and all the various forms of electromagnetic radiation that pass through the atmosphere around us and about which we are usually unaware.

Let's look at some specific examples:

People living near power plants or large power transmission lines often worry that the electronic and magnetic fields surrounding these structures might cause damage to themselves, their children, and their pregnancies. This has never been shown to be true.

Many people have similar concerns about exposure to television, radio, tape recorders, and the now ubiquitous cell phone. There have even been unsubstantiated reports that the use of cell phones, being held close to the head as they are, increases the risk of brain cancer. Such claims are totally false. In fact, the use of these sorts of common electrical devices by pregnant women has never been shown to increase the risk of miscarriage, or, for that matter, any other medical problem.

Over the last two decades, there has been intense research about the effects of one of the most common sources of electromagnetic radiation to which we are all exposed: television and computer screens. Many people have speculated that sitting in front of these screens for hours at a time, day after day, might prove dangerous. It has been suggested that such continuous exposure to the electrical and magnetic fields generated by these devises would cause an increase in the rate of cancer, birth defects, and miscarriages. Fortunately, multiple studies conducted both by medical researchers and public health officials have shown that this is not so. Three recent large-scale studies, one by the March of Dimes and one each from Finland and England, have confirmed this.

Electromagnetic radiation of a different sort is used in medicine, both for diagnosis and for treatment. *Diagnostic radiation* consists of x-rays, ultrasound waves, and intense magnetic fields such as are used in magnetic resonance imaging (MRIs). We have known for many years that x-ray radiation may be dangerous to pregnancy. That is why if you have an x-ray taken you will be asked whether you are pregnant. If you answer that you are or might be, either your lower abdomen will be shielded very carefully or the x-ray procedure will be canceled.

There are three ways that radiation can be harmful to a pregnancy. First, the energy of the radiation itself may injure or kill the fetus. Second, radiation may cause damage to the precursors of white blood cells in the fetus and increase the chances that the man or woman the fetus becomes will develop leukemia. Third, radiation, even in relatively small doses, may cause mutations in the fetal cells that will go on to become the eggs or sperm. Thus, when the fetus grows up and has his or her own children, those children could possibly have radiation-induced abnormalities.

TABLE 5.1 Typical X-Ray Procedures and the Amount of Radiation from Each

AVERAGE X-RAY EXPOSURE TO PELVIS FROM VARIOUS KINDS OF X-RAY EXAMINATIONS (IN RADS)

Skull	0.0001
Chest	0.004
Mammogram	0.01
Upper back	0.1
Lower back	0.3
Upper GI series (bowel x-rays)	0.6
Barium enema	0.8
Abdomen	0.3
IVP (kidney exam)	0.75
Hip	0.15

There has been much research into the question of exactly how much radiation is harmful for a pregnancy. Multiple studies have shown that this amount is somewhere between five and ten rads, the "rad" being the basic unit by which radiation exposure is measured. A rad is defined as the amount of energy transferred by x-rays to a certain amount of tissue in a certain period of time.

Fortunately, no one x-ray procedure results in exposure of more than 3.5 rads. Most simple procedures, such as the x-ray of an arm or leg or chest, expose the body to only a fraction of a one rad. So although you should not be exposed to radiation unnecessarily, if you need to have an x-ray taken during pregnancy, it is extremely unlikely that it would cause you to miscarry or that your fetus would be harmed.

Computerized axial tomography (CT scan) is just another way of taking x-rays, but one that involves higher doses of radiation. There are techniques for performing CT scans in pregnancy that decrease the amount of radiation used. Still, unless absolutely necessary, CT scans should be avoided in pregnancy.

Ultrasound examinations involve only sound waves. The safety of the energy levels of the sound waves used in ultrasound has been confirmed by the American Institute of Ultrasound in Medicine and by the National Institutes of Health. Because of their usefulness in pregnancy, ultrasound examinations are done frequently. Over the last thirty years, they have been performed on millions of fetuses. Some of these fetuses, because of special medical problems, have needed to have ultrasounds done weekly or even daily. Yet study after study has found that diagnostic ultrasound exposure does not increase the risk of miscarriage or cause any other sort of fetal damage.

Magnetic resonance imaging (MRI) machines form pictures of internal structures by magnetically exciting hydrogen atoms in the tissues examined. Via an extremely complex technical process, measurement of this magnetic alteration of hydrogen ions is converted into x-ray-type images. MRIs have not been found to be harmful to fetuses or to increase the risk of miscarriage. Indeed, as obstetricians have learned more about the safety of MRIs in pregnancy, MRIs are being used more and more often where in the past an x-ray or CT scan would have been employed.

As opposed to diagnostic radiation, *therapeutic radiation* is when some form of x-ray or sound wave is used for treatment. It is generally of two types.

One involves the use of high-energy x-ray radiation to treat cancers. These radiation treatments are usually given in multiple doses over weeks or months. Fortunately, this is a situation rarely encountered in pregnant women. Nevertheless, when a pregnant woman does have a cancer that requires x-ray therapy, the large doses of radiation employed are very likely to cause a miscarriage or fetal damage. In some cases, where radiation directly to the lower abdomen can be avoided, the abdomen can be shielded with lead aprons that can in large measure protect the fetus. In other instances, it is impossible to avoid significant radiation exposure to the pregnant uterus.

In these difficult situations, the pregnant woman so affected has to make a decision about her pregnancy before radiation therapy starts. She might choose to terminate the pregnancy. Alternatively, where a pregnancy is near the point of viability or where the mother chooses the continuation of the pregnancy over her need to receive radiation therapy, radiation treatment is postponed until after delivery, which is usually induced several weeks early.

The second type of therapeutic radiation involves the use of ultrasonic sound waves to treat muscular or joint injuries. Although not as much information is available about the safety of this higher-energy kind of ultrasound as there is about diagnostic ultrasound, there have been no reports that show that ultrasound used in this way poses a danger to pregnancy. Although it is probably a wise precaution not to employ such therapeutic ultrasound directly over a pregnant abdomen, its use over more distant muscular, joint, or bony tissues in pregnancy appears to be safe.

In addition to the danger of a pregnant patient's being exposed to radiation, female radiology technicians, radiologists, dentists, and other personnel performing diagnostic and therapeutic procedures with radiation-producing equipment are also concerned about their safety when pregnant. However, effective shielding and monitoring techniques have been developed that make such work safe. Aprons lined with lead, which are worn routinely by radiology personnel, protect against penetration from x-rays. The control panels at which radiologists and technicians sit as they control x-ray, ultrasound, and other equipment are shielded against radiation. Film badges that record the amount of radiation to which an individual has been exposed are checked at regular intervals. If, for whatever reason, exposure levels rise to anywhere near amounts dangerous to pregnancy, pregnant workers are reassigned temporarily to areas free of radiation exposure.

Take home message? If you are pregnant and need an x-ray, ultrasound, or MRI, you need have no concern for your safety or that of your fetus if proper precautions are taken. Just be sure you tell the doctor, dentist, or technician performing the test that you are pregnant or might be. This being known, either appropriate safeguards will be put into place or the test will be cancelled.

Cosmic Rays

Cosmic rays are another kind of radiation to which all people living on earth are exposed. They are random bursts of radiation originating in outer space that regularly penetrate the earth's atmosphere. Cosmic rays are powerful enough to injure human tissues and are thought to cause occasional genetic mutations in sperm and egg cells. Fortunately, however, no known association has been found between cosmic ray exposure and miscarriage.

Because cosmic rays are partially screened out by the thick layer of air in the atmosphere, it had been supposed that pregnant women who worked *above* much of the atmosphere—female flight attendants and female pilots—might have a higher incidence of miscarriage than women who work at ground level. However, multiple studies of pregnant flight attendants have shown that this is not so.

Physical Labor

"Put that box down—you shouldn't be carrying anything while you're pregnant." Although a cliché, I find this belief is still held by many of my patients, their husbands, and their families. The concern is that lifting or carrying or being on their feet too much while pregnant might cause them to miscarry. Is there any truth to this? Is physical labor dangerous to pregnancy? Will it increase the risk of miscarriage?

Surprisingly, very few studies have looked at this question. Those that have show no difference in miscarriage rates for women who regularly lift items weighing up to fifty pounds. Consistently lifting weights heavier than this may slightly increase their risk of miscarriage—but the data on this is not conclusive. What is known for certain is that the risk of having a premature baby is increased in women whose work involves intense physical activity.

In terms of the amount of time a pregnant woman stands on her feet, one study of pregnant midwives and another of pregnant flight attendants showed no increased risk of miscarriage compared to pregnant women of similar age and health who held sedentary jobs.

But more important in my mind than any studies on this issue is the obvious fact that the majority of women—whether pregnant or not—*do* spend their days lifting, carrying, or being on their feet. Yet there has never been a measurable difference in the miscarriage rate between women who work at desk jobs and women who work on farms, in factories, who teach or nurse, or who do the very physical work of childcare and housekeeping.

Nuclear Energy

Nuclear power plants offer the potential for the production of huge amounts of energy without the use of fossil fuels. However, the production of such energy involves radioactive byproducts and the remote but real possibility of a nuclear accident. Two such accidents have thus far occurred. One was at Three Mile Island, Pennsylvania, in 1979, the other in Chernobyl, Ukraine, in 1986. The only other large-scale exposure to radiation injury experienced by a general population occurred when atomic weapons were dropped on Hiroshima and Nagasaki in Japan in 1945 to bring an end to World War II.

We know from animal experiments with radiation and from the after effects of the Hiroshima and Nagasaki bombings of the harm radiation can do to early pregnancy: miscarriage, birth defects, and maternal injury. In addition, such radiation exposure greatly increases the odds that anyone thus exposed—including fetuses and children—will develop leukemia later in life.

Studies have been done on the risk of miscarriage following the Chernobyl accident, but the data have been conflicting. Some studies have shown an increase in the risk of miscarriage in women living in areas surrounding Chernobyl, but other studies have not. The lack of definitive answers is likely attributable both to the techniques used for collecting the data and to the variable levels of radiation exposure in the populations studied.

Wherever nuclear power plants have been built, they have aroused the concern of local residents. People living around such plants have wondered about the safety of the radioactive materials used to produce the power, about the byproducts of nuclear fission, and about the possibility of an accidental leakage of radioactive gases. These fears remain despite a multitude of federally mandated safety rules and regulations and despite the redundancy of safety features at these plants.

As far as pregnancy goes, however, there have been no reports either of an increased rate of miscarriage in residents of areas surrounding nuclear energy facilities or of an increase in miscarriages in workers at these facilities.

Airport and Building Security Systems

At airports and government buildings, we have all gone through metal detectors or other security equipment. Fortunately, the energy level of radiation and magnetism used in such equipment is so low that they pose no risk at all to the health of a pregnancy. This applies to those subject to searches with such equipment as well as to those who operate the equipment. Thus, if when you are pregnant you have to fly, or if you work in facilities where you have to go through metal detectors daily, you need have no concern about increasing your risk of miscarriage or otherwise harming your pregnancy.

Lifestyle

We have just taken a look at the risks to early pregnancy from factors that might be present at work. Let's now take a look at the other half of our lives. What effects on pregnancy are there from what we eat, how we play, and how we spend our leisure time?

Diet

Food is often a major source of concern for pregnant women. When you are pregnant, you will probably want to know that you are eating the right sorts of food in the right amounts to provide optimal nutrition for your baby. You will also want to avoid food or beverages that might be harmful.

Fortunately, on the subject of food I am able to reassure you with confidence: I can think of no food or beverage that you can buy in an ordinary market—with the exception of alcoholic beverages—that is harmful to your pregnancy or will increase your risk of miscarriage. Although there continue to be frequent media reports that one kind of food or another is harmful to pregnancy, such reports are almost always false or misleading. This is by no means to say that if you eat a diet exclusively of Twinkies throughout your pregnancy your health or the health of your baby might not be affected. What I am saying is that consumption of ordinary foods and beverages—even occasional junk food and snacks—will not harm your pregnancy.

The same applies to meals at restaurants. You cannot imagine how many times I have been asked, "Is it okay to eat Chinese food during my pregnancy?" My standard reply is, "Well, about a billion and a half Chinese people eat it every day and many of them are pregnant. It doesn't seem to do them any harm." Although said in jest, my basic point does apply: No food, beverage, or cuisine eaten or drunk by large numbers of people—again with the exception of alcohol—has ever been shown to be harmful to pregnant women or to increase their risk of miscarriage.

There is one category of food whose safety in pregnancy has recently been called into question. Various state and federal officials have warned that the mercury levels of certain more oily deep-sea fishes—swordfish, tuna, mackerel, bluefish—are higher than desirable. They recommend that pregnant women limit their consumption of these fishes to no more than one serving a week.

Although I pass along this warning to you, I do have to admit to some skepticism about it. Thus far in my years of practice I have never yet had a mother or a pediatrician report back to me that a baby had mercury poisoning thought to be due to maternal fish consumption. But I have urged my patients to take this new report seriously. If over the next few years data confirms this risk of mercury poisoning from fish, I will have to alter my statement about the safety of all foods for pregnant women.

Do certain food deficiencies increase the risk of miscarriage? The short answer is no. If you eat a diet deficient in proteins, minerals, vitamins, or calories, you will put *your* health in jeopardy and you may increase the chances that your baby will be born prematurely or underweight—but you will not increase your risk of miscarriage.

Are there any foods, beverages, or food additives that, if consumed in large quantities, will increase your risk of miscarriage? With foods and beverages, no. If by food additives, however, one includes vitamins and minerals, then the answer is less clear. We know that an excessive intake of vitamin A can cause profound birth defects. What is not known—because it has not yet been studied—is whether excessive amounts of vitamin A increase the risk of miscarriage as well.

The bottom line is that foods and beverages consumed in moderate proportions pose no harm to pregnancy. This holds for cuisine worldwide. Again, exceptions are alcoholic beverages and possibly certain kinds of fish.

Exercise

The effect of exercise on pregnancy is one of the most controversial areas in obstetrics. Depending on one's biases, studies can be found to support any point of view. The issue is an especially relevant and important one today since so many women—pregnant or not—exercise, sometimes extensively. Although the benefits of exercise are well known and continue to be supported by new research, the effect of *intensive* exercise on pregnancy is less well understood.

Why might intensive exercise pose a threat to your pregnancy? It is because of the physiologic changes that occur to your body both during pregnancy and during exercise.

In the nonpregnant state, only about 5% of your total blood flow goes to your reproductive organs—your uterus, tubes, and ovaries. During pregnancy, however, the blood flow to these organs increases to approximately 20% of the total. Your heart rate and respiratory rate also increase. During later pregnancy, the growing size of your uterus displaces your abdominal organs up toward your diaphragm and lungs, thus decreasing your lung capacity.

Exercise itself also induces physiologic changes. The normal distribution of blood flow to your internal organs shifts to supply more blood to your exercising muscles. Your respiratory rate increases, as does your central body temperature. If you exercise for an extended period of time, your blood can become acidotic, meaning that it is deficient in oxygen and contains unhealthy amounts of metabolic waste products and carbon dioxide.

Most important, when you exercise during pregnancy, your body has to make a choice. When the demands of your exercising muscles reach a critical level, your body is forced to shunt blood away from your pregnant uterus to those muscles. Various studies have confirmed that blood flow to the pregnant uterus decreases under these circumstances. The key question is whether this redistribution of blood flow will harm your fetus. Here the data are controversial. For every study that shows a decrease in the baby's heart rate when its mother exercises—a sign that the baby may not be receiving sufficient oxygen—there are studies that show no significant change in fetal condition. In addition, there is the experience of thousands of female athletes who have continued their exercise programs while pregnant, even to the extent of running in marathons, with no reports of an increased rate of miscarriage. In fact, the American College of Obstetricians and Gynecologists, in their guidelines on exercise in pregnancy, do not recommend any limitations on exercise because of the risk of miscarriage or because a woman has had previous miscarriages.

My own feelings on this subject are slightly different. I have no concerns whatsoever about moderate levels of exercise in pregnancy. Indeed, I have always encouraged it, both to help pregnant women keep their muscles in shape and because of how well exercise make them feel. I do have concerns, however, about more extensive levels of exercise in pregnancy. This is an issue that regularly comes up for me with my patients, for many of my patients are superb athletes used to performing at peak levels of physical fitness. Moreover, because they live in Boston (as do I), many are interested in running in the Boston Marathon each year. When my patients ask me about the safety of this level of exercise in pregnancy, here is what I say:

The heart can pump only a certain amount of blood to the body's organs at any one time. If during peak exercise your muscles are demanding more oxygen, thus requiring more blood supply, this can come only at the expense of the blood supply to your other organs. When you are pregnant, much of the blood is taken from your uterus. We know from human and animal studies that decreasing blood flow to a pregnant uterus decreases the oxygen supply to a fetus. At what level does this diminished oxygen supply produce harmful effects on a fetus? We do not know for certain.

In addition, we know that at a certain level of exercise anyone, man or woman, requires more energy than can be produced solely by burning carbohydrates and fat with the air we breathe in. At this point, our bodies go into *anaerobic metabolism*, an alternative means the body has of producing energy. This can be harmful for pregnancy because the byproducts of anaerobic metabolism are various acidic substances that can alter the chemical environment in a mother's blood. These acidic chemicals are passed across the placenta to the fetus with potentially dangerous consequences. Thus my cautiousness about extreme exercising in pregnancy.

So what answer can I finally give you to the question "Does exercising increase the risk of miscarriage?" At low and moderate levels it does not. At peak levels of exercising, however, we do not know for certain. Because of this uncertainty, I would discourage you from engaging in intense physical activity while pregnant.

Sports

Almost all sports are safe for women during early pregnancy. Pregnant women successfully bike, swim, skate, and play tennis, softball, and soccer. You can safely enjoy most water sports, winter sports, and competitive team sports. The only warnings that I would give you are the following:

1. Contact sports should be avoided in pregnancy because they can result in severe direct lower abdominal trauma. Such sports include football, hockey, rugby, and lacrosse.
2. You might wish to skip downhill skiing in years you are pregnant. The reason for this? Although skiing is not itself dangerous to pregnancy, the injuries that often occur while skiing may be. Unfortunately, all too often skiers injure bones, joints, and internal organs. These injuries often require surgery to repair. Along with surgery comes the need for x-rays, anesthesia, medications, and other medical interventions that could increase risk to a fetus. Every winter I get one or two calls from Vermont or New Hampshire after one of my pregnant patients has suffered a ski-related injury. Although almost all these women eventually do well, their concern about their

pregnancy during their injury and its aftermath is intense. Try cross-country skiing instead.

Injury

The human body is ingeniously designed from an engineering point of view. Its vital structures are well protected. The heart is encased in a bony rib cage. The brain is shielded by the thick bones of the skull. The female reproductive organs are surrounded by the immensely strong pelvic bones.

(I have no answer for why the scrotum is as exposed as it is. The standard explanation is that this exposure serves as an air-conditioning system for sperm, which do not function well at body temperature. However, this explanation of a trade-off between temperature control and total vulnerability never really made sense to me.)

Anyway, because of the protection afforded to the early pregnant uterus by the pelvic bones, it is extremely rare that a first-trimester uterus is ever damaged by abdominal trauma. Certainly a uterus in later pregnancy, when it has risen above the pelvic bones, can suffer injury. For instance, if a pregnant woman in her second or third trimester were struck forcefully in the abdomen, such as with a baseball bat, the blow could directly injure her fetus, cause separation of the placenta from the wall of the uterus, or even rupture her uterus. Catastrophic injuries such as gunshot wounds or stabbings can cause a miscarriage if the wound were to penetrate the uterus.

But the normal sorts of physical injuries that you might experience in early pregnancy, such as accidentally banging your abdomen against a counter, being involved in a minor automobile accident, or being kicked or hit in the abdomen by one of your other children, has never been shown to increase the risk of miscarriage.

You may wonder whether using seat belts is a good idea during pregnancy. You might be concerned that during an accident the seat belt will press too hard on your lower abdomen. This is a vitally important issue. The answer is unambiguous: *The use of seat belts has prevented more injury and deaths, both to mothers and their fetuses, than any miscarriages that might possibly have been caused by their use.* It has never been shown that seatbelts, when used correctly, increase the risk of miscarriage. Moreover, if you are seriously injured in an accident because you were not restrained by a seat belt, the injury itself and the medical procedures you might require will put your fetus at much higher risk than the pressure of the seat belt on your lower abdomen ever could.

Electrical Shocks

Electrical shock injuries in pregnancy are uncommon. Most instances discussed in the medical literature involve women in the second and third trimesters of pregnancy. There have been a few reports of women who have suffered significant electrical shocks in the first trimester. In several of these cases the women's fetuses did die, resulting in miscarriages. However, such reports have all involved major electrical shocks: lightening, high-voltage exposures, and so on. There is no information to suggest that lesser shocks, such as those that merely cause transient discomfort, are harmful to fetuses. Nevertheless, if you were to experience an electrical shock significant enough to make you jump or to cause skin injury while you are pregnant, you should either go to your nearest emergency room for evaluation or report the injury to your obstetrician.

Sexual Activity

Over the years I have noticed an interaction that often occurs on those visits when my pregnant patients come to the office accompanied by their husbands. As I usually do in all obstetrical visits, I ask my patient how she is doing, measure the growth of her uterus, and listen for her baby's heart. If this is the first time that the father has heard his baby's heart, this usually provokes much excitement and many smiles. My patient will then generally have several questions she wishes to ask me and we will go over these. Just as our meeting is about to end, a look will often be exchanged between husband and wife or the husband will make a small attention-getting cough. Then, hesitantly, my patient will ask, "Doctor, is there any danger in our making love while I'm pregnant? My husband is worried that he will hurt the baby."

This common question is a very reasonable one, for three reasons. First, during intercourse the head of the penis does come into contact with the cervix and lower part of the uterus, sometimes forcefully. Second, during female orgasm a woman experiences intense uterine and pelvic muscle contractions. Third, one of the components of a man's semen is a mixture of closely related chemicals called prostaglandins. Prostaglandins can cause intense uterine contractions, so much so that in pharmacologic form prostaglandins are often used to induce labor.

Fortunately, however, most forms of sexual activity are perfectly safe during pregnancy. Sexual activity has not been shown to contribute to miscarriage. This applies to intercourse in almost any position, to oral sex, and to masturbation.

An exception to this would be if, during the first four months of your pregnancy, you were to have vaginal bleeding or spotting. As we discussed previously, such bleeding is usually due to a minor detachment of the edge of the placenta from your uterine wall. If you were to experience such bleeding, you should decrease your level of physical activity until the bleeding has stopped for several days. You should also abstain from sex until your doctor tells you it is safe, which is usually from three to seven days after the last show of blood. Other than such a situation, however, sexual activity, including orgasm, is perfectly safe during pregnancy.

Contraception

Often, women in the earliest weeks of pregnancy do not know they are pregnant and continue to use contraception during intercourse. Once they learn they are pregnant, they may worry that the contraceptive agents they have used have either damaged their babies or increased their risks of miscarriage.

For the most part, such concerns are groundless. For women taking the birth control pill, those few women who become pregnant while on it have no higher rate of miscarriage or birth defects than any other pregnant women. As for spermicides, there was controversy some years ago about nonoxyl-9, the active agent in diaphragm gels and vaginal foam, as to whether or not it increased the risk of miscarriage or birth defects when pregnancy occurred following its use. However, scores of studies have shown that the risk of such outcomes was not increased. It is now clear that women who become pregnant when using spermicides in any form are at no higher risk of miscarriage or birth defects than any other pregnant women.

With intrauterine devices (IUDs), however, the story is different. But first I must give you a little bit of background.

For many years, IUDs had a bad reputation because of difficulties encountered with one of the earliest versions, the Dalkon Shield. The Dalkon Shield, popular between twenty and thirty years ago, appeared to increase the risk of pelvic infection in women who used them. However, current IUDs have proven themselves to be excellent and safe methods of contraception over the last fifteen years. The pregnancy rate for women who have an IUD in place is virtually the same as if she were on the birth control pill: less than 1%. Moreover, side effects from IUDs are minimal: less than 5% of women with them get cramping or heavy periods. The vast majority of women with IUDs find that after a few months they forget they have them in.

But in those very rare cases when a woman with an IUD does become pregnant, the risk of miscarriage is significant: 50%. There is also a very high risk of a severe infection developing in the uterus and pelvis. Thus, should a woman become pregnant while she has an IUD in place she should have the IUD removed immediately. The removal process incurs the same 50% chance of miscarriage that the woman who keeps her IUD in place has—but virtually eliminates the risk of infection, whether or not the pregnancy survives. If the pregnancy does not miscarry after the IUD is removed, the pregnancy almost always goes on normally from that point.

Travel

Travel is generally safe in pregnancy. Using normal modes of transportation such as car, airplane, train, boat, or bus, even those pregnant women who travel long distances over many days do not seem to have an increased risk of miscarriage. There are, however, two things that I should warn you about regarding travel during pregnancy.

First, I do not recommend that you travel to regions remote from good medical care, especially during early or late pregnancy. If you were to have vaginal bleeding, start to miscarry, or go into preterm labor, you would not have access to the sophisticated medical facilities you would need. Therefore, while travel in the United States, Europe, and most major cities in the world is fine during pregnancy, I do not feel that it is safe for you to travel to remote islands or to countries where obtaining good medical care might be difficult.

Second, I urge you while traveling to stretch your legs regularly. This is especially important in the confined spaces of airplanes, cars, and buses. During pregnancy, a woman's blood becomes hypercoagulable—that is, it forms blood clots more easily. Because of this, blood clot formation in the legs—thrombosis—is a common complication of pregnancy. It is especially common when pregnant women sit in one position for many hours such as occurs during traveling. By walking or otherwise regularly stretching your leg muscles, you can significantly decrease your risk of developing such blood clots.

Hot Tubs, Saunas, and Jacuzzis

Because their use would feel so wonderful to a woman made uncomfortable by pregnancy symptoms, I feel badly that I have to recommend to my patients that they not use hot tubs, saunas, and Jacuzzis during their pregnancies. Unfortunately, it has been shown in multiple studies with experimental animals that increasing a pregnant animal's core body temperature sharply increases its risk of miscarrying and of its offspring having birth defects. This is the reason why it is so important that if you get a fever during pregnancy you try your best to reduce it with acetaminophen (Tylenol) and a cooling bath.

Hot showers are safe for limited periods because in them a person's entire body is not continuously in contact with the hot water. Tub baths are safe to the extent that the bath water cools over time. If the bath were continually reheated by adding more hot water every few minutes, then, as with a hot tub, the risk of elevation of core body temperature would increase.

Heating pads and waterbeds are safe to use during pregnancy.

Stress and Anxiety

As a psychiatrist friend of mine once told me, "If you don't have stress and anxiety in your life, you're not paying attention." All of us are, of course, subject to stress and anxiety at home, at work, and in all our interpersonal relationships. Some circumstances engender more stress than others. Going through a divorce, having an ill child, losing a parent or spouse, and being fired or laid off from one's job are all common, intense sources of stress that can drive people to the edge of their ability to cope.

In the context of pregnancy, however, there is good news: *Stress does not seem to increase the risk of miscarriage*. True, over the years, multiple studies of people under stress have shown an increase in certain hormone markers. But it has never been shown that a rise in any of these hormones increases the risk of pregnancy loss.

Moreover, there is the evidence from the "natural experiments" of worldwide disasters that occur all too frequently. An example of this can be seen in the reports of birth statistics from various German-occupied countries during World War II. At that time, in countries such as Holland, people were living on starvation rations and suffered intense emotional and physical harassment. Yet although there was an increase in preterm births and although babies born during those years were smaller than average, the rate of miscarriage was no higher than it had been before the war.

Tobacco, Alcohol, and Drugs

We know that tobacco, alcohol, and drugs are bad for pregnancy. But do they increase the risk of miscarriage, and if so, why?

Tobacco

Smoking cigarettes has clearly been shown to increase the risk of miscarriage. This risk begins at the level of a half-pack a day—ten cigarettes. Above this level, the risk is dose-related, that is, the more a pregnant woman smokes, the greater her chance of having a miscarriage. The combination of tobacco and alcohol enhances this harmful effect. *How much* the risk of miscarriage is increased because of smoking in pregnancy has not yet been determined precisely. Estimates, however, range from a 30 to a 100% (two-fold) increase, resulting in a 26 to 40% miscarriage rate for pregnant smokers instead of the average miscarriage rate of 20% for nonsmokers. Smoking in pregnancy is also known to cause other major problems: premature birth, abnormally small babies, and an increase in respiratory problems in the children of smoking mothers.

The reason smoking increases the risk of miscarriage has to do with the contraction of blood vessels in the uterus and umbilical cord caused by nicotine. This condition has been demonstrated in many animal experiments. Contraction of these blood vessels of course decreases the amount of oxygen and nutrients that reach the fetus. It also interferes with the fetus's ability to eliminate carbon dioxide and other waste products.

Cigarette smoking also puts pregnancy at risk by increasing the amount of carboxyhemoglobin in the mother's blood. Carboxyhemoglobin latches onto oxygen more firmly than does regular hemoglobin. Thus, if a pregnant woman smokes, her carboyxhemoglobin-laden blood avidly retains its oxygen and does not transfer as much of it to her fetus as it would if she did not smoke.

Women who smoke should of course stop while pregnant. Abstinence would improve their health and be better for the health of their babies. But giving up the addiction to nicotine is not easy. Having observed over the years patients—and friends—who smoke, I know that it is extremely difficult for them to quit. Therefore, I try to make the recommendations I give them achievable ones. Here is what I tell them:

Try to quit smoking altogether if you can. But if you can't, at least reduce the amount you smoke to a bare minimum. Pick the few times each day—with breakfast, after dinner, just before bed—when you feel you absolutely have to have a cigarette. Try to limit your smoking to just those few times, at least during your pregnancy. Then after the pregnancy is over we can discuss how to help you stop smoking entirely.

Although the use of nicotine substitutes to help smoking works very well, its safety in pregnancy is unclear. The American College of Obstetricians and Gynecologists recommends using such agents in pregnancy only if prior attempts to stop smoking have been unsuccessful and if the pregnant smoker has been unable to reduce the amount she smokes to less than ten to fifteen cigarettes per day.

Caffeine

Although people who drink three or more cups of coffee a day usually do not think of themselves as "drug addicts," they are in fact probably addicted to caffeine. Caffeine is a drug in every sense of the word. It produces physical effects on our bodies and alters our mental state. When we don't have our normal supply of it, we often experience side effects such as headache and tremulousness. Of all the addictive drugs, however, caffeine is certainly the least harmful.

But does caffeine cause miscarriage? Multiple large-scale well-designed studies have shown that the consumption of two or less cups of coffee or tea every day does not increase the risk of miscarriage. Larger amounts than this *do* increase this risk.

Studies have shown that a safe amount of daily caffeine consumption in pregnancy is about 200 mg per day. Thus from the following we can estimate what would be an allowable amount of caffeine-containing substances per day for a pregnant woman:

- A cup of regular American coffee has approximately 100 milligrams of caffeine.
- Tea contains roughly half the amount of caffeine per cup as does coffee, or 50 mg.
- A serving of chocolate—from 6 to 8 ozs—or a can of regular cola contains roughly 50 mg per serving.

So feel free to continue to drink coffee or tea in moderation—up to two cups a day—while you are pregnant. But watch the cumulative effect of coffee, tea, colas, and chocolate so that you stay below the 200 mg a day caffeine threshold that is known to be safe.

Alcohol

As is true of cigarette smoking, there is clear evidence that alcohol consumption in anything other than the smallest quantities increases the risk of miscarriage. But what exactly constitutes "smallest quantities" is a matter of controversy. Some studies indicate that from one to two drinks a week are safe during pregnancy. Other studies indicate that any amount of alcohol increases the risk of miscarriage and has other injurious consequences for the pregnancy.

Alcohol is directly toxic to fetal cells, especially neurologic tissue. In addition, as with cigarettes, alcohol impairs blood circulation to the uterus, thus decreasing the amount of oxygen the fetus gets. Women who drink heavily in early pregnancy have higher than average miscarriage rates. Their babies are also at great risk for developing fetal alcohol syndrome—a pattern of birth defects that include growth restriction, behavioral disturbances, and structural abnormalities of the face. Just as worrisome but more subtle are the intellectual changes in the children of women who consume alcohol during pregnancy. Current studies show that even as little as two to three drinks a week over many weeks of pregnancy may cause a decrease in eventual intellectual capacity. Because of such studies, many obstetrical experts recommend against even low levels of alcohol consumption during pregnancy.

While certainly not an advocate of heavy drinking during pregnancy—or at any time—I'm not sure that a low level of alcohol consumption—one to two drinks a week—is as dangerous for pregnant women as it is currently thought to be. Certainly alcohol has the potential to harm many organs—the liver, the brain, the heart. But to cause such harm, one must consume large quantities of alcohol frequently over a long period. Usually this level of drinking is done at the expense of the ingestion of other healthy foods.

We know that in Europe and elsewhere in the world pregnant women regularly consume small quantities of alcohol. Despite this, I've never seen reports suggesting that there are large numbers of French or German or Italian men, women, and children who are intellectually impaired because of the alcohol consumed by their mothers during pregnancy. Interestingly, although most American studies looking at the role of alcohol consumption in pregnancy show harmful effects even for small amounts consumed, these results have not been replicated in most European and Australian studies.

The above discusses alcohol consumption when you know you are pregnant. But what if you had a few drinks before discovering that you were pregnant? Since alcohol is a common part of our culture, it is not at all surprising that many of my patients tell me at their first obstetrical visit that they had one or more drinks before they knew they were pregnant. Occasionally, a pregnant patient even admits to having been flat-out drunk. The key, I am able to reassure them, is the frequency of consumption. Fortunately, there is no evidence whatsoever that sporadic ingestion of alcohol—even an instance or two of heavy drinking—causes an increase in miscarriages or harms a fetus.

Recreational Drugs

Drugs, with the possible exception of marijuana, are known to be harmful in pregnancy. Some of this harm is caused by the drugs themselves. Some is due to the behaviors involved in acquiring and using these substances. Over the years, there has been much confusion about the effects of drugs on pregnancy. Some of this confusion has been deliberately fostered in a well-meaning but misguided attempt to scare pregnant women away from drug use. Let's take a look at what reliable information we do have on illicit drug use and pregnancy.

Some drugs do have direct harmful effects on pregnancy. Cocaine, for example, can cause intense spasm of blood vessels in organs such as the uterus and heart and result in decreased blood flow and oxygenation to these organs. In a pregnant uterus, this condition can cause fetal distress. In anyone, even star athletes, it can result in a heart attack.

Cocaine use in pregnancy has also been associated with placental abruption, a condition in which the placenta is sheared off the uterine wall. In late pregnancy, placental abruption can cause stillbirth and severe maternal bleeding. In early pregnancy, it can cause miscarriage.

Heroin and other narcotics cause addiction in babies while they are still in the uterus. After birth, these babies have to go through a long and difficult detoxification process. New drugs with the potential for damage to pregnancy—such as Ecstasy—come along regularly. But until sufficient data on their use in pregnancy is accumulated, we won't know specifically what their effects will be.

Drugs can also be harmful because of the circumstances by which they are obtained and consumed. The use of shared or dirty needles for injecting intravenous drugs is one of the leading causes of the spread of AIDS and hepatitis. Trading sex for drugs leaves women subject to physical abuse and the spread of sexually transmitted disease. Street drugs are often not sold in pure form and may contain substances that are either poisonous or can cause skin and blood vessel infections. Finally, the lifestyle of the drug user and the side effects that drugs produce, such as lethargy or agitation, can interfere with a woman's motivation and ability to obtain timely prenatal care.

It has often been stated in the past that the use of marijuana and LSD damaged the chromosomal structure of sperm and eggs, leading to birth defects and miscarriage. These claims are false. Although these two drugs can certainly cause family, employment, and social problems, there is no consistent evidence to show that they are directly harmful to pregnancy. I say this for two reasons.

First, there are no studies that show a definite relationship between LSD or marijuana use and miscarriage or congenital abnormalities. An old study—from 1972—showed "chromosomal breakage"—a type of chromosomal structural abnormality—in some cells of mothers and their babies when LSD had been used during pregnancy. But there was no increase in miscarriages or of babies in this group born with congenital abnormalities. In addition, the *sort* of chromosome structural abnormalities observed in this study have never been associated with birth defects.

Second, my career in obstetrics started just as the baby boomers were having their children. These survivors of the 1960s and 1970s were the greatest users of marijuana and LSD in history. Yet there is not the slightest bit of evidence that the pregnancies of these millions of former recreational drug users demonstrated an increased risk of miscarriage, preterm labor, or children with birth defects.

Conclusion

In this chapter I have looked at a variety of events and circumstances to which pregnant women are commonly exposed to see whether such exposures increase their risk of miscarriage. I have pointed out those areas in the home and work environment that have been associated with miscarriage, and I have discussed the areas that appear to be safe.

Despite all the risks I have discussed, it is vital that you not lose sight of the basic fact about miscarriages I keep going back to: The vast majority are caused by chromosomal miscombination at the time of conception. Pregnancies in which the fetus's chromosomes are normal generally do not miscarry despite any harmful environmental exposures a pregnant woman might have. Although in this chapter I have looked at circumstances in which the *risk* of miscarriage is increased, environmental and lifestyle issues remain an uncommon cause of the loss of an early pregnancy.

CHAPTER 6

The Influence of Health Problems on Miscarriage

AS I HAVE TRIED TO MAKE CLEAR SO FAR IN THIS BOOK, pregnancy—although a natural process—is a complex one. Many things have to go right for a healthy egg and sperm to be produced and to meet, and for the newly formed embryo to implant, grow, and thrive. Of course, the environment in which this all takes place—the mother—has to be healthy as well. Therefore, it should come as no surprise that if a woman has health problems her ability to maintain a pregnancy may be compromised.

In this chapter I will take a look at what effect a woman's medical problems have on her chances of having a miscarriage. I will also discuss how a father's health can affect miscarriage, although fortunately such effects are rare. All in all, health problems with parents are the cause of only a small minority of early pregnancy losses, approximately 2 to 3%. Nevertheless, if you or your partner has one of these conditions you should know what impact it might have on your pregnancy and whether your risk of miscarriage is increased.

Medical diseases

Pregnant women are subject to the same sorts of medical problems as are all women in the reproductive age group. But only certain diseases consistently have been seen to affect pregnancies and increase the risk of miscarriages. Below, I will discuss the most important of these.

Diabetes

Diabetes is one of the most common of all medical problems. Between 15 and 20 million Americans suffer from it to some degree. Approximately 7 to 8% of all adults either have diabetes or will develop it during their lives.

The basic problem in diabetes is that the body is not able to handle sugar in the blood properly. Sugar, along with other chemical substances, is the by-product of food digestion. As food is broken down in the bowel, sugar—along with fats, proteins, vitamins, and minerals—is absorbed into the cells of the bowel wall. From there it passes into the many small blood vessels that run through the bowel wall and on to the liver.

The organ that controls the level of sugar in the blood is the pancreas. It produces insulin, a chemical that causes sugar to be transported from the blood stream into cells throughout the body. In diabetes, however, either the pancreas does not produce sufficient insulin or the cells of the body become resistant to the insulin that is present, requiring more and more of it to keep blood sugar under control.

The reason diabetes causes so many medical problems is that exposure to high blood sugar levels over many years damages small blood vessels throughout the body—the "microvasculature." This results in decreased blood flow to the tissues served by these small blood vessels. Thus the tissues downstream from the damaged blood vessels receive an inadequate supply of oxygen and nutrients. They also accumulate waste products and excess tissue fluid, which is why people who have had diabetes for many years have an increased risk of heart attack—decreased oxygen to the heart muscle—and are prone to ulceration of the feet and legs—decreased blood flow and oxygen supply to these tissues.

If you have diabetes, it can threaten your pregnancy in several ways:

1. High blood sugar levels can have a direct toxic effect on your fetus. We know, for instance, that the less well controlled a diabetic's blood sugar levels are in pregnancy the higher is the chance either that a miscarriage will occur or that a fetus will die, resulting in a stillbirth. We also know that episodic high peaks of blood sugar can cause miscarriage or stillbirth.

2. Damage to the small blood vessels and capillaries of the placenta during the course of pregnancy can decrease oxygen and nutrient supply to the fetus. The cumulative effect of this damage is that later in pregnancy the ability of the placenta to nourish and supply oxygen to the baby diminishes significantly. This is why obstetricians deliver the babies of diabetic mothers before or right at term. The longer a pregnancy is exposed to excess sugar levels, the greater is the chance that placental function will deteriorate. This condition will eventually result in decreased transfer of oxygen and nutrients to the fetus and can lead to fetal distress or stillbirth.

3. Although babies of diabetic mothers can grow quite large, this is not a result of how well the placenta transfers nutrients. Rather, it is because the fetus stores the excess sugar it receives from the mother as fat. Thus, if your blood sugar levels are high, your baby could grow excessively large. This excess weight is why the cesarean section rate is higher for babies of diabetic mothers and why for these babies there is an increased rate of fetal injury during vaginal deliveries.

4. Babies born of diabetic mothers have a much higher rate of birth defects. This is most likely due to the effects of high blood sugar levels on the differentiation and migration of developing cells in the early embryo. While the birth defect rate for nondiabetic women is 3 to 4%, the rate for infants born to mothers with diabetes is 8 or 9%—more than double.

Until about forty years ago, your chances of becoming pregnant and having healthy children were dismal if you had diabetes. Even if you were able to become pregnant—not easy with diabetes—you would likely miscarry. If you were able to get past the miscarriage stage it was likely that your baby would die in the second or third trimester or that your baby would be stillborn following labor. If you actually did deliver a live baby, there was a significant chance that it would have a birth defect. Along the way, it was probable that you would become very ill with a serious medical problem such as kidney disease, high blood pressure, or severe diabetic shock (referred to medically as "diabetic ketoacidosis"). The latter comes about when excessive blood sugar levels increase the acidity of the blood. It was an unusual event for a healthy baby to be born to a well diabetic mother.

Since the advent of better techniques for monitoring blood sugar levels and for controlling these levels with insulin and other medications, the outlook for diabetic women wishing to become mothers has improved dramatically. If you have diabetes, your pregnancy still entails many risks. You still are subject to a higher rate of miscarriage, stillbirth, and birth defects, and you yourself could suffer serious illness. But these complications occur much less often than in the past. Diabetic women today can and do routinely have healthy pregnancies and normal children.

If you are a diabetic and you want to become pregnant, it is vitally important that your blood sugar levels be under good control before you conceive. Multiple studies have shown that if your blood sugar levels are normal before conception and during early pregnancy (the first twenty-one days), the chances that you will suffer a miscarriage or have a baby with birth defects approaches that of women without diabetes.

During pregnancy, "tight" control of blood sugars will reduce the risk of fetal death and excessive fetal size. It will also decrease your risk of experiencing the kind of pregnancy complications mentioned above: hypertension, kidney failure, and diabetic shock.

If you have diabetes, therefore, you should be in touch with an obstetrician *before* you try to become pregnant. In this way, you can be thoroughly evaluated before conceiving to see what, if any, other health problems you may have that might affect your pregnancy. Your blood sugar levels will be carefully monitored to see how well your body's blood sugar control mechanisms are functioning. If adjustments need to be made in your diet, if you need to be on medications that lower blood sugar, or if the doses of medications you are currently on have to be changed, this can all be done before you become pregnant. In this way, by the time you conceive, your blood sugars will be at normal levels and your risk of having a miscarriage or of your baby's being born with birth defects will be significantly reduced.

Two technical points: First, in addition to checking your blood sugar levels as part of your prenatal evaluation, you will likely also have blood drawn for a test called hemoglobin A1C. The hemoglobin A1C test measures the *average* of your blood sugar levels over the previous month. After all, what will affect your baby most when you become pregnant is not intermittent blood sugar spikes and dips but the average blood sugar level to which it is exposed over time.

Second, the main medicine used to control blood sugar levels is the same substance your body uses: insulin. The insulin used to treat diabetes comes from animal sources and is given by injection. It is almost exactly the same chemically as the insulin produced by your own pancreas. Insulin has been in general use for over seventy years. It has been used by millions of pregnant women and has not been seen to increase the risk of miscarriage, birth defects, or other pregnancy problems.

Until the late 1990s, it had been thought that the other category of medications that control blood sugar, oral medications, were not safe for use in pregnancy. However, recent research reports have begun to refute this. Tests performed on one such oral blood sugar lowering medication, glyburide, have shown it to be both safe in pregnancy and effective in controlling blood sugar in pregnant women. If further studies confirm these findings—and perhaps show that other oral blood-sugar-control medications are also safe—there will be several new options available for blood sugar control in diabetic pregnancies.

Thyroid Disease

Your thyroid gland lies directly over your voice box. It produces a hormone called thyroxine that plays a major role in controlling your body's metabolism. If your blood levels of thyroxine are too high—hyperthyroidism—your body goes into overdrive. It burns nutrients too quickly, causes your heart to race, and can cause you to have nervous tremors. If you produce too little thyroxine—hypothyroidism—your body behaves sluggishly. Reflexes slow, weight increases, and skin and hair thicken.

Both hyper- and hypothyroidism can cause problems in pregnancy. Hyperthyroidism can lead to preterm labor and can cause hypertension and cardiac disease in the mother. If hyperthyroidism becomes too severe, a shock-like state called "thyroid storm" may develop. Thyroid storm is marked by hypertension, severe vomiting and diarrhea, heart failure, and very high fever, all leading to general collapse.

*Hypo*thyroidism can cause excessive weight gain, separation of the placenta from the uterine wall (placental abruption), and stillbirth. Most important, hypothyroidism in pregnancy can lead to infants with impaired neuromuscular coordination and mental retardation.

Fortunately, it does not appear that hyper- or hypothyroidism in themselves put your pregnancy at increased risk for miscarriage. However, the conditions that *cause* the thyroid to be over- or underactive may do so. Let me explain.

There are several reasons why a thyroid gland can make too much or too little hormone:

1. The thyroid gland may grow larger than normal, thus increasing the number of cells producing hormone.
2. The control mechanism for thyroid production—the release of a protein called thyroid stimulating hormone (TSH) from the pituitary gland—may itself be over- or underactive. This would result in the thyroid gland's producing either too much or too little thyroxine.
3. A person's immune system may make antibodies against its own thyroid gland. Called Graves' disease, this condition is a relatively common cause of thyroid malfunction. The damage caused by the antibodies eventually depletes the number of thyroxine-producing cells. If the growth of new cells does not keep up with the rate of cellular destruction, the amount of thyroxine produced by the thyroid gland diminishes. The result is hypothyroidism.

For reasons that are not clearly understood, it is only when autoantibodies cause hyper- or hypothyroidism that the rate of miscarriage increases. Since this increase in miscarriage rate is not seen with other causes of high or low thyroxine levels, researchers have concluded that the autoantibodies—and not the level of thyroxine—are responsible.

What do you do if you have thyroid disease and want to become pregnant? Since thyroid abnormalities are one of the most common medical problems that my pregnant patients have, this question comes up frequently. The answer depends on what your thyroxine blood levels currently are and on exactly what kind of thyroid disease you have.

First, your level of thyroxine has to be adjusted into normal range. If it is too high, your thyroid gland's production of hormone must be suppressed. Several medicines can achieve this goal. There are, however, severe cases of hyperthyroidism not responsive to medical treatment. In such situations surgical excision of part or most of the thyroid gland may be necessary to control thyroxine production.

If your thyroxine level is too low, you will need to take thyroid medication to raise the level of thyroxine in your blood stream to normal.

Next, the *cause* of your thyroid abnormality must be determined and treated. The possibility of thyroid tumors must be ruled out. Your pituitary gland must be assessed to see whether it is producing the correct amount of TSH, the hormone that directly controls thyroxine production. Finally, the possibility of antibody-induced thyroid dysfunction must be checked and, if present, treated.

Fortunately, with proper evaluation and treatment of hyper- and hypothyroidism, your chances of having a normal pregnancy and of not miscarrying are exactly the same as those of any other woman.

Asthma

Asthma, like diabetes, is an extremely common disease. It is caused by the air passages in the lungs undergoing spasm more readily than normal. This results in wheezing and difficulty breathing. Severe asthma attacks can prevent the body from getting enough oxygen. However, with the excellent medications available today, most people with asthma are able to control their symptoms to the point that it rarely interferes with their lives.

What specifically causes someone to have asthma is not well understood. However, it is known that asthma is worsened by smoking, air pollution, and allergic irritants. Obviously, if you have asthma, it is important for you to avoid such exacerbating factors. It is especially important that you not smoke.

Fortunately, asthma does not increase the risk of miscarriage. In addition, the medicines used to treat asthma—inhalers, oral bronchodilators, steroids, and others—are all perfectly safe during pregnancy. Therefore, if you have asthma and want to become pregnant, you can be assured that your chances of having a miscarriage are no higher than that of other women.

Epilepsy

Epilepsy is a condition in which the electrical signals that control certain portions of the brain malfunction. When this happens, a flurry of abnormal nerve impulses are sent to the rest of the brain and to muscles and nerves around the body. These can cause seizures, loss of consciousness, tremulousness, incontinence of stool or urine, and tongue biting. During pregnancy, seizures result in decreased blood flow to the fetus.

Epilepsy is associated with an increase in the risk of miscarriage. One study, performed in Staten Island, New York, shows this unequivocally. The miscarriage rate of a large group of women with epilepsy was compared to that of their sisters who did not have a seizure disorder. The results of the study demonstrated clearly that the women with epilepsy had a higher rate of miscarriage than their nonepileptic sisters. Since the pairs of sisters were from the same genetic and environmental background, this natural experiment was able to test the effects of epilepsy on miscarriage as an isolated factor.

It has also been known for many years that the rate of birth defects in women with epilepsy is almost three times greater than normal: from 8 to 11% as opposed to the baseline rate of 3 to 4%. Most often, these birth defects are minor limb and facial abnormalities. Sometimes, however, they can be more serious conditions such as congenital heart defects, cleft lip and palate, and microcephaly—smaller than normal head size. Still, the vast majority of pregnant women who have epilepsy— roughly 90%—have healthy pregnancies and normal babies.

What we have not known until now is whether the increase in birth defects and miscarriages seen in epileptic women has to do with the epilepsy itself or to the potent medications that almost all epileptic women take to control their seizures. This question has been a subject of research for several decades. Recent studies, however, may have provided an answer to this question—although if you have epilepsy, the results are not encouraging: It appears that epilepsy *and* the medications taken to control seizures both increase the rate of birth defects and miscarriages.

But despite this increased risk to fetuses caused by antiseizure medications, the danger of seizures to the health of an epilectic mother and her fetus is so great that stopping these medications during pregnancy is not a safe option.

The bottom line? The vast majority of pregnant women with epilepsy do well in pregnancy and have healthy babies. But if you have epilepsy, you face an increased risk of miscarrying, and your child is at greater risk for birth defects. It is vitally important that you discuss these risks with both your obstetrician and your neurologist before becoming pregnant.

Hypertension

Hypertension—elevated blood pressure—is a disease that affects every organ of the body. Although generally seen in older men and women, it occurs often enough in women of childbearing age to be a major issue in pregnancy.

The good news is that women with hypertension are at no greater risk of miscarriage than other pregnant women. Hypertension can, however, cause serious problems in later pregnancy. Elevated blood pressure can result in kidney damage, heart failure, and, if severe enough, stroke.

More commonly, however, hypertension in pregnancy is associated with the development of a condition called toxemia, also known as preeclampsia, or pregnancy-induced hypertension. Toxemia generally occurs in late pregnancy and is characterized by elevated blood pressure, massive swelling, and large amounts of protein in the mother's urine. In years past, toxemia often progressed until the mother developed seizures or until the fetus was stillborn. Nowadays, however, toxemia is almost always detected early and serious complications prevented.

If you were diagnosed with toxemia, your obstetrician would take measures either to control your symptoms or, if your pregnancy was far enough along, to deliver you early. Ending the pregnancy is the only sure way to end the toxemic process. No matter what the gestational age of your baby, if measures such as bed rest and high blood pressure medication did not stop the progression of your toxemia, your baby would have to be delivered. Similarly, if fetal monitoring showed deterioration of your fetus's condition, early delivery would be necessary.

Colitis and Irritable Bowel Syndrome

Colitis and irritable bowel syndrome (IBS)—basically different degrees of the same disease—are common conditions in young women. They cause diarrhea, blood and mucus in the stool, and abdominal pain. Fortunately, colitis and IBS do not increase the risk of miscarriage and are not worsened by pregnancy. They are treated by diet or medications, the majority of which are safe for use during pregnancy.

In extreme situations, such as in Crohn's disease or ulcerative colitis, very strong medications such as methotrexate—also used to treat cancer—may be necessary. The toxicity of these medications can put a pregnancy at risk for miscarriage. But except for these unusual circumstances, if you have colitis or IBS, your risk of having a miscarriage or other negative pregnancy outcome is no higher than anyone else's.

Anemia

Anemia is not a disease in and of itself but rather is a symptom. It is defined as a decrease in either the number of red cells in the blood or in the total amount of iron carried by the blood. Both conditions have the same end result: reduced ability to bring oxygen to the tissues. The key issue with anemia is to find its cause. This could be inadequate blood production—something wrong with the bone marrow where blood is made—or an increase in blood loss, such as happens in chronic bowel bleeding or heavy menstrual periods.

Anemia does not increase the risk of miscarriage. If you have anemia, however, it makes being pregnant more difficult. It will increase your level of fatigue, it can make you short of breath, and it can make your body's job of oxygenating your tissues and those of your baby more difficult. The saving grace is that the fetus is very effective at getting what it needs. Its hemoglobin—the oxygen-binding component of blood—is designed to grasp oxygen more avidly than is your hemoglobin. Therefore, in the placenta, where the baby's and your blood flow side by side, the baby's blood extracts more than its share of oxygen from your blood.

If you have anemia, its cause should be sought out and corrected. In addition, your doctor will almost certainly start you on a regimen of iron supplements and multivitamins to build your blood level back up to normal. But even if you have moderate to severe levels of anemia, your risk of miscarriage is not increased.

Obesity

There are varying definitions of the term "obesity." The general consensus is that a man or woman is obese if he or she weighs more than 20% above the average for his or her height and build.

Obesity plays a significant role in reproductive system disorders and does increase the risk of miscarriage. In addition, obesity can interfere with hormone production, ovulation, and attempts to conceive.

There is another condition often found in women who are overweight which is also associated with reproductive difficulties: polycystic ovarian syndrome (PCOS). PCOS is marked by an imbalance in the production of the hormones necessary for ovulation—FSH and LH—and by the formation of multiple small ovarian cysts. Women with PCOS have difficulty conceiving and difficulty in sustaining early pregnancies.

While it is relatively easy to understand how PCOS can lead to miscarriage, why obesity in and of itself does the same thing is less clear. What is clear is that obese women both with and without polycystic ovarian syndrome have an increased risk of miscarriage.

Chronic Diseases

Many diseases, most of them fortunately not common, cause long-term illness and debilitation. Such conditions as kidney failure, chronic heart disease, tuberculosis, AIDS, and cancer deplete the body's resources and suppress bodily functions such as ovulation.

Surprisingly, women with all these conditions can and do become pregnant. However, the combination of pregnancy and chronic disease makes for extremely high-risk pregnancies. If you have such a chronic disease and are pregnant, most of the problems you will experience will involve the growth and well-being of your fetus in the third trimester. With the exception of AIDS, your having a chronic disease does not seem to increase your risk of having a miscarriage. Of course, if you are so ill that you do not ovulate, pregnancy will not be an issue. But if you do ovulate and conceive, your chances of having a miscarriage are not increased above normal.

Psychiatric Illness

Emotional and psychiatric illnesses are frequently seen in pregnancy, most often in women who have them and then become pregnant. These illnesses range in severity from mild depression over disappointing life events to profound schizophrenia requiring institutionalization. Although these conditions can be extremely debilitating for a pregnant woman, there is no evidence that they lead to miscarriage. Also, despite years of worry about the safety of psychiatric medications, it turns out that the ones used most commonly are not associated either with miscarriage or with birth defects. Even relatively new drugs such as Prozac, Zoloft, Paxil, and Celexa appear to be safe for pregnancy.

If you are pregnant and suffer from depression or other psychiatric illness, it is likely that whatever medications you are on can be continued during your pregnancy without fear of causing miscarriage or harming your baby. You should, of course, consult your psychiatrist and obstetrician about the specifics of your own situation.

One of the most common concerns pregnant women have is that severe emotional stress might harm their early pregnancy. As discussed in detail in Chapter 5, this is not the case.

Hereditary and Genetic Diseases

In the chapter on the genetic causes of miscarriage (Chapter 2), I briefly discussed various diseases linked to chromosomes. Such conditions as cystic fibrosis, phenylketonuria, Tay-Sachs syndrome, thalassemia, and sickle cell disease all cause major birth defects or severe childhood illness. As far as researchers have been able to measure, however, the damage caused by these diseases does not appear to act on fetuses early enough to cause miscarriage.

Certainly if you have a family history of a genetic disease, you need to find out more about it. This is best done by setting up a meeting with a genetic counselor. He or she will take a detailed family history and perhaps order laboratory tests for you and your close relatives. In this way, as much information as possible can be gathered about your risk of having children affected by a hereditary condition.

I am often told by my patients who have had a miscarriage that their mothers had similar problems "holding onto a pregnancy." They wonder whether miscarriages might "run in the family."

I am able to reassure them that they generally do not. The only exception is the unusual situation in which my patient or her partner has a chromosomal translocation. Such a condition might indeed have been inherited from a parent in whom it caused miscarriages. However, if your chromosomes are tested and found to be normal, a history of miscarriage or infertility in your mother will have no effect on your ability to become pregnant or to sustain your pregnancy.

Paternal Factors

Medical problems with fathers do not seem to increase the risk of miscarriage. This should not be surprising. Since the only contribution a man makes toward pregnancy is his sperm (some women swear that this is the only contribution men make toward childrearing as well!), once the sperm are released from his body the man's medical condition is irrelevant. He can affect pregnancy only by the chromosomal composition of the sperm he deposits or by infection carried in his semen. A man with significant medical diseases such as diabetes, thyroid disease, or cancer may be so debilitated that he is unable to make viable sperm or unable to ejaculate so that the sperm can reach an egg. But if he accomplishes both these tasks, the embryos formed from his sperm are no more likely to result in miscarriage than any other embryos.

Antibodies and the Immune System

In previous chapters I have discussed what antibodies are, how the body differentiates between "self" and "nonself," and how the immune system works. As medical scientists learn more about miscarriages, it is becoming increasingly clear just how large a role the immune system plays in whether a pregnancy will be successful. But because these issues play a larger role in causing *recurrent* miscarriages—defined as three or more consecutive miscarriages—I will discuss them in Chapter 7, which specifically deals with this topic.

Surgery

Women who are pregnant develop conditions requiring surgery as often as anyone else. Appendicitis, for instance, occurs as frequently in pregnant women as it does in nonpregnant women. Some conditions, such as inflammation of the gallbladder, actually occur more often during pregnancy. What happens to you if you need surgery when you are pregnant? Will it increase your chances of having a miscarriage? And what about anesthetic agents, pain medications, and postoperative therapies?

Fortunately, surgery does not increase your risk of miscarriage. This is true not only of the operation itself but also of the anesthetic agents given to you during your surgery.

The most common surgical condition affecting women in the reproductive age group is appendicitis. It occurs in approximately 1 out of 1,800 pregnancies. A woman's chances of having appendicitis are not altered because she is pregnant. However, because of the changing position of the appendix as pregnancy advances—it gets pushed up higher in the abdomen—appendicitis becomes harder to diagnose. This delay in diagnosis occasionally leads to an appendix rupturing before surgery is performed. The complications of infection, high fever, bowel obstruction, and direct inflammation of the uterus, tubes, and ovaries following a ruptured appendix can lead to miscarriage. Most of the time, however, appendicitis in pregnancy is diagnosed and treated promptly. In these cases the risk of having a miscarriage is not increased.

Likewise, surgery for most other conditions—gallbladder disease, ovarian tumors, hernias—does not increase the risk of miscarriage. In addition, the method of anesthesia used—general anesthesia, spinal anesthesia, intravenous sedation, or regional block—does not seem to matter. None of them has been shown to cause miscarriage.

The general safety of surgery in early pregnancy does not necessarily apply to surgery involving the reproductive organs. For instance, a woman who is seven or eight weeks pregnant might have ruptured an ovarian corpus luteum cyst. If she is in severe pain or has signs of significant abdominal blood loss, surgery would be necessary to remove the ruptured cyst and stop the bleeding. A miscarriage might result—but not because surgery had been performed. It would be because the source of progesterone maintaining the pregnancy—the corpus luteum—had been removed before the placenta has taken over progesterone production.

(In such a situation an attempt would be made to give the pregnant woman oral, vaginal, or intramuscular progesterone to replace that no longer made by the corpus luteum. If the pregnancy did not miscarry, progesterone would be administered until ten weeks gestation, after which time the placenta will have taken over the role as the main producer of pregnancy hormones. The progesterone supplementation would then be stopped.)

Over the last two decades, I and most other surgeons and gynecologists have been performing an increasing amount of surgery through laparoscopes. Laparoscopic surgery involves the placement of a long, thin telescope-like device into the abdomen through a very small (from half an inch to one inch) abdominal incision. Other similarly shaped instruments with specific functions—cutting, holding, cauterizing, and so forth—are placed into the abdomen through similar small incisions. Through the laparoscope I can perform many kinds of surgery: remove cysts, free adhesions, perform appendectomies, and much more. The major benefits to my patients are smaller, less painful incisions and decreased recovery time. One of the technical issues involved in using laparoscopes in the abdomen and pelvis is that it is necessary to lift the abdominal wall out of the way so that underlying structures can be clearly seen. This is done by filling up the abdominal cavity with carbon dioxide inserted through a small channel in the laparoscope. Since the carbon dioxide gas is under pressure, there has been concern that in pregnant women the pressure of the gas would exceed the pressure of the blood flowing into the uterus. This would decrease the amount of oxygen the fetus would receive during surgery.

Fortunately, however, it has been shown in multiple studies that as long as intra-abdominal gas pressures do not exceed certain carefully monitored levels, laparoscopic surgery is safe in early pregnancy and will not increase the risk of miscarriage. The safety of laparoscopy in later pregnancy is more problematic because in mid- or late pregnancy the size of the uterus makes placing instruments into the abdomen potentially dangerous. Thus I rarely use laparoscopy during these later stages of pregnancy.

Bottom line? If you have to undergo a surgical procedure during your pregnancy, you need not be concerned that it will cause you to miscarry.

Prudence dictates that pregnancy is not a time to have elective surgical procedures. But necessary surgery can and should be performed despite your pregnancy status. Surgery will not increase your risk of miscarriage.

Gynecologic Issues

A concern frequently voiced by my patients is that some previous gynecologic problem they have had may increase their risk of miscarrying. Let's take a look at some typical gynecologic conditions to see what risk, if any, they hold for pregnancy.

IUD

As discussed previously, an IUD is a plastic device, either covered with copper or filled with a slow-release progesterone, that is placed in the uterus to prevent pregnancy. It is as effective as the birth control pill in preventing pregnancy: 99%. Earlier types of IUDs often caused infections. Current IUDs rarely do.

If you have had an IUD in the past, your risk of miscarriage is not at all increased. It was once thought that having had an IUD might make it harder for you to become pregnant after its removal, but this also has been shown not to be true.

Unfortunately, if you become pregnant *while* you have an IUD in place, the story is entirely different. I have already discussed this situation in some detail in Chapter 5.

Previous Abortion (Pregnancy Termination)

Having had one or more abortions in the past will not increase your risk of having a miscarriage. The only possible exception to this is if your pregnancy terminations were performed relatively late—between sixteen and twenty-two weeks—so that the cervix had to be forcefully dilated to evacuate the tissue from your uterus. In this situation there is the slight possibility that your cervix was weakened in the process and that it is "incompetent"—unable to support the weight of a pregnancy as it progresses.

But since most abortions are performed in the first trimester, they do not damage the cervix. Millions of women have had one or more abortions and have gone on to have as many successful pregnancies and healthy babies as they wanted.

Previous Miscarriages

If you have had one or two miscarriages in the past, your risk of having another miscarriage is not increased. It is only when a woman has had three or more miscarriages that statistics show she has a higher than normal chance of miscarrying in the future. This, as mentioned previously, constitutes the condition called "recurrent miscarriage." I will discuss this condition in detail in Chapter 7.

The vast majority of women who have had one or two miscarriages go on to have as many healthy children as they wish. Your risk of *not* miscarrying in your next pregnancy is 80%, the same percentage seen in women who have never had a miscarriage. As I mentioned in the opening chapter, most of my patients who have two or more children have had a miscarriage or two along the way. Thus you should not think that having had a miscarriage means you will never be able to have children. This is definitely not so.

Endometriosis

Endometriosis is a condition in which menstrual blood backs up through the fallopian tubes during a period and implants on tissues inside a woman's pelvis. Each subsequent month under the hormonal stimulation of the menstrual cycle, these patches of endometrial tissue grow and bleed. They can eventually form blood-filled cysts and dense scar tissue. These in turn can cause severe pelvic pain and result in infertility.

Indeed, endometriosis is a major cause of infertility. But because the lesions of endometriosis are in the pelvis and not inside the uterus, they do not increase the risk of miscarriage *once you are pregnant*. If you have endometriosis and have been able to become pregnant, you have jumped the largest hurdle. Your risk of miscarriage is now no higher than that of any other woman.

Ectopic Pregnancy

An ectopic pregnancy is one in which the embryo implants somewhere other than the uterus. This can be inside one of your fallopian tubes, on the surface of an ovary, or in your abdominal cavity. Obviously, these structures were not made to house a pregnancy. Therefore, the growing fetal sac may cause the structure to rupture. Alternatively, the blood vessels from the growing placenta that implant into the tubal wall, the ovary, or the bowel surface may at some point cause massive internal bleeding.

Having had a previous ectopic pregnancy does not increase your risk of having a miscarriage. The ectopic pregnancy may have damaged your fallopian tubes or may have caused pelvic scarring. But such damage would affect only whether you could *become* pregnant—not whether you would stay pregnant once you have conceived. In fact, the major concern in any pregnancy following an ectopic is not that you would have a miscarriage, but that your chance of having a *repeat* ectopic pregnancy is relatively high.

Thus, if you have had an ectopic pregnancy in the past you should see an obstetrician as soon as you think you might be pregnant. Your doctor can then establish the location of your pregnancy—hopefully in the uterus—and the possibility of a recurrent ectopic pregnancy can be ruled out.

Medications

In this chapter we've discussed various medical conditions to see what impact they might have on causing miscarriages. But what about the medications used to treat these conditions? And how about other medications that pregnant women commonly use?

Generally the news is good: Very few medicines are known to cause miscarriage directly. The ones that do fall into two categories: those that cause severe constriction of small blood vessels, such as methergine (used to decrease uterine bleeding), and those that are extremely toxic to all tissues, such as anticancer medications. Multiple other medications may increase the risk of birth defects, usually by interfering with fetal cell development and migration. But few medicines directly cause miscarriage. Still, because each person's medical circumstances are unique and because each medication has its own set of side effects and complications, it is imperative that you always check with your doctor before taking medicine of any kind while you are pregnant or trying to become pregnant.

If we look at common categories of medications as they relate to miscarriage, some of which I have already discussed, we find the following:

- *Anti-seizure medications* may cause birth defects—clefts of the lip or palate, heart defects, shortened fingers—and, as discussed above, do slightly increase the risk of miscarriage.
- *Insulin* and oral medications used to treat diabetes do not cause miscarriage.
- All *asthma medications* are safe for pregnancy.
- *Pain relievers* such as Tylenol and the short-term use of narcotics such as Percocet, oxycodone, codeine, morphine, and Demerol in pregnancy are all safe. Analgesics in the aspirin family such as ibuprofen (Advil, Motrin, etc.) may slightly increase the risk of heart defects at birth, but do not cause miscarriage.
- Blood thinners such as *heparin* and *warfarin* do not cause miscarriage, but they can have other harmful effects on pregnancy. This is especially true if they are used long term as they are in women with a history of thrombosis—blood clot formation in major blood vessels. Heparin can cause pregnant women to lose calcium from their bones. Warfarin can increase the risk of facial and bone abnormalities in the fetus. It is fortunate that these anticoagulant medications do not cause miscarriage because they are vitally important for the prevention and treatment of several potentially serious medical conditions in pregnancy such as blood clots in the legs (thrombophlebitis) or lungs (pulmonary embolus).
- Most *antibiotics* are safe in pregnancy for women who are not allergic to them. This applies to antibiotics in the penicillin, erythromycin, sulfonamide, and aminoglycoside families. Some antibiotics—tetracycline, streptomycin, and perhaps ciprofloxacin—may cause birth defects such as discolored teeth, weakened bones, or deafness. But no antibiotic is associated with miscarriage.
- *Antidepressant medications*, especially the new generation of Prozac-like medications—SSRIs—are used by millions of people. Fortunately, there is increasing medical evidence supporting their safe use during pregnancy. They have not been associated with an increased risk of miscarriage.

- Over-the-counter medications for *colds, coughs,* and *allergies* do not increase the risk of miscarriage.
- Medications for treating *vaginal infections*—both yeast and bacterial—do not increase the risk of miscarriage.
- *Acne medications* are generally safe during pregnancy. Very important exceptions are those drugs derived from vitamin-A-like substances, such as isotretinoin (Accutane). These cause birth defects in a high percentage of pregnancies in which they are taken. They should definitely be avoided during pregnancy and for at least one month before trying to conceive. Although they pose a high risk for birth defects, none of the acne medicines, not even isotretinoin, is known to cause miscarriage.

Diagnostic Procedures

Women in early pregnancy are subject to the same sorts of illnesses, accidents, and injuries that all people are. Therefore, when you are pregnant you may find yourself in need of a medical test or diagnostic study. What effect might such tests or studies have on your pregnancy or your risk of having a miscarriage?

Generally speaking, very little. Let's look specifically at the tests you would be most likely to have:

- Blood tests, while uncomfortable, do not pose any risk to pregnancy and do not cause miscarriages.
- X-rays, as discussed in Chapter 5, are almost always safe. As long as the total dosage of radiation is less than 5 rads, there is no increase in the risk of miscarriage or birth defects.
- Ultrasound examinations pose no risk to pregnancy.
- Electrocardiograms measure the conduction of electronic pulses from the heart through the body. These have no harmful effects on pregnancy and do not cause miscarriage.

Assisted Reproduction

Over the last thirty years, the ingenuity of reproductive scientists has resulted in the development of techniques to treat infertility that are all but miraculous. These techniques have enabled many women who in the past never would have had children to become pregnant and have their own babies. However, many of these procedures and biological manipulations are complex and invasive. The question therefore arises whether these artificial means of achieving conception result in pregnancies at greater risk for miscarriage or birth defects.

It appears that early miscarriages, those occurring before seven or eight weeks, are more common in pregnancies conceived via assisted reproductive techniques (ART). Some of this increase is no doubt due to problems inherent in the egg and sperm of women and men who need ART. Another factor is the increased rate of multiple pregnancies that occur with assisted reproduction and the higher miscarriage rate all multiple pregnancies experience. The techniques themselves—egg retrieval via laparoscopy or needle aspiration, artificial insemination, hormonal manipulation of the ovulation cycle, and so on—do not seem to increase the risk of miscarriage once a pregnancy is established—after seven to eight weeks or so. But prior to this gestational age, pregnancies conceived via ART do have a higher rate of miscarriage than do spontaneous pregnancies.

Additionally, until now all data had indicated that there was no increase in the risk of birth defects in babies conceived via assisted reproductive techniques. However, very recent reports have claimed that there is a two- or three-fold increase in birth defects from such pregnancies. Since these results are from isolated studies, they have to be considered preliminary. We will have to await more studies and reports before we have a definitive answer to this very important question.

But even if eventually it were to be confirmed that an increased rate of early miscarriage or of birth defects occurred in assisted reproduction pregnancies, we still would not be able to state with certainty that they were caused by the reproductive technologies themselves. For the fact that a woman and man have had to avail themselves of artificial fertilization techniques likely indicates that they have some inherent abnormalities of egg, sperm, or intrauterine environment in the first place.

Moreover, despite the possibility of increased risks with these pregnancies, the fact is that were it not for assisted reproductive technologies those women and men who require them to conceive would in most cases not be able to become pregnant at all. Certainly a higher early miscarriage rate for such couples is better than no chance of pregnancy. And even if it were to be shown that there was some elevation in the risk of birth defects in these babies, the vast majority of couples who become pregnant via assisted reproduction have babies that are entirely normal.

Pregnancy-Related Medical Procedures

What effect do tests and procedures routinely performed during prenatal care have on the risk of miscarriage?

It is standard practice during a first obstetrical visit to assess the size of the uterus by physical examination and to do a Pap smear if one has not been performed recently. Occasionally I will get a call from a patient a few days following such an examination saying that she is miscarrying. Naturally enough, the woman wonders whether the examination or Pap smear brought on the miscarriage.

The answer is clearly "no." We must remember that 20% or so of all pregnant women will miscarry. Thus, if an obstetrician examines newly pregnant women day after day, the odds are that some of these women will have their miscarriages in close proximity to that exam. Observations of millions of pregnant women over many years have shown that neither routine pelvic examination nor Pap smear will disturb a healthy pregnancy. If a miscarriage occurs shortly after such an examination, it is coincidental. The miscarriage would have happened anyway.

Chromosomal Testing

Amniocentesis and chorionic villous sampling are procedures for evaluating the chromosomal status of a fetus.

Amniocentesis is generally performed at fifteen or sixteen weeks gestation. It involves inserting a long thin needle into the uterus through the abdominal wall and withdrawing amniotic fluid. Fetal cells are then extracted from the amniotic fluid and "cultured"—grown in a special medium to increase their numbers. When a sufficient amount of cells is available, the cells are prepared for chromosomal analysis.

Chorionic villous sampling, performed anywhere from the tenth to the thirteenth weeks of pregnancy, involves the actual biopsying of tissue from the placenta. This is done through a needle placed either in the

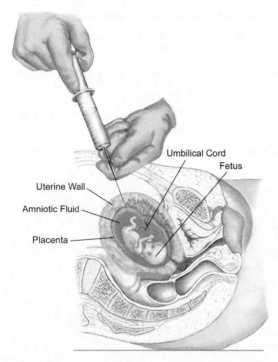

Umbilical Cord

Fetus

Uterine Wall

Amniotic Fluid

Placenta

FIGURE 6.1   Amniocentesis

vagina or through the abdominal and uterine walls. Since the cells in the placenta are already present in large numbers, they do not have to be cultured as is the case with amniocentesis. Thus the results of the chromosome studies can be obtained more quickly.

Both of these procedures involve insertion of an instrument directly into vital pregnancy structures, yet both have been proven to be relatively safe. In amniocentesis, putting the needle through the wall of the uterus and amniotic and chorionic sacs results in a miscarriage only 1 in 200 times, equivalent to a 99.5% safety record. With chorionic villous sampling the rate of miscarriage is either the same as amniocentesis or slightly higher, depending on which study you read. Thus, although both of these procedures can occasionally cause miscarriage, the odds of this happening are small.

Herbal Remedies and Alternative Medicine

Nontraditional medicine has become very popular in the United States, echoing its popularity throughout the world. But because most of these alternative medical therapies have not been subjected to the same sorts of evaluation that mainstream Western medical techniques have, it is hard to assess how well they do or don't work or whether they pose any dangers to pregnancy. Here are some of the things we do know about them.

Acupuncture

Although its mechanism of action is not well understood, acupuncture appears to offer many benefits to pregnant women. The procedure has clearly been shown to relieve morning sickness and may also be effective in diminishing the aches, pains, and discomforts of pregnancy. Acupuncture has also been effectively used for pain relief in labor.

There is no evidence that acupuncture increases the risk of miscarriage. There are even claims that the stimulation of certain acupuncture points can be used to "treat" miscarriages and help prevent them from occurring. These claims have not yet been substantiated.

Herbal Remedies

It's hard to make definitive statements about the effects and safety of herbs on pregnancy or miscarriage. Since the Food and Drug Administration does not classify herbal products as medications, the manufacturers of these products do not have to submit safety or efficacy data for review. But it is known that many of the herbs used therapeutically do have potent pharmacologic actions, not all of them innocuous. The following is a list of potentially harmful effects caused by common herbal remedies:

- *Echinacea* has anti-inflammatory properties and has been shown to cause sperm damage in animals.
- *Black cohosh* contains a chemical that acts like estrogen. It is known to increase the risk of miscarriage.
- *Garlic and willow barks* have anticoagulant (anticlotting) properties.
- *Gingko* can interfere with brain chemistry (MAO) and has anticoagulant properties.
- *Pennyroyal* is known to increase the risk of miscarriage.
- *True licorice* contains glycyrrhizin, which can have hypertensive effects.

- *Ginseng* interferes with MAO (brain neurotransmitter) physiology.
- *Soy products* contain estrogen-like phytoestrogens.

Whether these effects in and of themselves cause or contribute to miscarriage is not known. But because we know so little about these herbal remedies and because of the sorts of effects listed above, I do not recommend their use in pregnancy.

Chiropractic Manipulation

Many women feel that chiropractic treatments help them with the aches and pains that are sometimes associated with pregnancy. Fortunately, the physical manipulations involved in chiropractic medicine do not increase the risk of miscarriage. Because ligaments can be looser than normal during pregnancy, it is possible for joints to be strained during chiropractic manipulations. But when performed by an experienced chiropractor knowledgeable about pregnancy, this rarely occurs.

Conclusion

In this chapter I have looked at various commonly occurring medical, surgical, and gynecologic conditions to assess the roles they might play in causing miscarriage. During this discussion, the subject of "recurrent miscarriage" has come up several times. It's now time to take a look at this phenomenon in greater detail.

CHAPTER 7

Recurrent Miscarriage

FOR ANY COUPLE, HAVING A MISCARRIAGE IS A TREMENDOUSLY sad, usually unexpected event. Yet, some couples have more than one miscarriage. They may experience failed pregnancies two, three, or even more times. Every obstetrician has such patients in his or her practice. The repeated disappointments they experience make them some of the unhappiest patients we see.

During my own years of practice I have, unfortunately, had many such patients. I remember three of them particularly well.

The first was a smart, well-respected academic—as well as a superb athlete—who started trying to become pregnant when she was in her late thirties. She had no problems conceiving. Yet each time she did so, she miscarried.

She tried again and again. Each time she became pregnant, our hopes would rise after the sixth or seventh week of pregnancy, only to be disappointed when she called me to say that she had started bleeding and cramping. Yet none of the tests I performed on her was able to isolate a specific cause for her miscarriages.

She gave it one last shot when she was forty-two. We held our breaths as each week went by. When she made it to ten weeks, we were encouraged. By fourteen weeks, we allowed ourselves to be cautiously optimistic. She was actually going to have a baby! And she did: a wonderful little boy who has delightfully transformed the lives of her and her husband.

The story of the second patient starts off with many similarities—but its ending is very different. When I first met this woman, she already had one healthy baby. But thereafter she had a tremendously hard time becoming pregnant again and, once pregnant, keeping her pregnancies going. She struggled for four years with this combination of having difficulty conceiving followed by miscarriages when she did.

Finally, after four consecutive miscarriages, she became pregnant again and this time had an uneventful pregnancy. Everyone in our office was thrilled to see that she was at last going to have her much-desired second baby. She had a normal, uncomplicated labor and delivered a healthy baby girl.

I should more accurately say an *apparently* healthy baby girl. Over the first six months of life, the child's growth and development began to slow down. She was late for the normal milestones of turning over, sitting up, beginning to crawl. She was eventually diagnosed as having a rare genetic syndrome with multiple defects of her internal organs and with severe neurologic abnormalities. She will likely never walk or speak, and she has only a limited life expectancy.

The third and last of these special patients of mine was an Asian woman who worked in our hospital cafeteria. She and her husband had been trying for eight years to have children, without success. Being first-generation immigrants and also having only limited proficiency in English, they had not known the ins and outs of seeking medical care. Thus, they had not availed themselves of an obstetrician or fertility specialist during their years of unsuccessfully trying to have a baby.

After reviewing this woman's reproductive history and performing some basic tests, it quickly became apparent to me what her problem was: She did not ovulate regularly. I worked with her over several months with ovulation induction medications without being able to correct the problem. When I realized that she would need more sophisticated help than I could provide, I referred her to a colleague who is a fertility specialist.

He started her on treatments with different, more potent medications to induce ovulation. After three cycles, she did conceive—but had a very early miscarriage. Encouraged that she had finally been able to become pregnant, she elected to continue the hormonal treatments. But over the next three years, although she became pregnant three more times, she miscarried with each one.

Frustrated and drained by her years of infertility followed by multiple miscarriages, she finally told me that she and her husband no longer had the emotional strength to continue trying to have a baby. She decided to stop the fertility treatments and to adopt a child.

Thus far in this book, I have discussed mainly routine miscarriages, the sorts of sporadic miscarriages that occur in 20% of all pregnancies. But the examples I have given above are of a different phenomenon, that of *recurrent miscarriage*. Recurrent miscarriage is defined as three or more miscarriages in a row.

Now having even two miscarriages in a row is not that unusual: The chances of having a single miscarriage are 20%. The odds of having two miscarriages in a row are 4%. This means that although one in five women who become pregnant will have a miscarriage, one in twenty-five will have two miscarriages in a row—not so rare an occurrence. But the odds of having three consecutive miscarriages drop precipitously to less than 1%. To have this many miscarriages in a row merely by random chance is extremely unlikely. And, in fact, it turns out that when women have three or more miscarriages in a row it usually is *not* due to random chance. Thus we see that the distinction between *sporadic miscarriages* and *recurrent miscarriages* is not merely semantic. These two categories of miscarriage usually have different causes. They therefore require different treatments.

In Chapter 2, we discussed at length the usual cause of sporadic miscarriages: a miscombination of the chromosomes of the egg and sperm at conception. But this is a much less frequent cause of recurrent miscarriages. More often recurrent miscarriages are caused by anatomic abnormalities, hormonal inadequacy, hereditary chromosomal abnormalities of the parents, and so on—all the causes *other* than chromosomal miscombination we have discussed. So for instance, although 60% of *sporadic* miscarriages occur when chromosomes fuse incorrectly at conception, this is the cause of only 10 to 15% of *recurrent* miscarriages. And while sporadic miscarriages are only rarely caused by anatomic abnormalities, recurrent miscarriages frequently are.

Another difference between sporadic and recurrent miscarriages is their prognosis for future successful pregnancies. A woman who has had one or two miscarriages still has an 80% chance of having a successful pregnancy the next time she conceives. But a woman who has had three consecutive miscarriages, has only a 60% to 70% chance that her next pregnancy will "make it"—and her odds decrease with each subsequent miscarriage.

That recurrent miscarriage is truly a different condition having different causes than sporadic miscarriage is further demonstrated by the following:

1. Women who experience recurrent miscarriages have a more difficult time becoming pregnant than women who have had sporadic miscarriages.
2. There is a higher-than-average rate of birth defects in babies born to women with a history of recurrent miscarriage.
3. Women who have recurrent miscarriages have higher rates of other pregnancy complications such as preterm labor, placenta previa (the placenta covering the cervical opening to the uterus), and breech position at delivery.

A further difference between sporadic and recurrent miscarriages is the gestational age in pregnancy when they occur. Sporadic miscarriages most often happen in the early or middle part of the first trimester. This is because the embryos involved usually lack complete, correct copies of the chromosomal instructions necessary for their further development. Thus these embryos cannot grow past a certain early stage.

Since chromosomal miscombination is much less often a cause of recurrent miscarriages, the instructions for early fetal development are usually present. These pregnancies therefore usually make it to a later stage of development before succumbing to whatever factor eventually does cause them to miscarry.

The above description of recurrent miscarriage sounds pretty scary. If having a miscarriage is bad, the possibility of having miscarriage after miscarriage is terrifying, enough so that—like the third patient I described—many couples refuse to try becoming pregnant again after having several miscarriages. Yet even with couples who have recurrent miscarriages, the ultimate odds of their achieving a successful pregnancy resulting in a live baby are still very good: from 60 to 70%.

What does this mean for you? It means that even if you are unfortunate enough to qualify for the category of "recurrent miscarriage," your odds of eventually having a full-term pregnancy and a healthy baby are still excellent. In fact, statistics clearly show that the majority of women who have had three miscarriages in a row at some point in their reproductive careers go on to have one or more healthy children.

The Causes of Recurrent Miscarriage

Above I have explained the differences between sporadic and recurrent miscarriage. Now let's examine the difference in their *causes*.

Chromosomal Causes

Most *sporadic* miscarriages are caused by misalignment and miscombination of the chromosomes of the egg and sperm, the phenomenon of "nondisjunction" discussed in Chapter 2. This kind of miscarriage recurs with a predictable frequency. The various forms these miscombinations take—extra individual chromosomes, extra sets of chromosomes, missing chromosomes, missing or extra sex chromosomes—are random, accidental occurrences. We do not understand all the reasons why these "nondisjunctions" occur. The only real correlation of which we are sure is that trisomies—three copies of one specific chromosome such as the trisomy 21 that causes Down syndrome—are seen more frequently in older mothers.

This is not so with recurrent miscarriages. As mentioned above, the majority of recurrent miscarriages are caused by factors *other* than random chromosomal miscombination. In fact the only chromosomal abnormalities seen with consistent frequency in recurrent miscarriages are *translocations*.

You may remember from Chapter 2 that translocations are permanent abnormalities of a person's genetic material. They are caused by chromosomes exchanging DNA during the reproduction of sex cells: eggs and sperm. If an embryo inherits DNA from an egg or sperm containing a translocation, there is a significant chance that the cells of the embryo will contain abnormal chromosomal material—and that the pregnancy will end in miscarriage. The reason is simple: The genetic material containing the translocation will cause the cells of the embryo to have either too much or too little DNA. If part or all of a chromosome is duplicated, the embryo will have three copies of it. As in Down syndrome or trisomy 13 or 18, this situation is not compatible with normal life. If, on the other hand, part of a chromosome is missing, the embryo will have only one copy of whatever genes were on the missing segment. This produces a monosomy, also incompatible with life, except in the case of the X chromosome.

Chromosomal translocations are the cause of only 0.3% of sporadic miscarriages. However, they are present in fully 5% of recurrent miscarriages. This makes sense. Couples who have a miscarriage because they have the bad luck to have an accidental chromosomal miscombination are unlikely to have that same bad luck with a subsequent pregnancy. But a couple whose eggs or sperm permanently contain chromosomal translocations are bound to produce embryos with those translocations over and over again.

Environmental Factors

The environmental factors that cause recurrent miscarriages are the same as those that cause sporadic miscarriages. Obviously, if you are exposed to the same toxic factors each time you are pregnant, these factors will likely repeatedly exert their negative effects on you. Thus, if you persistently smoke, drink, consume large amounts of coffee, or are exposed to toxins at work or at home, your risk of recurrent miscarriage increases.

Hormonal Factors

Many fertility specialists feel that inadequate production of progesterone by a woman's corpus luteum can cause both infertility and miscarriage, especially recurrent miscarriage. These doctors believe that such underproduction of progesterone leads to insufficient development of the endometrial lining tissue of the uterus—thus inhibiting implantation—and to inadequate general hormonal support of an early pregnancy. In the former case, the pregnancy will never truly get started. In the latter, the embryo will miscarry. These experts feel that the tendency to have inadequate corpus luteum function is a recurrent phenomenon and that it leads to recurrent miscarriage.

But as I discussed in Chapter 3, this theory is not totally convincing. First, gynecologic researchers have not been able to consistently identify "undergrown" endometrial lining tissue in women who supposedly have inadequate corpus luteum syndrome. This, after all, is one of the ways by which inadequate corpus luteum supposedly causes infertility and miscarriage.

Second, it has never been shown that giving progesterone to women who supposedly have inadequate corpus luteum function decreases their risk of miscarriage. If inadequate progesterone production was indeed the cause of infertility and miscarriage in these women, then giving progesterone supplementation should correct the problem. Despite multiple studies attempting to show this, however, none have been successful in doing so.

Nevertheless, advocates of the theory of corpus luteum inadequacy attempt to diagnose this entity by measuring progesterone levels and by doing biopsies of endometrial lining tissue in women who have a history of recurrent miscarriages. Women who have had irregular periods—therefore, irregular ovulation cycles—are especially likely to be tested in this way. If the doctors performing the tests detect what they see as evidence of corpus luteum deficiency, they either administer supplemental progesterone—in the form of pill, shot, or vaginal suppository—or they attempt to make whatever corpus luteum is present function better. They do this by stimulating a "stronger" ovulation with clomiphene, an ovulation enhancer.

The issue of corpus luteum inadequacy as a cause of miscarriage remains one of great controversy among fertility experts.

Polycystic Ovarian Syndrome

Another condition thought by some infertility experts to cause recurrent miscarriage is polycystic ovarian syndrome (PCOS), which we discussed briefly in Chapter 6. This is a complex condition marked by obesity, excessive hair growth, acne, and irregular ovulation that results in irregular periods and infertility. Its causes are obscure and are currently the subject of intensive research. Something—abnormal hypothalamic or pituitary function, resistance to insulin—results in the unbalancing of the monthly cyclic ebb and flow of reproductive hormones. When this happens, multiple ovarian follicles—egg precursors—develop simultaneously. Each of these follicles produces hormones. This results in the continuous production of estrogen, progesterone, and *androgens*—male-type hormones—instead of the normal pattern of the rise and fall of hormones usually seen each month. The increase in androgen production results in excessive hair growth, weight gain, acne, an increased risk of heart disease, and even male balding patterns.

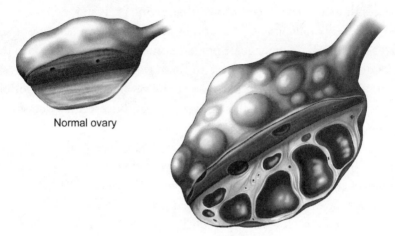

Normal ovary

Polycystic ovarian syndrome

FIGURE 7.1   Polycystic Ovarian Syndrome

Those experts who think that polycystic ovarian syndrome leads to recurrent miscarriage feel this way because (1) luteinizing hormone (LH)—one of the hormones produced by the pituitary gland—is chronically high in PCOS; and (2) elevated luteinizing hormone levels are known to be a cause of miscarriage.

Yet many obstetricians, myself included, are not convinced about the role PCOS supposedly plays in causing recurrent miscarriage. We certainly all agree that it is a major factor in infertility. But the evidence purporting to link it to recurrent miscarriage is not totally persuasive. For instance, studies have shown that women with recurrent miscarriage who had elevated LH levels and had those levels lowered by treatment with medications suffered no fewer miscarriages after such treatment. As with the inadequate corpus luteum story, if the correction of the supposed problem does not solve that problem, it casts doubt on the validity of there being a cause-and-effect relationship.

Moreover, if a woman with PCOS does ovulate and conceive, then at least in *that* cycle her level of LH and FSH, the hormones controlling ovulation, must have been normal. So if she were to miscarry it is hard to argue that "elevated LH" was the cause.

Anatomic Causes

Anatomic causes of miscarriage account for only a small percent of sporadic miscarriages. However, they are the cause of fully 12 to 15% of recurrent miscarriages. This makes sense. If you have a certain uterine anatomy, it would not spontaneously change from pregnancy to pregnancy. If abnormalities of your reproductive structures are such that they have caused you to miscarry once, the process is likely to repeat itself— or at least have a greater chance of doing so.

In Chapter 3, I explained how the tubular embryonic urinary structures on both sides of the fetal abdomen eventually combine to form the uterus and fallopian tubes. I explained how this process occurs in two phases. The first is the actual merger of the lower ends of these tubes to form a central midline structure. The second is the resorption of the inner, middle layers of these now-combined structures.

Most of the anatomic defects that lead to miscarriage are the result of the failure of this second phase of uterine formation, resorption. It turns out that defects in fusion, resulting in two separate uteruses, are still compatible with successful pregnancy outcomes. It is the defects in resorption of the tissue in the middle of the newly unified uterine cavity— the septum—that result in most anatomically caused miscarriages. I have already discussed the two reasons for this:

1. The fibrous septum has a minimal blood supply. If an embryo implants on the septum, the septum's ability to increase its blood flow to supply the embryo as it grows is extremely limited.
2. The fibrous septum is covered with only a thin layer of endometrial tissue. It does not provide a lush, nourishing site for embryo implantation.

Another cause of recurrent miscarriage is *cervical incompetence*. This occurs when congenital weakness, damage from cervical surgery, or trauma during delivery leave the cervix too weak to remain closed and hold in a growing pregnancy. Because exactly when an incompetent cervix will begin to open up depends on the weight of the pregnancy pushing down on it, miscarriages caused by cervical incompetence generally occur later in pregnancy than miscarriages caused by other factors. Obviously, the cervix that is unable to hold in a pregnancy at twenty weeks in one pregnancy will most likely be unable to do so in a subsequent pregnancy. Only if cervical cerclage stitches are placed in the weakened cervix early in pregnancy can this tendency to premature cervical dilation and miscarriage be prevented.

Anything that causes the uterus to develop an abnormal shape can also cause recurrent miscarriage. This situation can be the result of events during prenatal life, such as the T-shaped uterus caused by mothers taking DES during pregnancy, or the growth of fibroids in the walls of a woman's uterus later on in her life. As discussed in Chapter 3, abnormal uterine shape can result in recurrent miscarriage either because of inadequate room for a fetus to grow or because the embryo implants on tissue such as a fibroid that is inadequate to support its growth.

Infection

The same bacteria, viruses, and other organisms that can cause routine miscarriages can also cause recurrent miscarriages. Thus, if you were to contract an infection with a miscarriage-causing organism and were not treated, you could suffer repeated miscarriages because of it. Fortunately, there are no specific infections that are particularly linked to recurrent miscarriage.

Antibodies, the Immune System, and Hereditary Clotting Disorders

One of the major reasons for the intense interest of medical scientists in the immunology of pregnancy is that it offers the hope of finding a category of miscarriages that can be prevented. We know that the majority of miscarriages are caused by chromosomal miscombination at conception. Physicians have no way of intervening in these sorts of miscarriages— and it is not clear that we ever will. The immune system, however, *is* amenable to medical manipulation. Research on the immune system over the last 125 years has resulted in such lifesaving therapies as immunizations against contagious diseases and the ability to transplant organs between individuals. Thus there is hope that further understanding of the immunologic aspects of pregnancy might allow intervention and treatment for at least those miscarriages caused by immunologic factors.

The basic biological issue is this: The fetus is made up of chromosomes that are half "self"—from the mother—and half "foreign"—from the father. Generally, the mother's immune system would reject tissues containing "foreign" structures. But in pregnancy this does not happen. A condition called "immune tolerance" develops in the mother that prevents this rejection and allows the fetus to grow.

Immune tolerance is thought to arise from "blocking antibodies" produced by the mother in the earliest stages of her pregnancy. Their production is initiated by chemical messengers secreted along with her other pregnancy hormones. These maternal blocking antibodies latch onto those tissue markers of the embryo that are recognized as foreign. In some way yet undefined, these blocking antibodies protect the embryonic tissue from destruction by the lymphocytes of the mother's immune system.

If anything interferes with the maternal production of blocking antibodies, the mother's "killer lymphocytes"—the soldiers of her immune system—recognize embryonic tissue as half foreign and destroy it. This would, of course, lead to miscarriage.

An "experiment" that occurs spontaneously in nature goes a long way toward proving this blocking antibody theory. You and I and everyone have specific biochemical markers on the various cells of our bodies that differentiate our cells from those of everyone else. These markers are called *human leukocyte antigens*—HLAs. However, some people's HLAs are so similar to each other that their bodies would not immediately recognize each other's tissues as foreign.

The natural experiment is this: It is known that some miscarriages occur because the HLA markers of the mother and the father are *too* similar. Because of this similarity, the mother's immune system does not immediately recognize that half of the HLA markers in the embryo—those derived from the father—are in fact "foreign." The mother's body therefore does not produce the blocking antibodies to protect the embryonic tissues containing them. As the mother's killer lymphocytes eventually determine that some of the HLA markers in the embryonic tissue *are* foreign—and are not protected by blocking antibodies—the lymphocytes set about destroying them. This is likely one of the reasons pregnancies between close relatives so often end up as miscarriages.

An undeveloped "immune tolerance" is not the only means by which malfunction of the maternal immune system can cause miscarriage. As will be discussed below, some immune disorders lead to miscarriage by directly injuring embryonic or fetal tissue. In other disorders, microscopic blood vessels and the capillaries of the placenta become filled with blood clots that block the flow of oxygen and nutrients to the fetus.

Antiphospholipid Syndrome

Antiphospholipid syndrome is one of a group of closely related medical conditions that can lead to miscarriage. Its nature has only recently been discerned and it is currently the subject of much research.

In this syndrome, the mother, for reasons unknown, makes antibodies to specific chemical structures in her own body called phospholipids. These phospholipids are components of many important organs and tissues and are especially prominent in the walls lining blood vessels. The two major antiphospholipid antibodies are anticardiolipin and lupus anticoagulant.

How do anitphospholipid antibodies cause miscarriage? It has to do with the complex biochemistry of the lining of blood vessel walls. There is a family of chemicals in the walls of blood vessels that we have already discussed as a component of semen, the prostaglandins, that can cause blood vessels to squeeze shut. In antiphospholipid syndrome, the action of antibodies on the phospholipids in the blood vessel walls causes these prostaglandins to be released. This induces blood vessel spasm. In addition, the effect of antibodies on the blood vessel walls causes platelets in the blood to clot. The spasm of blood vessels and the platelet-initiated blood clots block small blood vessels throughout the body, including those in the placenta.

Antiphospholipid syndrome in pregnant women affects not only the fetuses but also their mothers. The fetus suffers because blockage of the small blood vessels in the uterus and placenta decreases the amount of oxygen and nutrients it receives. This can result in miscarriage in early pregnancy and stillbirth or undernourishment later in pregnancy.

For the mother, the disruption of the lining of her blood vessels can provoke serious medical problems. These include hypertension—blood vessel spasm causing a rise in blood pressure—and large blood clots in major blood vessels. Such clots have the potential to break free and to be carried by the blood stream into the lungs, causing pulmonary embolus, or into the brain, causing a stroke.

Fortunately, antiphospholipid syndrome is an uncommon condition. It causes less than 1% of routine miscarriages. But antiphospholipid syndrome is seen much more frequently in women who suffer recurrent miscarriage. It is thought to be responsible for fully 15% of these miscarriages.

Lupus Erythematosis

Lupus erythematosis, or "lupus," is a generalized autoimmune disease. An individual with lupus makes antibodies to many of his or her own tissues. When tissues are attacked by these antibodies, a host of responses are initiated, including the formation of blood clots in small blood vessels, prostaglandin-induced blood vessel spasm, and destruction of tissues by lymphocytes. The damage caused by lupus antibodies eventually leads to kidney failure, crippling arthritis, and damage to almost every organ of the body.

If you have lupus, the degree to which it will affect your pregnancy depends on how severe your case is and whether you are currently in remission. Unfortunately, lupus often worsens during pregnancy. This can result in a flaring up of your symptoms and the deterioration of your kidney function. Lupus can also cause severe toxemia of pregnancy, a threat not only to your health but also to that of your baby. Lupus definitely increases the risk of miscarriage.

Although many women who have lupus can and do have successful pregnancies, it is not something to embark upon lightly. You need to be fully informed about the medical problems being pregnant with lupus may present to you and your fetus. If you have lupus, make sure that you consult both your obstetrician as well as the doctor treating your lupus before you became pregnant. It is important that you be in the best possible health before conceiving. This usually means waiting for a remission.

Inherited Thrombophilias

Our understanding of inherited thrombophilias is so new that even many obstetricians do not know much about it. But this condition is certainly changing the way medical scientists think about miscarriage and late pregnancy loss. It is also providing insights into the causes of the blood-clotting complications women may experience during pregnancy and while on the birth control pill.

It turns out that some individuals have a genetic predisposition to low levels of certain proteins that are essential for preventing blood from clotting inappropriately. The names of some of these proteins are protein C, protein S, antithrombin III, and factor V Leiden. The absence or diminished presence of these anticoagulation proteins predisposes blood to form microscopic clots throughout the body. This deprives tissues downstream from these clots of oxygen and nutrients. Because this clotting phenomenon can affect the uterus and placenta, women with these inherited biochemical deficiencies have a miscarriage rate that is from three to four times higher than normal.

Although these protein deficiencies account for only a small percentage of miscarriages—from 1 to 3%—they constitute one of the causes of miscarriage that may be medically preventable. Various techniques for treatment are being investigated at the current time—anticlotting medications such as heparin or aspirin and steroids to counteract immune effects—but the final answer is not yet in.

These protein deficiencies are also of vital interest because of the non-pregnancy medical problems they can cause. It is now thought that many episodes of stroke, pulmonary embolus, and heart attack may be due to clots brought on by these inherited disorders. Some experts have even warned that all women planning to go on the birth control pill should be tested for these deficiencies. Since the birth control pill increases the risk of stroke or heart attack by increasing the tendency for blood to clot, the absence of anitclotting factors in a woman on the pill would put her at especially high risk. So if such birth control pill candidates tested positive for these inherited clotting disorders, the pill would be withheld from them.

Sporadic vs. Recurrent Miscarriage: Why Should We Care?

At the beginning of this chapter, I pointed out that the importance of distinguishing between sporadic and recurrent miscarriage was that these conditions had different causes, different treatments, and different long-term outlooks. Sporadic miscarriages most often occur because of random chromosomal miscombination. Recurrent miscarriages are usually caused by some nonrandom, potentially treatable condition. After a sporadic miscarriage, the odds of the next pregnancy being totally normal are extremely high, approximately 80%. In recurrent miscarriage, the chances that another subsequent miscarriage will occur are from 30 to 40%.

For you as a patient, whether your miscarriage is sporadic or recurrent will determine if it makes sense to pursue a "work-up"—a set of medical tests looking for a specific cause for your miscarriage. If you have had only one miscarriage, the chances that such testing will identify a specific cause are very low. If, however, you have had three or more consecutive miscarriages, then the odds of learning useful information from such postmiscarriage testing are dramatically increased.

Whether your miscarriage is sporadic or is part of a recurrent pattern will also determine how likely it is that a medical or surgical treatment can increase your chances of having a successful pregnancy in the future. If your miscarriage was sporadic due to misalignment of chromosomes, then no specific therapy is likely to help. If, however, you have had recurrent miscarriages, the probability is greatly increased that a specific anatomic, immunologic, or other *treatable* cause will be diagnosed. You could thus undergo therapy—surgery, anti-inflammatory medications, antibiotics, and so on—with the reasonable expectation of eliminating or decreasing the risk of miscarriage from that cause.

Finally, if your miscarriage history places you in the category of recurrent miscarriage, you can at least take solace in the knowledge that you are in a position to actively seek diagnosis and treatment. You do not have to wait passively, trusting only to luck that the outcome of your next pregnancy will be different.

Conclusion

Thus far I have talked in some detail about what miscarriages are and what causes them. I have also discussed the phenomenon of recurrent miscarriage and seen how it differs from the much more common sporadic miscarriage. You are now prepared to take the next step: to begin looking specifically at what you can do if you do have a miscarriage not only to ascertain its cause but to decrease your risk of having another one. Over the next several chapters we will look in detail at four specific areas:

1. How the causes of miscarriage are diagnosed
2. To what extent these causes can be treated
3. What those treatments are
4. What results we can expect from these treatments

But just before exploring these issues, let us take a moment to step back from the medical and scientific aspects of miscarriage and look at a vitally important topic: the emotional and psychological impact of having a miscarriage. Alice Domar, Ph.D., a nationally known psychologist and an expert on the psychological aspects of women's reproductive issues, discusses this critical subject in the next chapter.

CHAPTER 8

Coping with the Emotional Pain of Miscarriage

BY ALICE DOMAR, PH.D.

MARIA WAS A HEALTHY, OUTGOING THIRTY-FIVE-YEAR-OLD when she married Bob. Although he was eight years younger than she, they were both anxious to have a baby. So, shortly after they returned home from their honeymoon, Maria and Bob started trying to conceive. Much to their delight, Maria became pregnant immediately, and they were exuberantly happy. "Seeing that positive pregnancy test was one of the happiest moments of my life," says Maria, a physical therapist.

As the pregnancy progressed, Maria and Bob talked often about their baby. Would it be a boy or a girl? Would it have Maria's straight blonde hair or Bob's brown curls? The couple imagined their child as a newborn, a toddler, a preschooler. They even tried to imagine their child as an adolescent, and Bob joked good-naturedly about sending the child off to college at his alma mater. Together they discussed names and made plans about how they would decorate the nursery. Little by little, their attachment to their baby and to the idea of being parents grew.

Another patient, Suzanne, reacted completely differently when she discovered she was pregnant. "As soon as my doctor confirmed the pregnancy, I started to worry," says Suzanne, a thirty-eight-year-old schoolteacher. "My sister had had a miscarriage the year before, so I was very reluctant to feel secure about the pregnancy until after the first trimester." Suzanne agonized over whether the fetus was healthy, whether it was growing normally, whether it had chromosomal abnormalities. When her morning sickness was bad, she worried that her vomiting might hurt the baby, and when she didn't feel nauseous, she worried that it was a sign that the baby wasn't developing properly. When she went to the bathroom she would tense up, concerned that she would look down and see spotting. She and her husband Jerry refused to allow themselves to become attached to the baby or to dream about their future as a family.

Unfortunately, bad luck struck for both Maria and Suzanne. At Maria's eleven-week checkup, no heartbeat could be found. An ultrasound confirmed her doctor's suspicions: The fetus had failed to develop.

Suzanne, on the other hand, began to bleed and cramp during her eighth week. The next day, it was confirmed that she, too, had suffered a miscarriage.

Miscarriage is an immensely grueling experience, whether you are a dreamer like Maria or a worrier like Suzanne. It's awful whether your miscarriage occurs in the first trimester, as most miscarriages do, or in the second, after you may have already started to show and to feel the baby move. No matter how far along you are, whether it's your first child or your fourth, or whether you have allowed yourself to become attached to your baby or tried very hard not to, experiencing a miscarriage can be a devastating blow that causes intense emotional anguish, sadness, and grief. A miscarriage is not just the death of a fetus; it is the loss of a dream.

Your sorrow may be compounded by the fact that we live in a society in which the emotional pain of miscarriage is often not recognized or honored, and the grief of the miscarrying couple is not given credence. "You can just get pregnant again," well-meaning friends may say. "It's a blessing—the fetus was probably malformed anyway." They might remind you that miscarriages are fairly common. "Everyone has them," you might be told. "What's the big deal?" The big deal is that even if you can become pregnant again easily, even if the fetus was malformed, even if a lot of women do have miscarriages, those things don't take away the pain you feel because you will never hold that child in your arms.

During my sixteen years as a psychologist, I have counseled hundreds of women who have had miscarriages. Some have had just one miscarriage, and others have had as many as nine. By working with them—and, sadly, by suffering a miscarriage of my own—I have learned that it is an incredibly painful, emotionally wrenching experience. But I've also discovered that there are a number of strategies you can follow to help you cope and emerge psychologically strong from this difficult experience. In this chapter, I'll share my insights with you on the emotional impact of miscarriage, as well as some techniques that help couples heal after losing a pregnancy.

Shock

One of the first feelings many women experience when they miscarry is shock. Even women who are worried about miscarrying still feel shock when they suffer a pregnancy loss. Whether your miscarriage announces itself with blood and pain or with a still, silent image on an ultrasound screen, it is an absolutely stunning experience. To see blood flowing out of you when you are pregnant (although it's important to remember that blood doesn't always necessarily equal miscarriage) or to have an ultrasound and not see a heartbeat is a horrible bombshell. Women are not only shocked that they've lost their baby; they're shocked about what goes on during a miscarriage. If you are bleeding and cramping, you're probably amazed by the pain. I remember being astonished by how much my miscarriage hurt. If you find out about your miscarriage during either a scheduled or an emergency ultrasound, not only must you cope with the horror of discovering that the fetus is dead—and may have died weeks ago—but you may then undergo a dilatation and curettage (D&C), a procedure in which the cervix is opened and tissue is gently scraped or suctioned from the inside of the uterus. Alternatively, your doctor may recommend that you let nature take its course and allow your body to push out the pregnancy tissue when it is ready, sometimes days or weeks later. (Ironically, women who wait for their bodies to expel the pregnancy tissue may still feel pregnant for a while, which is always difficult and occasionally leads to false hopes that the doctor was wrong, and that the baby really is alive.) My patients often tell me that it is incredibly difficult for them to know that the baby they thought was viable may actually have been dead for weeks. It frequently leads them to question themselves—how can I be a good mother, they may ask themselves, when I couldn't even tell that the baby inside me was dead? No, it's not logical, but emotions often aren't.

Couples are also shocked by how helpless they feel. I remember one of my patients telling me that, after she miscarried, she held the tiny fetus—which was less than an inch long but which, even at that tiny size, looked distinctly like a baby—and felt so frustrated that she could do nothing at all to save her unborn child. She couldn't rush to the hospital or perform CPR or administer a medication. All she could do was hold it in her hand. She'd never felt so helpless in her life.

Although miscarriage is usually a rude shock, some women are more prepared for it than others. I've found, as I've counseled women who have lost pregnancies, that about half of them never had even the slightest idea that miscarriage was a possibility, either because they don't know anyone who has miscarried or because they had never read the statistics: Roughly 20% of all pregnancies that are far enough along for a woman to know that she is pregnant end in miscarriage. These women conceived, celebrated their positive pregnancy tests, and assumed that everything would go smoothly. The other half of my patients—either because they had suffered a miscarriage before, knew someone who had, or knew through reading that miscarriage was a real possibility—had been hypervigilant during their pregnancies and were less stunned when their miscarriage occurred.

I find that the women who don't have a clue about how commonly miscarriages occur tend to have a tougher time dealing with the initial experience than those who are educated about it. They were totally emotionally unprepared for it, and when it happened, it was like a bolt of lightning coming from out of the blue. Knowing this, I certainly don't advise women to become nervous Nellies about miscarriage, but I do think it behooves them to learn the facts about miscarriage either before they conceive or early in their pregnancies so that they know what to expect if it does happen. Don't get me wrong—women who have prepared themselves to some degree still grieve, just as unprepared women grieve. But for the vigilant women, the initial impact of the miscarriage may not be quite as devastating.

Grief

After confronting the shock of your miscarriage, feelings of grief begin. Grief is a difficult emotion, particularly for people who have little experience with it. Often, a miscarriage is your first encounter with loss and the feelings of grief that loss brings. When someone dies, your world feels as if it has been turned upside down, and your mind fills with emotions that range from sadness to loneliness to fear or even anger.

It's tempting to hide from feelings of grief, but it's far better that you mourn instead. One way to do this is simply to *allow* yourself to mourn. (Just for clarity, let me define the words *grief* and *mourning*. Grief is the feeling you have inside after a loved one dies; mourning is the social response you have to your grief.) People who try to bottle up grief and not share it with others through mourning are the most likely to have emotional problems later on. Give yourself permission to share your grief with others.

Keep in mind that our society tends to discount miscarriage, so your feelings of grief and rituals of mourning may not be honored by people who don't understand the emotional impact of miscarriage. My patients are forever telling me that people dismiss their miscarriages with an attitude of "just get over it and move on." That's ridiculous. This was not just a collection of cells. It was a baby. Your baby. To lose this baby is a death, and you can't let anyone tell you differently.

Although your feelings of grief will subside over time, you might feel raw until after your baby's due date. I have patients and friends who remember the due date of the baby for the rest of their lives. Indeed, women in their fifties, sixties, and seventies have told me that they still remember and feel sad on the due dates of babies they miscarried twenty, thirty, or forty years ago. Anticipate that the time of your due date may be difficult. Plan to treat yourself gently that day.

The pain will subside eventually, but it may never go away completely. I know that I still feel sadness over losing the baby I miscarried—I always will. And I have a patient who's had five children but still feels empty when she thinks about the baby she lost.

You may feel extra sad when you're with a friend or a family member who conceived around the same time as you and whose baby is due the same month yours was. It's important that you not feel ashamed of these reactions or guilty about them. They are valid and legitimate, and once you start talking with other women who have miscarried, you'll find they're quite common, too. One of my patients found that she had to completely avoid her best friend, whose due date was a week or so after hers had been. After her own loss, she just felt too sad and too uncomfortable to watch her friend's pregnancy progress normally. When my patient's friend delivered her baby, my patient was able to resume her friendship and even enjoyed being with the child. But during the pregnancy, it was just too painful. And that, as I told my patient, is fine.

Naturally, there is a line between normal grief and extreme grief, and if you are feeling extreme emotions you should be evaluated by a mental health professional. Be on the lookout for signs of depression, such as loss of interest in usual activities, change in sleep patterns, changes in appetite or weight, increased use of drugs or alcohol, marital discord, social isolation, thoughts about death or suicide, and persistent feelings of hopelessness, pessimism, guilt, bitterness, or anger. But don't think that feeling sad about your miscarriage is abnormal. It's not.

On the other hand, if you are relatively unaffected by your miscarriage and feel very little grief, that's okay, too. Don't feel that you should be mourning if you're not upset. Some people never become emotionally attached to the fetus. This sometimes has to do with how easily you conceived, your age, whether you have other children, and so on. If you become pregnant accidentally or very easily, for example, you may be able to take some solace in the belief that you can probably become pregnant easily again. But if you're older, if you have struggled to become pregnant, or if the lost pregnancy was the result of a long, difficult, expensive fertility treatment, the miscarriage may be extra painful.

People who say they don't feel anything after a miscarriage probably don't. They may have really good coping mechanisms or perhaps they experienced significant losses in the past. Possibly they are young enough to feel they have years of childbearing time ahead of them. Or it may just be the nature of their personality. Whatever the reason, if you don't feel grief, that is fine. The most important thing is to accept whatever feelings you do have without judgment or guilt.

Out of Control

We twenty-first-century Americans are used to being in the driver's seat. We're accustomed to being in control of our careers, our personal lives, and yes, even our fertility. That's why one of the hardest things for a couple to cope with after a miscarriage is the feeling that they are not *really* in control after all. This is particularly hard for women, who, because of the availability these days of birth control and abortion, grow up believing they have absolute power over when they will or will not become mothers.

At first, many women have trouble accepting that a pregnancy is not completely under their control, and after miscarrying, they may seek to retain feelings of control by blaming themselves, even when their doctors assure them they are not at fault. These women examine every moment of their pregnancies looking for a cause for the miscarriage. "Why did I drink a glass of wine when I knew I was pregnant?" they may ask themselves. "Why did I lift a heavy box? Should I have slept more? Should I have worked less overtime?" They may settle on something—drinking coffee, catching a head cold—and obsess about it, blaming themselves for behaving in ways that endangered their pregnancies. They may also blame their husbands for initiating sexual encounters, even though there is no evidence whatsoever that intercourse can impact the developing fetus in a healthy woman. They simply can't accept that the vast majority of miscarriages just happen—not because of the mother's behavior but because of chromosomal problems, uterine abnormalities, hormonal issues, or other factors that are beyond their control.

As discussed earlier, some lifestyle choices do raise a woman's risk of miscarriage. Those include smoking, drinking alcohol and caffeine, and exposing oneself to certain industrial chemicals. If you took part in any of those behaviors, there is a small chance that they may have contributed to your miscarriage, although it's more likely that chromosomal problems caused the fetus not to develop. You may feel guilty about this, but there's nothing you can do about it now other than move on to your next pregnancy with a pledge to make better, more healthful choices. If you have trouble putting your guilt behind you, seek the guidance of a mental health counselor or therapist who will help you learn to forgive yourself.

Women sometimes blame their negative thoughts for causing a miscarriage. A woman who is ambivalent about being pregnant and then miscarries might jump to the incorrect conclusion that her downbeat thoughts about the pregnancy somehow may have caused the miscarriage. Her doctor may tell her that this is impossible, but still, she may feel intense guilt about her thoughts.

I've found that part of the healing process for a woman who blames herself or her husband for the miscarriage falls into place when she finds the strength to release control and accept that there is nothing that she, her husband, or her doctor could have done to prevent it. This isn't easy, but if a couple can move to this point, healing can begin.

Your Husband

As you cope with your miscarriage, you may find that your husband (or partner) is not reacting to it in the same way that you are. He may seem less upset, and that can be infuriating to a woman. But there are reasons for the detachment some men show when their wives miscarry.

There are exceptions, of course. Some husbands are terrifically understanding and supportive, and they grieve as deeply as their wives. In general, however, men are less attached to a pregnancy than women, particularly an early pregnancy. I believe the reason for this is that even though the child is as much his as yours, because the baby is housed within your body and not his, he feels less connected to the pregnancy. He is, literally, an outsider. This often begins to change when a man hears the baby's heartbeat, sees images of it during an ultrasound, and feels kicking when he rests his hands on his wife's belly. But since 75% of miscarriages occur in the first trimester, before there are heartbeats to hear or pictures to see or kicking to feel, the pregnancy ends before the father ever really has a chance to become attached to it. A woman feels pregnant—she's the one who misses periods, experiences morning sickness, has sore breasts. She's the one who feels so fatigued that she's ready to fall into bed at 7:00 P.M. But for a man, pregnancy, especially very early pregnancy, is entirely abstract.

As a result, miscarriage seems sometimes less devastating for a man than for a woman. And when it is, a difficult situation can occur. You're grieving, crying, feeling sad, and your husband is getting on with his life, going to work, picking up where he left off. You may feel he's insensitive for not being upset. And he may think you're overreacting. So not only are you dealing with a miscarriage, which may be the first loss you've experienced as a couple, but you're confronting the fact that you're reacting to this loss in completely different ways. This can be really hard.

There are other scenarios as well. Your husband may seem unaffected because he wants to be strong for you, but in fact he's aching inside. Or he may hold himself together while you're a mess, and then when you start to feel better, he'll fall apart. Or he simply may not know how to express his sadness. Because so many men were told as children not to cry or to show emotion, they just bury their pain instead of expressing it.

If your husband does show emotion, he may not have the same feelings as you. While you're sad that you lost your baby, he may feel guilty for putting you through a pregnancy (I know, it's irrational, but irrational thoughts are a normal reaction in a situation like this). If you experienced a lot of pain, he may be angry because you had to go through all that. He may be frustrated because he could do nothing to protect you and his unborn child. Or he may feel helpless and alienated because the world of childbirth is a very female world in which men don't always feel comfortable or welcome.

Try to leave the lines of communication open with your husband so that he can express his feelings in a way that is most comfortable for him. Encourage him to talk, and make sure that when you talk to him about your feelings, you give him opportunities to open up, too. And when he does share his emotions, listen carefully without interrupting. If he doesn't open up, either because he can't or because he truly doesn't feel the grief that you feel, try to accept it without blaming him. It doesn't mean he's a bad guy or that he's going to be a negligent father. I've seen patients, furious with their husband's lack of sadness after a miscarriage, later be amazed by what fantastic fathers their husbands are. It may just be that the pregnancy didn't seem real to him, so losing it didn't seem real, either.

If your husband can't adequately help you through this difficult time, you need to seek support elsewhere. Talking to other people about it is very helpful and therapeutic. And if you think you and your husband would benefit from couples therapy, ask your physician to refer you to a therapist or counselor experienced in treating couples who have experienced pregnancy loss.

How to Cope

There are a variety of techniques that you and your husband can use to survive the emotional pain of miscarriage. The following skills are helpful for managing any emotional upset, but I find they are particularly useful for men and women who have experienced miscarriage. Keep in mind that not every strategy is right for every person. Try them all, and use only what helps you.

Relaxation

When you are upset, your body reacts biochemically and physiologically. Your heart rate increases, your blood pressure rises, your breathing becomes shallow and rapid, your muscles tense up, and your endocrine system unleashes a flood of stress hormones. The best way I know of to interrupt this fight-or-flight reaction, as it's known, is by eliciting the relaxation response, a physical state of deep rest that occurs when you are completely relaxed. The relaxation response, which was first identified by Harvard cardiologist Herbert Benson in the 1970s, counteracts and interrupts the biochemical and physiological responses I have listed above, and allows the body to return to a calm, relaxed state. When a person elicits the relaxation response, heart rate, blood pressure, breathing rate, stress hormone levels, and muscle tension all sustain a measurable drop.

There are many ways to elicit the relaxation response—meditation, yoga, body scan, progressive muscle relaxation, prayer, guided imagery, mindfulness, and autogenic training, among others. (I discuss each of these methods fully in my book *Conquering Infertility*.) I advise my patients to do some form of relaxation exercise, either alone or with the help of a relaxation tape, for twenty to thirty minutes once a day (or twice a day during periods of acute stress). Eliciting the relaxation response daily helps bring calm and peacefulness not only during the relaxation session but also throughout the day. I recommend relaxation during any time of distress, but it is particularly useful after a miscarriage. Relaxation helps you calm your mind, let go of the damaging effects of stress on your body, and find inner peace and strength.

Mini-Relaxations

Performed throughout the day, mini-relaxations, or "minis," as I like to call them, help recapture, in just a few seconds, a feeling of peace. They help you shift from shallow to deep abdominal breathing, and they give you an opportunity to gather the emotional resources you need to cope with a difficult situation.

There are several ways to do a mini, but this is the easiest: Simply take a deep breath, slowly counting one, two, three, four. Pause briefly. Then exhale, slowly counting four, three, two, one. Repeat a few times.

You can do minis anytime, anywhere. When your mother-in-law makes an insensitive comment about your miscarriage, do a mini. When you walk past the baby clothes section of a department store, do a mini. When you call your doctor to ask him or her questions about test results, do a mini. Some of my patients have told me that they do dozens of minis a day. They're a fantastic way to survive a difficult time.

Journaling

Research shows that writing intensely about an upsetting situation can help alleviate some of the pain caused by that situation. And I can tell you from the experience gained in my clinical practice that journaling is a fabulous tool for women who have experienced miscarriages. Writing about your miscarriage allows you to explore your thoughts, anxieties, anger, and sadness. It can also help you uncover solutions and emotional strength that may be lying buried within you. Like meditation, journal writing allows your mind to focus quietly and completely on accepting a painful situation such as a miscarriage.

I recommend this journaling process: For four days in a row, set aside twenty or thirty minutes to write about what's bothering you. Don't worry about handwriting, grammar, spelling, or using complete sentences; the point is to explore what you're feeling. You might feel worse after the first or second day, but hang in there, because it will probably get better. Research shows—and my clinical experience backs this up—that people who journal in this fashion feel worse before they feel better. If you don't improve after the fourth day, try writing again for a fifth and sixth day. Then, if you still feel burdened by your thoughts, journaling may not be enough for you, and you may need to talk to a therapist instead.

Don't limit yourself to sentences and paragraphs. Patients of mine have found it comforting to write poetry, speeches, even songs. Some of my patients have penned long letters to their unborn children in which they write at great length about the love they feel and their hopes and dreams for their children. For many women (and men, too) writing a letter to an unborn child helps them feel close to the child in an almost spiritual way.

Cognitive Restructuring

This is a technique that helps you to interrupt the cycle of negative thoughts that can loop through your mind. After a miscarriage, or any traumatic event, certain recurring thoughts or phrases may begin circulating through your head. "I should have been more careful," is a common one. So is: "This miscarriage is my fault." By using cognitive restructuring, you can defuse the power of such thoughts and free yourself of their destructiveness.

Here's how to do cognitive restructuring. First, identify one common negative thought pattern that plays in your head. Next, ask yourself the following questions about that thought:

1. Does this thought contribute to my stress?
2. Where did I learn this thought?
3. Is this thought logical?
4. Is this thought true?

These questions allow you to face your negative thought, discover its origins and effects, and put it to the test of logic. Let's ask our four cognitive restructuring questions about this statement: "The miscarriage was my fault."

Question 1: Does this thought contribute to my stress?
Answer: Certainly. Taking on the responsibility of having caused a pregnancy to fail is an enormous stressor.

Question 2: Where did I learn this thought?

Answer: Think about it—why do you think this? Did your mother have a miscarriage and blame it on herself? Did your mother-in-law tell you that you should have taken more time off from work in the first few weeks of your pregnancy? Is it just an idea you picked up somewhere years ago that you've never let go of?

Question 3: Is this thought logical?

Answer: No, it's not. Your doctor told you the miscarriage was not your fault—do you think your mother and your mother-in-law know more than a physician?

Question 4: Is this thought true?

Answer: Absolutely not. You did everything you could possibly do to ensure a healthy pregnancy. Research has shown that the primary causes of miscarriage—chromosomal abnormalities—cannot be influenced by maternal behavior.

By using cognitive restructuring on all your negative thought patterns, you can, over time, replace negative, destructive thoughts with positive, nurturing thoughts. In the above example, you can change the thought, "The miscarriage was my fault," to something like, "I did everything I could to have a healthy pregnancy, but some things are out of my control. This was not my fault."

Social Support

Having the love, support, and understanding of the people around you can be a tremendous help after a miscarriage. I remember, after my miscarriage, being astounded at the outpouring of love from family and friends. My in-laws, who were out of the country at the time, called twice a day to check on me. Friends and neighbors brought casseroles. My mother's rabbi, whom I don't know very well, called to check on us. And there were so many flowers in my living room that I ended up giving bouquets to friends. (I also began to associate the smell of cut flowers with miscarriage; I wouldn't allow flowers in my home again for a full year, when I became pregnant again and had seen the baby's heartbeat on ultrasound.)

Social support can do wonders for a couple after a miscarriage, but not all couples receive the support they need during this difficult time. There are several reasons for this. First, many couples wait until the end of the first trimester to announce their pregnancy. Since most miscarriages occur during the first trimester, family and friends probably did not even know that the couple had conceived, much less that a miscarriage had occurred. When family and friends do find out, it may be difficult for them to know how to deal with the situation. Thus for you, if your family and friends did not know that you were pregnant they are unlikely to be as emotionally attached to the pregnancy as you were. Being caught off-guard, they may not be able to muster the resources and support that you might need and wish them to provide. Second, many people are uneducated about miscarriage, the emotional strain it triggers, and the reasons for it. This lack of understanding can cause otherwise well-meaning people to make hurtful, misinformed comments. Third, we as a society are not particularly good at dealing with death and grieving in any form. Friends and family may not know how to help you, and, as a result, may say nothing or may try to just return to business as usual, commenting on whatever they watched on television last night or read in the paper this morning rather than seeking to console and support you.

Here's how you can get the support you need: speak up. You can't expect people to read your mind and know what you need and then be disappointed and angry with them when they don't come through for you. Tell people what you need, and ask them to help and support you. If you need your mother to bring over dinner for a week because you're too upset to cook, ask her. If you need your sister to stop telling you about all the people she knows who miscarried, tell her. If you need your best friend to come over for a few nights and just sit with you while you cry on her shoulder, ask her. In my experience, most people are more than willing to help, but they often need guidance. Don't think that you're selfish for asking people to help you. Your family and friends probably want to help, but don't have a clue how to do it.

If you haven't told anyone about your pregnancy, consider sharing the news of your miscarriage anyway. You need the people you love to help you through this. And you need to rely on people other than your husband since he may be limited, for one reason or another, in how much support he can give you. At the same time, don't forget that your husband may need some extra support right now, too, and that you can't fill all his support needs. Men are sometimes less willing to open up about the grief they feel after a miscarriage, but you can help your husband by putting him in touch with other men whose wives had had miscarriages—maybe you can send him over to watch a football game with the husband of a friend who miscarried. Even though he may seem less affected by it than you, he still needs support.

You'll probably find that as you tell people about your miscarriage, stories will begin pouring out from friends, family—maybe even your mother—about miscarriages they suffered. When I miscarried, people came out of the woodwork to share their stories, and it helped me so much. I can't tell you how many times I heard, "I had one, too," when I talked about my miscarriage with family, friends, and coworkers. I had no idea that so many people I knew had miscarried. Even one of my closest friends confided that she had suffered a miscarriage a few years back and hadn't told anyone about it. Sharing these stories and seeing that these women were able to survive miscarriage, most of them going on to give birth to beautiful, healthy children, was a very therapeutic experience for me.

Joining a miscarriage support group can be a wonderful, nurturing experience. Check with your local hospital, women's health clinic, or OB/GYN office to see whether there are miscarriage support groups near you. If you can't find one, try to build your own—ask your doctor to pass your name and number along to a couple of other patients who recently had a similar experience.

I do advise against joining ordinary grief support groups, which tend to consist of people who have lost husbands, wives, or older children. Also, I wouldn't recommend a support group for women who have had stillbirths—unless you miscarried very late in your pregnancy—because you might not receive the type of understanding that you need in such a group.

If your miscarriage occurred in the second trimester, try to find other women who had second-trimester miscarriages to support you. Again, a good way to do this is to ask your doctor to match you up with other women who have had a similar experience. Talking to other women who have suffered the same sort of loss as you have and who truly understand what you are going through can go a long way toward helping you heal.

If you find that you can't get the support you need from family, friends, or a support group, a visit to a therapist, clergy member, or grief counselor may help you.

It might help you next time you become pregnant to consider sharing the news of your pregnancy early, rather than waiting for the end of the first trimester. When you tell family and friends that you're pregnant, they become emotionally invested in the pregnancy. If you were to have another miscarriage, you're much more likely to get support from them. This isn't the right choice for everyone, but for some, it is.

Self-Nurturance

Women in our society spend so much time taking care of others that they often forget to take care of themselves. I am an advocate of self-nurturance for all women, but especially for women who have sustained a loss or undergone a tragedy. After you miscarry, you might be tempted to throw yourself back immediately into your other nurturing roles—wife, daughter, sister, friend, perhaps even mother to your other child or children. Naturally, you can't abandon these people, but you also can't ignore your own needs. Now is the time to nurture yourself as carefully and as thoroughly as you nurture all the other people in your life.

Spend half an hour a day doing something that is just for you. Read a trashy novel. Have a tea date with your best friend. Shop. Take yourself out for an ice-cream cone and a walk in the park. Light a candle, put your favorite classical music CD on, and just listen. Whatever you do, you'll be caring for yourself and showing yourself the love and nurturing that you show others all day long.

Nurture your relationship with your husband, too. This is called *couple nurturance*. Take long walks together, do activities that you both enjoy, plan a weekend getaway, or just do some extra cuddling as you're watching television or hanging out reading the newspaper. Pamper yourselves and create time that you can relax together and reaffirm the love you have for one another.

Another way to nurture yourself is to stay away from events or situations that may cause you pain. If a friend is having a baby shower a week or two after your miscarriage and the thought of being around a room full of chirpy women drives you crazy, then don't go to the shower. If a cousin

who conceived around the same time that you did is having a christen-
ing ceremony for her new baby, and the thought of going brings you to
tears, then skip it. Write a note, send a gift, and take care of yourself. As
a colleague of mine always says, sometimes the best way to nurture yourself is to say "no" to others.

Commemoration

Many couples feel comfort and healing when they commemorate their
baby's life and death in some way. After my miscarriage, my husband and
I planted a bush in our baby's honor and held a small private ceremony,
just the two of us, as we planted it. Other couples might make a donation
in their child's memory or write a letter to their baby and bury it with the
roots of a tree. Some commemorate their baby's existence in some other
way. One of my patients, who had suffered three miscarriages, placed
candles surrounded by sand into three paper cups and wrote a baby's
name on each cup. In a ceremony in a forest where they had spent many
happy hours hiking, the couple played music, read poetry, and then
placed each of the cups into a stream and watched them float away. As
the cups drifted downstream, the couple cried and hugged as they said
goodbye to their children.

Whatever you choose to do, a commemoration of some kind is a ges-
ture that acknowledges your baby existed. It can also give you and your
husband a sense of closure.

Waiting

Physically, most women tend to heal pretty quickly after a miscarriage,
and your physician may okay your trying to become pregnant again soon.
I would urge you, however, to wait until after you have healed emotionally before embarking on another pregnancy. Don't rush back to your
daily routine with the hope that doing so will help you forget your pain.
The best way to heal is to allow yourself to feel the pain and, eventually,
to learn to cope with it.

I've seen many patients have a miscarriage and then rush to become
pregnant again. When they do this, though, they don't leave themselves
time to grieve appropriately and completely. Even if they go on to have
successful pregnancies, they often find, years later, that they still hold

within them the pain and sadness of having miscarried. This pain may lie dormant for a while, but it can resurface when another heartbreak or loss occurs. I've seen miscarriage patients who have a particularly hard time when a parent dies, not just because they are mourning the death of the parent, but because they never properly mourned the death of their unborn child and still harbor feelings of anger, sadness, or self-blame.

It's so important to grieve your lost child before moving on to the next pregnancy. Don't push yourself to feel okay about your miscarriage. If you feel better about it, that's fine, go ahead and try to become pregnant again. But if you feel sad, weepy, and are having difficulty around pregnant women, that's okay. You need to accept that you've experienced a loss and you need time to heal. Keep in mind, of course, that if deep feelings of sadness persist for a while, you should check in with your OB/GYN or a mental health professional to see whether you're suffering from depression. A miscarriage, like any emotional upheaval, can trigger depression even in a woman who has not previously had depression. Also, if you've had a loss in the past and you didn't mourn appropriately, a miscarriage may trigger depression or deep feelings of sadness over your previous loss.

As you give yourself time to mend, take extra care of your body. Eat nutritious foods—lots of fruits, vegetables, whole grains, and an occasional indulgence of ice cream. Exercise if your physician approves. Take mindful walks or try a yoga class. This is the time to give yourself a break and to nurture your mind, body, and spirit. A miscarriage is an enormous loss, and you owe it to yourself to take the time you need to heal.

CHAPTER 9

To Test or Not to Test

EARLIER IN THIS BOOK I TOLD YOU THAT THE TWO MOST commonly asked questions after a couple has a miscarriage are:

"Why did it happen?"

and

"Did I do anything to cause it?"

In the previous chapters, we have looked in detail at the answers to these questions. We have examined all the different factors that can cause miscarriage. We have discussed at length the fact that the majority of miscarriages are caused by random chromosomal misalignment—something totally out of your control. And we have examined the way women and men respond emotionally to the crisis of having a miscarriage.

The next two most frequently asked questions—usually asked after a couple has had time for reflection—are the following:

"Should I undergo testing to see whether there was a specific cause for my miscarriage?"

and

"What can I do to prevent myself from having a miscarriage the next time I become pregnant?"

These questions have a different focus. As opposed to looking back at the pregnancy that was lost, these questions seek information about diagnosis and treatment that can be used in subsequent pregnancies.

What Is a Miscarriage Workup?

In this chapter, I will discuss whether it makes sense for you to undergo diagnostic testing—a "miscarriage workup"—after you have had a miscarriage. A miscarriage workup is an information-gathering process. It involves the taking of an in-depth medical history, a comprehensive physical exam with emphasis on the reproductive organs, and a series of blood, imaging, and other tests. The goal of the workup is to see whether there is a specific cause for your miscarriage(s) other than the spontaneous miscombination of chromosomes that is the most common cause. If such an abnormality is identified, then it may be possible to offer you a specific treatment or procedure that will improve your chances of a successful pregnancy in the future.

As we shall see, some parts of a miscarriage workup are easy and cheap, such as taking a medical history and undergoing a physical examination. Other parts are more expensive, time-consuming, and uncomfortable. In describing the components of the miscarriage workup, I have been more comprehensive than selective. It is rare that a physician will employ all the tests I describe in this chapter in evaluating any one patient.

Who Should Undergo a Miscarriage Workup?

Whether you should undergo a miscarriage workup after you have a miscarriage depends on what the odds are that you will learn something useful from it. If you have had a single first-trimester miscarriage, it's likely that its cause was chromosomal miscombination. The odds are slim that an extensive miscarriage evaluation will uncover something of use to you in future pregnancies. However, if you have had multiple miscarriages or if you have had a "late"—second trimester—miscarriage, then the odds of finding a potentially correctable cause for your miscarriage are greater—and would justify going ahead with the workup.

Here are two other reasons why it might make sense for certain couples to undergo a miscarriage evaluation:

1. Some of the chromosomal causes for miscarriage, such as translocations, involve permanent chromosomal abnormalities in one of the parents. Such chromosomal abnormalities not only cause miscarriages but also may cause birth defects in a fetus that survives to term. Therefore, if your doctor thinks there is a significant chance that your miscarriage was caused by such an inherited chromosomal abnormality, it

would certainly be worthwhile for you and your partner to have your chromosomes tested. By so doing, you can help determine the odds that you might carry a chromosomally abnormal fetus in a subsequent pregnancy. The chances that either you or your partner have an inherited chromosomal abnormality are greater if you have had recurrent miscarriages, late miscarriages, or miscarriages in which examination of the fetal tissues has revealed obvious abnormalities.

2. A second reason why it might make sense for you to have a miscarriage evaluation, even if you have had only one miscarriage, is if you are so anxious about having another miscarriage that you do not feel you can proceed with another pregnancy until you have ruled out every possible treatable cause, no matter how low the yield of such testing is likely to be. If undergoing the time, expense, and discomfort of a miscarriage evaluation is the only way it will be emotionally possible for you to go ahead with your next pregnancy, then you should undergo such testing.

How Expensive Will a Miscarriage Workup Be?

As mentioned, taking a medical history and performing a physical examination are relatively inexpensive. Other tests, such as hormonal blood testing, chromosomal analysis, and X-rays or ultrasounds will be more expensive, the tests ranging in cost from $100 and $1,000 apiece. If exploratory surgery is necessary, the cost of the workup increases significantly. With pre- and postoperative care, anesthesia, and the surgery itself, the bill can amount to as much as $4,000 to $10,000.

Whether the cost of these tests is covered by your health insurance plan will depend on the specifics of your plan and various health care "mandates" in place in your state. A health care mandate is a requirement under a given state's laws requiring insurance companies in that state to provide certain kinds of coverage. Massachusetts, for instance, is one of the few states that mandates that all health insurance plans in the state pay for infertility evaluation and treatment. In most states, insurance companies do *not* provide coverage for these sorts of tests. Certain components of a miscarriage evaluation, such as tests looking for specific diseases like lupus or diabetes, are usually covered. However, tests related specifically to miscarriage or infertility, such as hysterosalpingogram (to evaluate whether fallopian tubes are open) or laparoscopy (to visually examine pelvic organs) usually are not paid for by most plans.

In my opinion, your decision to undertake a miscarriage evaluation should not be based upon whether your insurance plan covers such tests. Your decision should be based on (1) whether such testing is appropriate for you; and (2) the lengths you are willing to go to try to avoid having another miscarriage.

As is probably clear, I am an advocate of miscarriage evaluations only for those couples in whom there is a reasonable chance of finding a specific treatable cause for their miscarriages. I do not advocate miscarriage testing for the vast majority of women who have one or two miscarriages because there is little chance that such testing will reveal anything significant or useful. We also know that most women will have successful pregnancies the next time they try to conceive no matter what tests or treatments they do or do not undergo.

But for couples with a history of recurrent or late miscarriage or a known medical problem that might lead to miscarriage, such testing can be extremely important. If a correctable cause for your miscarriage is found, taking appropriate action to redress the problem may prevent subsequent miscarriages. Just because insurance companies for their own financial reasons have made decisions about what they will or will not cover should not, I feel, affect whether you decide to be tested if your indications for such testing are appropriate. Unless your financial situation makes it totally impossible for you to afford such tests, you should consider a miscarriage evaluation *in appropriate circumstances* as one of the best long-term investments you and your spouse can make toward achieving lifelong goals for the family you have always wanted to have.

Will the Tests Be Painful or Uncomfortable?

Some will, some won't. Physical examination involves only a minimum of discomfort for most women and men. The same is true for blood work. Hysterosalpingogram—described in more detail below—can be quite uncomfortable. Of course, any diagnostic surgical procedure you undergo may involve more extensive and sustained pain and discomfort.

How Long Does Such an Evaluation Take?

Many of the tests performed during a miscarriage workup have to be performed at specific points in your menstrual cycle. Therefore, at least one month—one full cycle—is required. Usually, however, a miscarriage evaluation takes a bit longer due to scheduling problems either you or your doctor might have.

A question I am often asked is whether performing a miscarriage evaluation will delay a couple from trying to become pregnant again. Other than the one or two cycles in which the testing is taking place, the answer is no. Since testing can begin following the first period after a miscarriage, any delay will be minimal.

The Miscarriage Workup

What exactly is your doctor seeking to learn when he or she performs a miscarriage workup?

Previous Miscarriages

Although most of the information gathered in a miscarriage evaluation focuses on your current health and that of your spouse, much of importance can also be learned from previous miscarriages you have had. For instance, did it take you a long time to conceive in the pregnancy that miscarried? If so, you may have ovulation difficulties or you may have been experiencing recurrent early miscarriages before you knew that you were pregnant. Did your miscarriage occur in the second trimester? If so, factors other than accidental chromosomal miscombination are more likely to have caused it.

When you have recurrent miscarriages, examination of the tissue from the miscarriages can shed light on whether there are parental chromosomal translocations or other heritable chromosomal abnormalities present. Thus, if you have had three or more miscarriages—some doctors do this after two—it is likely that the tissue passed or removed from your uterus will be sent for chromosomal analysis. Such tissue must be preserved in saline—a saltwater solution that has chemical similarities to human blood—as opposed to the normal formalin in which tissue specimens are generally placed. Formalin preserves tissue, but in so doing causes tissue death. This would prevent the cell growth necessary for chromosomal evaluation.

Many of my patients having miscarriages for the first time want to have the tissue from their miscarriage tested. I have to tell them that such testing almost never reveals anything useful. I explain to them that the cause of most miscarriages, especially first miscarriages, is accidental chromosomal miscombination. Therefore it is a foregone conclusion that testing tissue from such miscarriages *would* reveal chromosomal abnormalities in most cases—but not the kinds that are likely to recur in subsequent pregnancies or that can be prevented.

I also explain that to test the tissue of every miscarriage that occurs, at a cost of approximately $800 to $1,200 per test, would even further bankrupt our national health care system without producing beneficial results.

The other circumstance in which it makes sense to have a laboratory evaluation of miscarriage tissue is in second-trimester miscarriages. Much can be learned by examining the tissue that is passed because structural abnormalities, skeletal defects, and other indications of inheritable birth defect syndromes can sometimes be discovered. The information derived from such testing will enable you to have as much information as possible when making decisions about your next pregnancy. Such decisions may include whether you should have an amniocentesis or chorionic villous sampling, whether—and when—to have specialized ultrasound examinations, and even whether you should try to become pregnant again. If evidence of an inherited chromosomal abnormality in either you or your spouse is uncovered, you may want to consider the use of either donor sperm or donor egg when next trying to conceive. You must know, however, that more than 50% of the time, examination or autopsy of fetal tissue from a miscarriage *does not* reveal a specific cause to explain why the miscarriage or fetal demise occurred.

Medical History

The most important part of a miscarriage evaluation is a comprehensive medical history of both you and your spouse. Below are questions you are likely to be asked.

YOUR PREGNANCY HISTORY

Have you ever been pregnant before?

Did you have any difficulty becoming pregnant?

Have you ever used assisted reproductive techniques?

> *Why does your doctor want to know this?* Because the causes of infertility and miscarriage are often the same, information about any infertility problems you have had may shed light on the cause of your miscarriage.

What were the outcomes of your pregnancies?

Did they end in living children, miscarriages, or stillbirths?

> *Why does your doctor want to know this?* A history of frequent miscarriages or stillbirths may be a sign that you have one of the causes of recurrent miscarriage such as an inheritable chromosomal abnormality or a hereditary clotting disorder.

Were they full-term deliveries?

Did you have a vaginal delivery or a cesarean section?

During those deliveries, did you experience any vaginal or cervical lacerations?

> *Why does your doctor want to know this?* Answers to these questions might indicate an increased risk of cervical weakness in subsequent pregnancies.

Have any of your children ever had congenital anomalies?

Have you ever had preterm labor? At what gestational age?

Did you have contractions with the preterm labor or did the baby just "fall out"?

> *Why does your doctor want to know this?* Your doctor is looking for evidence of incompetent cervix.

Did you experience bleeding during previous pregnancies?

> *Why does your doctor want to know this?* This may indicate the presence of hormonal inadequacy, polyps or fibroids in the uterus, or uterine structural abnormalities.

Did you have invasive testing such as amniocentesis or chorionic villous sampling during the pregnancy that ended in miscarriage?

> *Why does your doctor want to know this?* Your miscarriage may have been caused by such an intervention.

PREVIOUS MISCARRIAGES

How many miscarriages have you had?

How far along were the pregnancies when they miscarried?

How did the miscarriages "present"?
- Was there cramping and bleeding?
- Was there a gush of fluid?

Did you experience severe pelvic pressure?

How was the miscarriage treated?

Did you pass the tissue on your own or did you have a D&C to help you empty the uterus?

Were laminaria—seaweed dilators—ever used?

> *Why does your doctor want to know this?* Such information may show that there has been damage to the uterus or cervix.

Did you have live babies in between or before your miscarriages?

Was any specific cause for your miscarriage(s) ever determined?

THERAPEUTIC ABORTIONS

How many abortions have you had?

At what stage of pregnancy were the abortions performed?

What was the technique used? Suction curettage? Mini labor?

Were laminaria used?

> *Why does your doctor want to know this?* Again, this raises the possibility of structural damage to uterus or cervix.

MENSTRUAL HISTORY

Are your periods regular?

How old were you when you had your first period?

Do you get menstrual symptoms such as breast tenderness, bloating, or PMS with your cycle?

> *Why does your doctor want to know this?* The answers to these questions provide information about whether or not your cycles are ovulatory. They also provide clues to whether you are pro-

ducing normal amounts of estrogen and progesterone each cycle.

Do you have severe pain with your periods?

> *Why does your doctor want to know this?* Severe period pain is one of the cardinal symptoms of endometriosis.

How long and how heavy is your period bleeding each month?

> *Why does your doctor want to know this?* This may shed light on whether you have polyps or fibroids in your uterus.

VAGINAL OR PELVIC INFECTIONS

Have you ever had a vaginal infection? If so, what have they been diagnosed as being—yeast, bacteria, or something else?

Do you get them frequently or only intermittently?

How have they been treated? Did the treatments work?

> *Why does your doctor want to know this?* As was discussed previously, bacterial vaginal infections can cause miscarriage.

Have you ever had a pelvic infection, one involving tubes, ovaries, or uterus?

If you have, was any specific organism diagnosed as having caused it? Gonorrhea? Chlamydia?

Were you hospitalized for treatment of this infection or were you treated as an outpatient?

Have you ever had surgery either to diagnose or to treat such an infection?

What was found and what procedures were performed?

Have you ever been diagnosed as having damage to your fallopian tubes or uterus because of such an infection?

Have any of your sexual partners ever been diagnosed as having gonorrhea or chlamydia?

> *Why does your doctor want to know this?* For three reasons. The first is to make sure that you are not currently infected because this could be dangerous should you become pregnant again. The second reason, more important for obstetrical care than miscarriage evaluation, would be for your doctor to know that there might be

scar tissue in the pelvis left over from the infection. Such scar tissue could make performing a cesarean section or other pelvic surgery more difficult. The third reason is to let your physician know that Asherman syndrome—scarring caused by damage to or infection of the uterus—might be present.

SEXUAL HISTORY

How frequently do you have intercourse?

If you are trying to become pregnant, do you time intercourse to when you think you ovulate?

Does work or travel interfere with the timing of intercourse?

Are there any problems either with sex drive or sexual function with you or your partner?

Does ejaculation take place during full penetration?

Do you use any lubricants or spermicides during intercourse?

> *Why does your doctor want to know this?* The answers to these questions will tell your doctor whether any relative infertility you might have is merely due to the lack of opportunity to become pregnant or whether true infertility factors are at work. We have already seen how the causes of miscarriage and infertility can overlap: Miscarriages may recur repeatedly but do so at such an early stage that it appears no pregnancy has ever taken place.

After your "reproductive history" has been taken, your doctor will want to know about your general medical background with special emphasis on those conditions that are known to contribute to miscarriage.

Medical Problems

Are there conditions for which you are or have in the past been under the care of a physician?

Do you have any ongoing medical problems?

Have you ever been diagnosed as having diabetes, lupus, or hypertension?

Are there any medicines that you take every day?

Have you ever had surgery? What kind? Were there any complications? Did you even have an infection following one of your surgeries?

Have you ever had a tubal pregnancy? Have you ever had a fallopian tube or ovary removed for any reason?

Have you ever been told that you have congenital anomalies or birth defects?

Have the results of any of your medical tests or diagnostic studies ever come back abnormal?

Have your Pap smears always been normal?

Family History

Because so much of who and what we are is determined by our genes, it is important that we look carefully at family history to see whether there is a pattern of birth defects or evidence of hereditary chromosomal abnormalities that could contribute to miscarriage. As part of your miscarriage workup, therefore, you will be asked about members of your family who might have had birth defects and whether any of your relatives have a history of hereditary diseases. Your doctor will want to know whether anyone in your family or that of your spouse has had frequent miscarriages or prolonged infertility. Because many diseases are seen much more frequently in specific ethnic or racial groups—Tay-Sachs disease in Jews, sickle cell anemia in people of African descent, and so forth—you will be asked about the ethnic background of your family members. Of special interest will be whether your mother had any difficulties with her pregnancies. How many years were there between her children? Did she have any miscarriages? If so, how many? Was she ever given medication such as diethylstilbestrol (DES) during her pregnancies in an attempt to prevent miscarriage?

Finally, the issue of *consanguinity* will be discussed. Consanguinity is when people with some degree of blood relatedness conceive children together. It has long been known that when close relatives reproduce with each other there is a marked increase in the rates of miscarriage, stillbirth, birth defects, and hereditary diseases in their offspring. This likely accounts for many of the early societal prohibitions against marriage with close relatives.

Why do consanguineous pairings result in such poor reproductive outcomes? Almost all individuals carry some deleterious recessive genes, of which there are thousands of different types. Recessive genes cause birth defects when both copies of the gene in a pair of chromosomes are abnormal. In this situation, there is no "normal" copy of the information for which that gene is supposed to code. Since an unrelated man and woman are not likely to have inherited the same set of deleterious recessive genes, it would be rare for one of their children to inherit two of the same abnormal copies of a specific gene. However, if the deck is stacked—if a child's chromosomes come from *related* parents whose gene pools have some of the same recessive genes because they derive from the same ancestors—then the odds change. Thus, it is much more likely that the children of consanguineous marriages will be born with recessive gene defects or diseases.

Let me give you an example to show how information from your medical history can point the way to specific testing that might not otherwise be considered and might thus result in a missed opportunity for diagnosis.

There exists a condition known as Fragile X syndrome, the most common form of inherited mental retardation. It is caused by unstable DNA on specific sites of the X chromosome. It is possible to test for Fragile X syndrome by performing an analysis of the pattern of amino acids on the X chromosome. Yet Fragile X syndrome is a rare enough condition that it is not tested for routinely. You or your spouse might be a carrier of Fragile X genes—but neither of you would routinely undergo chromosomal analysis to determine this before having a baby.

A careful family history, however, might reveal several instances of mental retardation in either one of your families. Your obstetrician would thus be alerted to the need to check for the possibility that either you or your spouse carry the Fragile X gene. If follow-up testing proved this gene to be present, amniocentesis could be performed during your pregnancy to look specifically for evidence of this abnormality in the fetus. If it was found, you would be offered the option of pregnancy termination. Had the detailed family history not been taken, the suspicion never would have been raised that you or your spouse could be Fragile X carriers and the option of diagnosing the condition in your fetus would not have been offered.

Environmental History

The environment in which you live and work will determine if you regularly come into contact with any substances that could increase your risk of miscarriage. Thus the next area you will be questioned about is your environment and your personal habits:

Where do you live? Is it in an urban, rural, or suburban area? Are there factories, farms, or other facilities in your neighborhood that might expose you to chemicals or other pollutants?

What kind of work do you do? What sort of facility do you work in? Are you exposed to environmental toxins or any obvious noxious gases or fumes at work? Is there marked physical or emotional stress on the job?

What kind of physical shape are you in? Do you exercise? How much and how often? Do you do triathlons or the occasional walk around the block?

Do you participate in sports involving physical contact? Do you participate in any potentially dangerous activities such as rock climbing, skiing, flying, scuba diving, or parachuting?

Of what does your diet consist? Do you consume any unusual foods in large quantities? Given recent warnings about mercury levels in deep-sea fish such as swordfish, how much of such fish do you eat? Do you have any dietary restrictions?

Do you smoke?

How much alcohol do you drink?

What over-the-counter medications do you take regularly?

Do you use recreational drugs?

What are your hobbies? Do you develop your own pictures, make stained-glass artifacts, or participate in activities that might expose you to chemical toxins?

How about travel? Have you been to areas where you may have been exposed to parasites or infections such as malaria, hepatitis, or yellow fever? Have you had any recent vaccinations?

Have you been exposed to radiation, either for medical testing or at
work? If so, how much? If exposed to radiation at work, do you wear
a film badge to check the amount to which you are exposed?

The information supplied in answer to the above questions will give
your doctor a good idea whether you have any unusual or abnormal exposures or risk factors that might increase your chances of having a miscarriage. Such information will also help direct your doctor toward other
lines of inquiry and will help him or her determine which of the various
tests available to you should be performed.

Physical Examination

The next aspect of the miscarriage workup is a comprehensive physical
examination with special attention given to the thyroid gland and reproductive organs. A complete physical examination is necessary because several conditions that can increase the risk of miscarriage have
physical correlates. Some examples of these are specific rashes in lupus,
thyroid enlargement or nodules in thyroid disease, and uterine fibroids.

First, your blood pressure and weight will be checked. In addition to
being a sign of cardiovascular disease, elevated blood pressure may also
be caused by conditions such as adrenal or thyroid gland abnormalities.
A significant gain or loss of weight not only may be a clue to the presence of a serious disease but also may indicate why a woman does not
ovulate regularly. Inadequate body fat can interrupt the normal ovulation cycle by suppressing the pituitary gland. Excessive body fat may be
an indication of polycystic ovarian syndrome.

Your head, neck, mouth, and eyes will be examined. Then your thyroid gland will be felt to check for enlargement and to determine
whether any nodules are present. Your breasts, heart, and lungs will be
checked. Your abdomen will be "palpated"—examined carefully by
hand—with specific attention being paid to the presence of abdominal
masses or enlargement of the spleen or liver.

Next, the reproductive organs will be evaluated. Physical examination of the male is more often done in infertility than in miscarriage
evaluations. However, when such an examination is done in the male,

the penis, scrotum, and testicles are examined, looking in particular for evidence of genital infection, unusual lumps or masses on the testicles, or the presence of scrotal varicose veins. Varicose veins release more heat than thinner normal veins. This heat in turn increases the temperature in the scrotum and testicles where sperm are produced. Warm environments impede sperm production and quality. It has been shown that in men with low sperm counts, or nonmotile—inactive—sperm, tying off scrotal varicose veins can improve sperm number and motility.

In the female, the vagina, cervix, uterus, tubes, and ovaries are examined. Special attention is paid to the shape of the vagina and cervix to rule out the possibility of congenital or trauma-induced abnormalities. They are also checked for evidence of vaginal or cervical infection.

The size and shape of your uterus will then be checked by "bimanual" examination. This is the examination in which the doctor places one hand in your vagina and the other hand on your lower abdominal wall. Between the two hands, the size and shape of your uterus, tubes, and ovaries are evaluated. An enlarged uterus could indicate that you have fibroids, or even that you are pregnant. Enlarged ovaries could indicate an ovarian cyst or tumor. Enlargement of your fallopian tubes could indicate a tubal abscess or a hydrosalpinx—a scarred, fluid-filled tube resulting from a previous tubal infection.

After having learned as much as possible about your reproductive health from your medical history and physical examination, the next part of your miscarriage evaluation will involve evaluating your internal chemical environment via blood tests.

Blood Work

Blood flows to every cell of the body. Not only does it supply each cell with nutrients and oxygen but it also picks up the cells' secretions and waste products. Thus, the chemical analysis of blood allows us to measure the physiologic state of our cells—as determined from their waste products and secretions—and to evaluate what they have and have not been producing.

As part of your miscarriage evaluation, you will have several blood tests taken. Some of these can be performed at any time and may be drawn at your initial visit. Other tests are dependent upon where you are in your menstrual cycle or when you have last eaten. These need to be drawn at specific times in relation to the onset of your last period or after an overnight fast.

The first tests drawn will check your general health. These include a complete blood count—CBC—and a chemistry profile, a smorgasbord of tests that gives an overall assessment of how well your liver, kidneys, and other organs are functioning. In addition, you'll likely be asked to give a urine specimen for urine analysis and culture. This checks for urinary tract infection, diabetes, and kidney disease.

Other blood work will be obtained to check for the presence of specific diseases that are known to be associated with miscarriage. You will probably have blood tests performed to check your baseline blood sugar—a "fasting blood sugar"—and to determine how well your body handles a sugar load, a "glucose tolerance test." As the name implies, the fasting blood sugar test is drawn after not eating all night and before eating in the morning. The glucose tolerance test is drawn one to two hours after drinking a special sweet drink that contains a fixed amount of sugar. When you eat, your pancreas normally increases its production of insulin to help you digest the sugar portion of the sugar, protein, and fat into which all food you eat gets broken down. In diabetes, either the pancreas cannot produce enough insulin to meet the demands of the sugar load in your blood or your body has become "insulin resistant"—does not respond properly to the insulin that is there. Either one of these conditions leads to chronic elevated levels of sugar in the blood—the definition of diabetes—that eventually induces the sort of microvascular disease described in Chapter 7.

The presence or absence of thyroid disease is determined by evaluating three things:

1. Thyroid stimulating hormone (TSH)
2. T3 and T4, the two forms of thyroid hormone
3. Antithyroid antibodies

TSH is normally produced in the pituitary gland. It induces the thyroid gland to produce thyroid hormone. TSH is suppressed if adequate amounts of thyroid hormone are present in the blood. However, if there is inadequate thyroid hormone, the pituitary gland produces more TSH to stimulate an increase in the thyroid gland's output. Thus the TSH level is the body's own measure of whether its thyroid hormone level is normal.

The T3 and T4 tests are direct measures of the amount of thyroid hormone in the body. The antithyroid antibody test checks for the presence of autoimmune antibodies against thyroid cells. As you may remember from Chapter 6, antithyroid antibodies are directly associated with miscarriage. Such antibodies not only indicate the presence of thyroid disease but also indicate the propensity for the body to make antibodies against its own tissues.

Lupus erythematosis is another autoantibody disease. In lupus, antibodies are made to a variety of tissues resulting in damage to multiple organs of the body. Several different antigens associated with lupus can be measured in the blood. Those most commonly checked for are antinuclear antibodies (ANA) and "anti-native DNA antibodies." Unfortunately, these antibodies are not specific to lupus and are also often present in other autoimmune diseases such as rheumatoid arthritis and scleroderma. Therefore, the diagnosis of lupus, although suspected by positive ANA and anti-native DNA antibody tests, is in the end made by a combination of history and physical examination findings together with laboratory tests.

The blood's ability to clot properly is assessed in several ways. The first is by a blood platelet count, which often is a part of the CBC mentioned above. Platelets are the components of blood that first respond to cuts and lacerations. They form an initial, temporary clot to which the other clotting factors in the blood adhere. The mixture of platelet "plug" and clotting factors forms the permanent clot.

In addition to measuring platelets, the blood clotting abnormalities that cause the hypercoagulability disorders discussed in Chapter 7 are sought. These are:

1. Deficiencies in proteins C and S
2. Congenital abnormality of factor V Leiden
3. Partial thromboplastin time
4. Bleeding time—the stop-watch measured time it takes an intentionally made cut to clot

All these affect or measure the ability of the body's complex clotting system to function correctly. As we have seen, conditions that result in excess clot formation in small vessels in the placenta can lead to miscarriage.

The presence or absence of antiphospholipid syndrome is evaluated by checking the blood for the presence of anticardiolipid antibodies and lupus anticoagulant.

You may also be tested for blood mercury and lead levels, depending on specific risks in your home and work environment and in the geographic area in which you live. As we have discussed, elevated levels of these "heavy metals" can be toxic to a developing embryo and result in miscarriage.

Evaluation of Reproductive System Hormonal Function

A vital element in evaluating how well prepared your body is to conceive and successfully carry a pregnancy is an assessment of your reproductive hormones. This is done in several ways.

First, your follicle stimulating hormone (FSH) level will be measured on day three of one of your menstrual cycles. The level of FSH will reveal the status of your "ovarian reserve"—how many eggs you have left in your ovaries and how well they function. If you have adequate egg stores and the cells of the follicles surrounding these eggs are potent enough, they will produce sufficient estrogen and progesterone to suppress your FSH production. If your supply of eggs is low—as it sometimes is in women in their late thirties and early forties—your follicle stimulating hormone level will not be suppressed. An elevated day three FSH level does not bode well for a woman's ability either to become pregnant or to sustain a pregnancy.

Other hormones may also be tested as part of your miscarriage evaluation:

1. Serum progesterone.
   As described previously, progesterone is produced in the second half of the menstrual cycle by the corpus luteum. The corpus luteum is formed from those cells remaining on the ovary at the site of ovulation. Progesterone is essential for the support of early pregnancy.

An adequate progesterone level in the second half of your cycle confirms that you have ovulated and that your postovulation corpus luteum is producing adequate amounts of this hormone. Thus if your doctor wants to check your serum progesterone value, you would have blood drawn approximately one week before your next expected menstrual period.

2. Androgen levels.

Androgens are predominantly male hormones that are present at low levels in all women. Half the androgens in women are produced by the ovaries while the other half are produced by the adrenal glands. If your androgen levels are elevated, whether through ovarian or adrenal gland overproduction, your ovulation cycle may be interrupted and your production of estrogen and progesterone reduced. Elevated androgens can also negatively affect the quality and consistency of your cervical mucus. The condition of cervical mucus is important in allowing sperm to swim through the cervix up to the uterus during attempts at getting pregnant.

3. Serum prolactin.

Prolactin is a hormone made in the pituitary gland. There are several reasons why a woman's serum prolactin might be elevated. Rarely such elevation indicates the presence of a pituitary tumor and a CT or MRI scan will be ordered to determine if this is the case.

Because the pituitary gland produces the stimulatory hormones that induce the production of many other hormones—thyroid, adrenal steroids, estrogen, progesterone—malfunction of the pituitary gland interferes with the normal workings of many physiologic processes in the body. Such malfunction can also prevent ovulation and conception and increase the risk of miscarriage.

Chromosome Testing

An essential part of any miscarriage evaluation is to establish that your chromosomes and those of your spouse are normal. Thus you will both have blood tests to ascertain this. White cells will be taken from those blood specimens and specially processed. The result will be a "karyotype"—a composite analysis of the physical structure of a person's chromosomes—for both of you.

TABLE 9.1   Normal Values for Blood Tests*

TEST	NORMAL
Hematocrit (Hct)	35–45%
(Measure of % of blood that is red cells)	
White blood cell count	3.8–10.8
(Rough measure of infection status)	
Platelet count	140–400 thou/uL
Fasting blood sugar	65–95 mg/dl
Blood sugar 1 hr after glucose drink	65–180mg/dl
Blood sugar 2 hrs after glucose drink	65–155 mg/dl
Thyroid stimulating hormone	0.3–5.5 uIU/ml
T3	60–181 ng/dl
T4	4.5–12.0 ug/dl
Serum prolactin	2.8–26.7 ng/ml
Protein C	70–140% of normal
Factor V Leiden	65–150% of normal
Protein S	70–140% of normal
Bleeding time	2–9.5 min
Partial thromboplastin time	22–35 secs
Blood mercury	0–10 ug/L
Blood lead	0–9 ug/l

*Typical values. The "normal" values for each laboratory differ.

To produce a karyotype, the white cells extracted from blood specimens are placed in tissue culture. This is a special chemical medium that
allows cells to continue to live and grow outside the body. When as part
of their growth cycle the cells divide, this division is stopped midway to
completion by treating the cells with colchicine, a compound that para-
lyzes cell growth. The point in the cycle selected for this interruption of
cell division is when the chromosomes are at their thickest and are most
easily identifiable. All 46 chromosomes of several selected cells are pho-
tographed through a microscope. Pictures of these chromosomes are then
pieced together like a jigsaw puzzle. The chromosomes are arranged by
pair on a display page so that each of the 46 chromosomes in the 23 pairs
can be examined for structural integrity. This is the karyotype. (See Figure 2.1 on page 26.)

The karyotypes of several cells from each white cell culture are
checked against each other for consistency to make certain that the
chromosomes arrayed in the karyotype are representative of that person's
overall chromosomal makeup. If any structural abnormalities of the
chromosomes are seen in the karyotype, these are identified and labeled.

Thus if your karyotype shows that you are missing an X chromosome— Turner's syndrome—or that you have a balanced translocation, this may explain why you had a miscarriage or why you and your partner have had trouble becoming pregnant (see page 37).

Over the last thirty years, laboratories across the country and around the world have developed the ability to detect several thousand gene-mediated diseases. Some of these diseases, such as Tay-Sachs syndrome, are relatively well known. The majority are exceedingly rare, and often only one or two laboratories in the world can test for a specific disease. If your family has a history of a hereditary disease, it may be that your chromosomes can be tested to see whether you are a carrier of this disease. The ins and outs of which diseases can be tested for and which laboratories are able to do this testing are complex and ever-changing. When such questions arise, they are best handled by genetic counselors. Your obstetrician can direct you to qualified genetic counselors in your area.

Assessment of Ovulation

Whether you ovulate normally and the "quality" of your ovulations are vitally important factors in determining how successful you will be in reproduction. Of course, the first step in becoming pregnant is for you to make an egg. But as you now know, the entire hormonal environment of your reproductive system after you ovulate each month depends on the "potency" of your ovulation, that is, on the health of the egg and the ability of the cells that surround it to produce necessary hormones. These are key factors that must be assessed in any miscarriage evaluation. There are several means by which this can be done, some of which we have already discussed.

The first means of determining whether you are ovulating is the simple and exceedingly reliable method of inquiring about your menstrual history: If you have regular monthly periods, you are almost certainly ovulating.

Next is the measurement of basal body temperature. We have discussed previously that a woman's body temperature rises from approximately one-half to one degree above her average temperature following ovulation. This is due to the rise in progesterone level in her blood that occurs at this point in her menstrual cycle.

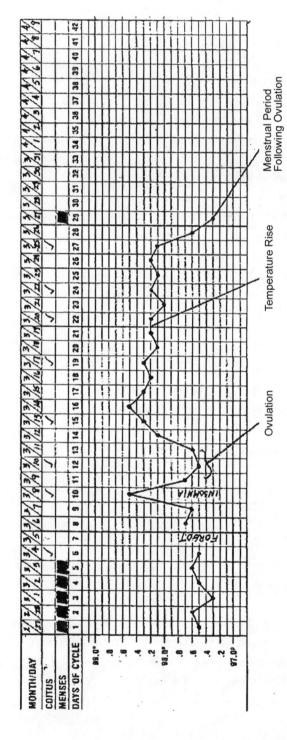

FIGURE 9.1   Basal Body Temperature Chart

You can measure your basal body temperature by taking your temperature first thing in the morning while still in bed and then charting it. Over the course of a monthly cycle you will see that the values you plot will start at one level and then rise from one-half to one degree in mid-cycle to a second, higher level. These elevated temperature readings will persist until the cycle's end. If your chart does not show this sort of consistent rise in basal body temperature in the second half of your cycle, you probably did not ovulate that month.

As discussed above, your serum progesterone level will be measured one week before your next expected menstrual period. If it is above a certain level—and that level varies with each laboratory—ovulation in that cycle will have been confirmed. Blood estrogen levels are sometimes also followed during the first half of the menstrual cycle to assess how well the growth of your egg follicles is progressing. A rapidly rising estrogen level indicates that normal follicular growth and preparation for ovulation are taking place.

Another way to assess the presence or absence of ovulation is the ovulation predictor kit. These kits, which can be purchased in any pharmacy, measure the surge of luteinizing hormone (LH) that occurs at mid-cycle. As discussed in Chapter 2, a burst of LH is released from the pituitary gland approximately twenty-four hours before ovulation. This is what triggers the mature egg-containing ovarian follicle to rupture and release its egg. The buildup and surge of this LH can be measured in urine.

Each kit contains small plastic sticks with immunochemically sensitive patches on them. You dip one of the sticks into your "first morning" urine each morning. The "first morning" urine is used because it is the most concentrated of the day and thus has the highest level of hormone in it. If a measurable amount of LH is present in the urine, the patch will change color. When this change is seen for the first time in a given cycle it means that ovulation will take place within twelve to thirty-six hours. Ovulation predictor kits are usually used by couples to indicate when it is best for them to have intercourse to maximize their chances of becoming pregnant. But it can also be used as part of an infertility or miscarriage evaluation to verify that ovulation is occurring.

For women who do not ovulate regularly and for those women who are using potent medications to induce ovulation, the growing follicles in the ovary can actually be observed and followed by ultrasound examination. When one or more follicles reach a critical size, it indicates that ovulation is imminent, thus confirming that ovulation is going to occur and alerting couples about the best time to attempt to conceive.

Finally, endometrial biopsy, discussed previously, can give proof positive that ovulation has occurred. The endometrial lining of the uterus undergoes specific changes when exposed to estrogen and progesterone. Its appearance will be different depending on whether it has been exposed to estrogen alone or to both estrogen and progesterone. Since progesterone is only present in the body following ovulation, evidence of progesterone-type changes in the endometrium demonstrates conclusively that ovulation has occurred. Whether one can precisely define the *adequacy* of progesterone production on the basis of endometrial testing is, as discussed in Chapter 7, in dispute.

Testing for Infection

Because infections of the female genital track are much more likely to cause miscarriage than infection in the male, most testing for infection will be done on the female partner. The testing that is done on semen is discussed below.

In women, testing for infection is performed by taking a culture of vaginal and cervical secretions. Your physician will place a sterile cotton or nylon swab into your vagina and cervix and collect specimens with them. These swabs are then put into a growth medium and sent to the laboratory. In the laboratory, the specimens are incubated in special solutions known to foster the growth of certain organisms. The ones we are most interested in are those we discussed back in Chapter 4 as being suspected of leading to miscarriage: gonorrhea, chlamydia, mycoplasma, and ureaplasma.

Depending on your medical history and any recent exposures you may have had, you may have blood tests performed looking for antibodies, both recent and long standing, to such conditions as hepatitis, cytomegalovirus, HIV, syphilis, toxoplasmosis, chickenpox, and German measles. You will remember that IgG antibodies against a specific infection indicate that immunity was acquired in the past while IgM antibodies indicate recent, perhaps ongoing, infection.

I have already mentioned that new studies have reported that bacterial infections of the vagina—bacterial vaginosis (BV)—may increase the risk of miscarriage. Thus your vagina will be evaluated for the presence of bacterial vaginosis by looking for a frothy, fishy-smelling, gray, yellow, or green vaginal discharge and by doing a microscopic examination of the vaginal discharge.

Semen Analysis

It is unlikely that male factors, other than hereditary abnormal chromosomes, contribute much toward the occurrence of miscarriage. Nevertheless, there is controversy amongst experts in the field as to whether the following semen factors might cause miscarriage: abnormal sperm shape and size, the presence of white blood cells or bacteria, and evidence of antibodies.

What is the significance of these factors?

1. Abnormal sperm shape and size may be caused by abnormal chromosomes, which could lead to miscarriage.
2. The presence of white blood cells in semen is usually a sign of infection. Such an infection could spread to the cervix and uterus. Depending on the organism causing the infection and the inflammatory response it evokes, this infection could induce a miscarriage.
3. Although antibodies in semen are more likely to cause infertility than miscarriage, there is the possibility that the presence of such antibodies could create an inflammatory response in the uterus. Such a response would diminish the chances for successful implantation of an embryo.

Because of the lack of consensus about the significance of the above factors, semen analysis is not always performed as part of a miscarriage evaluation.

Imaging Studies

Imaging is the term used by radiologists to describe all the means available to them for picturing internal structures. It incorporates x-rays, CT scans, ultrasound examinations, and magnetic resonance imaging. As with the history taking, physical examination, and blood work described above, the imaging that will be performed will focus on those conditions known to contribute to miscarriage.

Imaging studies can provide a more precise evaluation of the size and shape of your pelvic organs than can be gained by physical examination alone. For this reason you will almost certainly undergo either a hysterosalpingogram (HSG) or a sonohysteroscopy as part of your miscarriage evaluation. Both these tests can show whether you have:

- a septate or bicornuate (double) uterus,
- uterine fibroids,
- adhesions present between the uterine walls—Asherman syndrome, or
- any other uterine or tubal structural abnormalities.

In addition the HSG can outline the internal shape of the uterine cavity and can determine whether or not your fallopian tubes are open, the latter more important in infertility investigations than in a miscarriage workup.

Hysterosalpingograms were described briefly in Chapter 3. A sonohysteroscopy is the performance of an abdominal or vaginal ultrasound examination of the uterus after filling it with fluid via a catheter threaded through the cervix. The fluid separating the uterine walls increases the sensitivity of the ultrasound examination.

Usually at the completion of either test your physician or the radiologist will review the findings of the test with you. Any cramping you experience usually dissipates five to fifteen minutes after the procedure is over. In HSGs, the dye in the pelvis is absorbed by your body over several days.

Other tests may sometimes be needed to further define the shape of your uterine cavity or to follow up on an abnormality of your uterus, tubes, or ovaries suspected by physical exam, HSG, or sonohysteroscopy. These tests may include magnetic resonance imaging (MRI) or computerized axial tomography (CT scan). Such tests can often aid in determining the exact size or position of uterine fibroids or determine more precisely the nature of a congenital or acquired uterine anomaly.

Occasionally, your doctor will need information about the inside of your uterus that can be acquired only by direct visual examination. If you require such an exam, your doctor will recommend that you undergo a hysteroscopic procedure. As discussed previously, hysteroscopy is a minor diagnostic operation in which a very thin scope is placed into the cervical and uterine cavities so that these structures can be observed directly or via a camera and television monitor (see Figure 3.2 on page 60). By viewing the inside of the cervix and uterus in this way, specific lesions or surface abnormalities can be seen, thus facilitating diagnosis. Hysteroscopy can be performed in the office or surgical outpatient setting. It can be done with minimal anesthesia or a brief general anesthetic depending on the goal of the procedure and the preferences of you and your doctor. Hysteroscopy can also be used to surgically correct various problems—but more on that in Chapter 10.

The need for evaluation by other operative means such as laparoscopy or exploratory abdominal surgery is rare in a miscarriage evaluation. It is true that such surgery would enable your physician to see scar tissue in the pelvis, damage to fallopian tubes, ovarian abnormalities, and the presence of endometriosis. But these factors are of much more importance in determining causes of infertility than they are in evaluating why a woman has had miscarriages. Thus, fortunately, the need for invasive abdominal and pelvic surgery in a miscarriage workup is rare.

Cervical Evaluation

The main reason for evaluation of the cervix is to rule out cervical incompetence. This is the condition in which the cervix is so structurally weakened that it cannot hold in the increasing weight of a growing fetus. Most cases of cervical incompetence are diagnosed by a history of a "silent"—symptomless—second-trimester miscarriage as described in Chapter 3. The diagnosis can also be made—or confirmed—by ultrasound examination during early pregnancy. If the diagnosis is made, a woman can have a cervical cerclage (described in Chapter 10) placed before the cervical weakness results in miscarriage. Unfortunately, there are currently no reliable tests for incompetent cervix that can be performed when a woman is not pregnant.

Controversial Theories

Since miscarriages occur as frequently as they do and since they affect the lives of so many people, the phenomenon of miscarriage is of tremendous interest to medical researchers. Almost every month, therefore, there are new reports of diagnostic tests and proposed new treatments for miscarriage. As with any new development in medicine, things almost always look more optimistic initially than they do later. Thus many of these new tests and proposed treatments for miscarriage, when evaluated over time, do not live up to the initial claims made for them. Because you will hear about such tests and treatments as you do further reading or Web research on the subject of miscarriages, I will present a couple of examples of such controversial tests and treatments and discuss their current status.

Embryotoxic Factor

It had been thought by a prominent group of researchers in Boston that they had found an immunologic factor in blood that was present much more frequently in women who had experienced miscarriages than in women who had not. They felt that this factor was the causative agent of many miscarriages. These researchers initially claimed that by identifying this *embryotoxic factor* in women, it could be treated and the risk of miscarriage reduced.

Unfortunately, other laboratories have tried to identify and measure embryotoxic factor but have been unable to do so. Now, as a general rule, any scientific hypothesis or theory needs to be verifiable by others if it is to be accepted by the scientific community as a whole. Thus the inability of researchers at other institutions to duplicate the initial work on embryotoxic factor has called the theory's validity into question. Until and unless other investigators can reproduce the results obtained by the Boston research group, the role of embryotoxic factor in the diagnosis and treatment of miscarriage will remain unsubstantiated.

Antipaternal Cytotoxic Antibodies

Another proposed cause of miscarriage is that of antipaternal cytotoxic antibodies (ACAs). It has been suggested by a few research laboratories that some pregnant women make cell-killing—"cytotoxic"—antibodies against certain cell markers in their babies. These cell markers are those derived from their father. The mother's cytotoxic antibodies supposedly bind with baby's cell markers and induce killer lymphocytes to destroy the cells containing these markers.

But further research has shown that these so-called antipaternal cytotoxic antibodies are present as often in women who have successful pregnancies as they are in women who miscarry. It is currently felt by the majority of investigators in the field of miscarriage studies that antipaternal cytotoxic antibodies are not a significant cause of miscarriage.

The above is in no way intended to educate you about the intricacies of immunology as it relates to miscarriage. Rather, it is to alert you to the sorts of claims you may run across in your reading, on the Web, and when talking to friends. You may encounter reports of new diagnostic or therapeutic techniques claiming either to definitively determine the cause of miscarriages or to provide a new, guaranteed cure for them. Such claims should be regarded cautiously and with a certain amount of skepticism.

Conclusion

In this chapter I have described in some detail the tests you may undergo in attempting to find out why you have had a miscarriage. I have particularly tried to point out when and in what circumstances such testing is and is not appropriate.

The key thing to remember about a miscarriage evaluation is that despite how precise it all may sound, we are just beginning to understand why most miscarriages occur. Regarding the random miscombination of chromosomes that is the basis for the majority of miscarriages, we do not know why this occurs in 20% of all pregnancies and not in the other 80%. As for the other causes of miscarriage, we do not know why some women with uterine infection, uterine septum, and so forth, will have a successful pregnancy while others with the same factors will miscarry.

We must never forget that most women who have a miscarriage will go on to have a successful pregnancy the next time they conceive whether or not an evaluation is performed or treatment is administered. Therefore in deciding who should and who should not undergo extensive testing it is important to go back to the basic question that should guide all decisions about medical diagnostic testing: Given the cost, time, and discomfort involved, is the performance of these tests likely to be rewarded by useful information or an improved outcome?

CHAPTER 10

Preventing Miscarriage

IN THE PREVIOUS NINE CHAPTERS I HAVE EXPLORED WITH you various aspects of the subject of miscarriage. Among other things, you now know what miscarriages are, what causes them, and what tests are appropriate for you to undergo if you have had one. It is now time for us to confront the most important question of all: How can you prevent a miscarriage—or at least significantly decrease the chances of having one—in your next pregnancy?

The answer to this question is not straightforward. It depends on the kind of miscarriage we are talking about. Remember, there are two major categories of miscarriages: those caused by sporadic, accidental miscombinations of chromosomes and those caused by a variety of other specific problems—anatomic, immunologic, and so on. Whether a miscarriage can be prevented depends on what caused it.

Moreover, the question "How can we prevent miscarriages?" assumes that it is easy to tell just when a miscarriage has been prevented. Unfortunately, this is not always easy to determine. If we are talking about miscarriages that have a specific cause, such as diabetes or a weakened cervix, it is not too hard to compare how groups of women with these problems do in subsequent pregnancies with or without treatment. But for those women whose miscarriages are in the "sporadic" category—the great majority of miscarriages—determining whether a treatment works is more complicated.

It is more complicated because of the key fact about miscarriages I have discussed repeatedly in the preceding chapters: The success rate for *any* pregnancy following a sporadic miscarriage is about 80%. Thus, any proposed treatment for sporadic miscarriage would have to have a success rate considerably in excess of 80% for us to know that the treatment had made a difference. This is a high hurdle a proposed therapy must jump for it to prove itself worthwhile.

So when we ask the all-important question, "Can miscarriages be prevented?" we must specify two things. First, we must distinguish the kind of miscarriage we are talking about. Second, we must understand our limitations in knowing whether a treatment has been successful.

Spontaneous Sporadic Miscarriages

Spontaneous sporadic miscarriages constitute the vast majority of miscarriages. By definition, they do not have a specific identifiable cause such as infection, abnormal uterus, or immune disorder. They may occur during your first pregnancy or may happen after you have had one, two, or more normal babies. Most of these sorts of miscarriages, as we have discussed in detail, are due to random chromosomal miscombination at some phase of the reproductive process. They result from spontaneous errors in chromosome replication, chromosome pair splitting, and the chromosomal recombination that takes place when egg and sperm fuse at conception. These are natural, spontaneous phenomena.

Unfortunately, there is currently nothing you can do to prevent these sorts of miscarriages. We have as much control over the specifics of chromosome replication in our eggs and sperm as we have over the specific behavior of any cell in our bodies: none. Just as we cannot determine how one of our hair cells or liver cells or muscle cells will grow and divide, we cannot affect the microscopic behavior of eggs and sperm. We can try to eliminate those causes of miscarriage that we do understand. We can try to treat specific problems that we know lead to miscarriage. But we cannot as yet manipulate or alter the spontaneous behavior of chromosomes as cells replicate, split, and recombine to form an embryo.

This is not to say that someday we won't have control over this behavior. Even now assisted-reproduction specialists can insert a specifically chosen sperm directly into an egg cell. It is also currently possible, as part of an in vitro fertilization cycle, to take one cell from a very early embryo and analyze its chromosomes, the preimplantation genetic diagnosis discussed in Chapter 2. From this analysis, the decision can be made whether the embryo is healthy enough to be implanted into a woman. Other methods to evaluate whether the chromosomal content of an embryo or fetus is normal are amniocentesis and chorionic villous sampling. But as with the analysis of a single cell from an embryo, such techniques only allow us to evaluate chromosomes from *existing* embryos. From these results, our only option is to decide whether or not to terminate a pregnancy. These techniques do not give us control over the health of the chromosomes in the egg or sperm that will direct the development of the fetus.

So although it is possible to evaluate chromosomes at a very early stage of embryo formation, no technique currently exists that will eliminate chromosomal miscombinations in spontaneous reproduction. Chromosomal miscombinations will continue to occur—and will continue to cause miscarriages.

Treatable Causes of Miscarriage

Although it is true that the majority of miscarriages—those caused by sporadic chromosomal miscombinations—cannot be prevented, there is a significant group of miscarriages whose causes are potentially treatable. In the last chapter we looked at the various ways in which we can try to diagnose why a miscarriage has occurred. We can thus try to determine for any particular miscarriage whether it has a specific identifiable cause—thus is potentially treatable—or whether it is in the "nontreatable" group. In the pages that follow, I will look at what can be done to try to prevent the occurrence of those miscarriages in the "potentially treatable" group.

Chromosomal Causes of Miscarriage

Couples diagnosed as having an inherited chromosomal abnormality as the cause of their miscarriage face some of the same problems in trying to prevent recurrent miscarriage as do couples who have had a "sporadic" miscarriage. That's because such couples currently have no way of determining which of the genes in their 23 pairs of chromosomes—the normal ones or the inherited abnormal ones—will wind up in the egg or sperm that becomes fertilized when they conceive. Moreover, we are all stuck with the genes we are born with. Currently, there is no known way to change the chromosomal composition of our cells. And even if we had the expertise to know which sperm or eggs from among all the sperm or eggs we produce were healthy ones, the mere process of trying to se-lect them out would likely damage them.

We can determine who is at risk for inherited chromosomal abnor-malities by the diagnostic techniques discussed in Chapter 9. Your fam-ily history, your personal reproductive history, and laboratory analysis of your chromosomes are vital factors in this evaluation. Genetic counsel-ing can help shed light on the specific conditions you are at risk for and what your odds are of having one of them. This information can help you decide whether you wish to try again to become pregnant and what tests you wish to have once you are pregnant.

Infections

In Chapter 4 we discussed the role of infections in causing miscarriage. We saw that although not all infections increase the risk of miscarriage, there are many that do. We also discussed the mechanism by which in-fections can cause early pregnancy loss: the creation of a hostile envi-ronment for implantation and growth of the early embryo, inflammation of the placenta, and direct toxic effects on the fetus. In addition, we saw how the symptoms and side effects a mother may experience when she has an infectious disease—elevated temperature and acidosis of her blood—can harm her early pregnancy.

Let's take a look at some of the infectious conditions you might expe-rience and then review what dangers they do or do not pose and how such dangers can be avoided or treated.

Colds and Flus

Except for the possibility of fetal injury from elevated maternal tempera-tures, colds and flus do not lead to miscarriage.

Vaginal Infections

Yeast infections: Although irritating and very uncomfortable, yeast in-fections do not cause miscarriages.

Bacterial vaginosis: Until very recently, bacterial vaginal infections were not thought to contribute to miscarriage. It had been suspected for many years that bacterial vaginal infections might increase the risk of preterm labor in pregnant women. Only very recently, however, have researchers found evidence that the inflammation in the birth canal, cervix, and lower uterus caused by bacterial vaginosis does, in fact, increase the risk of miscarriage.

If you have bacterial vaginosis, you can and should be treated, especially during early pregnancy or if you are trying to conceive. A variety of antibiotics effective against bacterial vaginosis are safe for use during pregnancy. The ones most commonly employed are clindamycin and metronidazole, both of which come in oral and vaginal forms. By eliminating bacterial vaginosis, you will lower your chances of having a miscarriage.

Urinary tract infections: Unless it were to turn into a severe kidney infection, a urinary tract infection during pregnancy will not cause you to miscarry.

Childhood Viral Illnesses

Chickenpox (Varicella): This common childhood disease can cause miscarriages and birth defects if acquired during pregnancy. Fortunately, you are probably already immune to chickenpox from having had it as a child. If you are not immune, a chickenpox vaccine is now available, and you should arrange to have yourself vaccinated with it. Unfortunately, since the chickenpox vaccine is a "live virus" vaccine, inoculation for chickenpox cannot be performed during pregnancy. Its administration during pregnancy could allow the chickenpox virus to pass from the mother to the fetus, potentially causing fetal injury or death.

To know whether you are immune to chickenpox, you need to know for certain that you have had it at some point. If you don't know, you should have your blood tested to determine whether you have antibodies to chickenpox. "Knowing for certain" means your direct memory of having had chickenpox, having been told by your parents or siblings that you had it, or getting access to your childhood medical records.

If you are pregnant and are not immune to chickenpox, you need to avoid situations in which you might become exposed to it. If you are a schoolteacher, nurse, or work with children, you should consider discontinuing such work for the duration of your pregnancy. Before going on visits, you should call ahead to find out whether there is anyone where you are going who has chickenpox or has been exposed to it.

If you are pregnant, not immune, and find that you have contracted or been exposed to chickenpox, you need to contact your doctor immediately. There is a medicine called varicella-zoster immunogloblin—VZIG—that can help lessen the severity of a case of chickenpox and perhaps—although this has not yet been definitely proven—reduce the chances of miscarriage or birth defects. VZIG is usually distributed by Red Cross blood banks. Your doctor will know how to put you in touch with them. Afterward, your fetus will be followed carefully with ultrasound examinations to see whether it has suffered any ill effects from exposure to the chickenpox virus.

Fifth disease: This is a common childhood illness caused by the parvovirus. The symptoms, as discussed in Chapter 4, are fever, joint pains, and an all-over reddish rash. Often there is a red "slapped cheek" facial appearance as part of the rash. As with chickenpox, you are probably already immune to fifth disease. But if you are not immune and become infected with the parvovirus while you are pregnant, it can sometimes cause a miscarriage or stillbirth.

Unfortunately, there is currently no way either to prevent or to treat fifth disease. There is no vaccine for it. And there also is no specific medication to cure it once acquired. The illness has to run its course over three to seven days. But, as with chickenpox, you can take precautions to avoid it.

One important step is to find out whether you are immune to fifth disease before becoming pregnant. You can do this by having blood tests done at your doctor's office. If you are not immune, attempt to avoid situations in which you might become exposed to it. Such situations would be anywhere children gather: school classrooms, nursery schools, medical facilities dealing with children, and so forth.

But even while presenting such advice, I must acknowledge a major problem with it: It is not realistic. For many women—teachers and nurses especially—are at risk for acquiring fifth disease because their work involves children. Interestingly, official recommendations about fifth-disease avoidance for women in high-risk jobs have been ambiguous. This is probably because, in any given year, relatively few women become infected with fifth disease and suffer consequences from it despite the many pregnant women exposed to it. What *you* should do if pregnant and faced with the possibility of exposure to fifth disease at work is a decision that you should make together with your spouse, doctor, and employer.

If you contract fifth disease during pregnancy, your doctor will advise you to have serial ultrasound examinations to look for evidence of fetal injury. Of special concern is the possibility of fetal anemia leading to fetal heart failure. If your fetus were to develop anemia, you would probably be offered the option of an intrauterine fetal blood transfusion, a procedure that can be lifesaving for your fetus.

German measles (Rubella): German measles was the first of the viral illnesses shown to cause miscarriage and birth defects. As with other childhood viral illnesses, there is no specific treatment for it. The best and only approach to prevent miscarriage and fetal damage from German measles is for pregnant women to avoid getting it. Toward this end, almost all children in developed countries are inoculated against rubella. This is important for two reasons. First, if you are immunized you will not get the disease. Second, if the majority of individuals in a community are immunized, there will be fewer outbreaks of German measles that could injure the fetuses of those few women who are not immune.

If you are considering becoming pregnant, it is vitally important that you know or find out whether you are immune to German measles. If you are not, get inoculated before you become pregnant. After inoculation, you should not become pregnant for three months.

If you are not immune to German measles and become pregnant, you must do your utmost to avoid situations in which you might come into contact with anyone who has German measles. This means foregoing travel to areas where there is not universal immunization and checking ahead when visiting people to make sure that there have been no outbreaks of German measles in those households. Given almost universal inoculation to rubella in the United States, the risk of a nonimmune pregnant woman's acquiring German measles here is much less than that of her getting chickenpox. However, in any community there are those who are not immune to German measles—immigrants, the poor, people who just never had the shot—who could be a source of infection.

Measles and mumps: The same dangers and precautions that apply to chickenpox and German measles also apply to regular measles (variola) and to mumps, even though these conditions are much rarer in adults. As with chickenpox and rubella, there is no treatment for measles and mumps, and they do increase the risk of miscarriages and birth defects, even if only slightly. The best way to prevent acquiring them in pregnancy is to be immunized against them. Most women born in the United States or in other medically advanced countries will probably have received such immunization as children. If you did not—or if you are not sure about it— you need to have your blood tested to determine whether you are immune.

Coxsackievirus (Hand, foot, and mouth syndrome): This common childhood illness is marked by fever and by blisters of the hands, feet, and mouth—thus its name. It lasts from two to four days and usually occurs in mini-epidemics in schools and camps. It is not commonly seen in adults. In you were to become infected with coxsackievirus while pregnant, your chances of experiencing either a miscarriage or damage to your fetus because of it are extremely small.

Cytomegalovirus (CMV): Usually acquired by contact with infants and young children, CMV is most commonly seen among nurses, nursery school workers, and others who work with youngsters. As was discussed in Chapter 4, only 15% of women have symptoms when they are infected by CMV. These symptoms, when present, are fatigue, fever, sore throat, swelling of the lymph nodes, and enlargement of the spleen and liver.

Cytomegalovirus infection can cause miscarriage and is known to result in severe fetal injury such as deafness, damage to vision, and mental retardation. As with most viral infections, the initial episode is the most harmful. However, with CMV, even recurrent infections have been known to cause birth defects and miscarriage. If there is any good news about cytomegalovirus infection in pregnancy, it is that only from 1 to 4% of susceptible women will become infected when exposed to CMV, and that even then less then 5% of the infants of these infected mothers will suffer injury.

Unfortunately, there is no vaccine available to prevent CMV infection and no specific treatment for it if it is acquired. Because the risk of infection even for women who work with infants and children is low, it has not been recommended that women who are pregnant or planning to become pregnant avoid such work. Our best hope is that development of a cytomegalovirus vaccine, currently underway, will soon be completed.

Information about infections such as CMV can be frightening. Such phrases as "fetal injury" and "no known prevention or treatment" are ominous. But it is important to keep things in perspective. Even though CMV is the most common infection an infant can acquire during pregnancy, it is still a rare event. In my twenty-two years of practice, for example, I have delivered only one baby who had an obvious CMV-related injury. So although we need to know about CMV and be vigilant in detecting it when it is present, CMV-infected infants are not seen frequently and this condition is not something you should be extremely worried about.

Sexually Transmitted Diseases

Herpes: Herpes infections can cause harm to a pregnancy in two ways. The first and most serious is if a woman acquires herpes for the first time while pregnant, a primary infection. If the infection occurs in early pregnancy, it will cause a miscarriage anywhere from 5 to 40% of the time. Infection of the fetus in later pregnancy from passage of the herpes virus through the placenta is rare, and only occasional cases have been reported.

At the time of delivery, if a baby comes into contact with sores on its mother from a *primary* herpes attack, the baby has a 40% or more chance of becoming infected. Such infections are serious. An infant who acquires herpes from delivery can suffer injuries to the eyes, the brain, and other organs.

Fortunately, *recurrent* herpes attacks can cause harm to a fetus only if the sores are present *while* a woman is in labor. If a baby is delivered directly over recurrent herpes sores, there is a 1 to 2% chance that he or she will become infected.

But such generalized herpes infections in babies are rarely seen today. First, if you have herpes sores present at the time you go into labor, your obstetrician will probably perform an immediate cesarean section to prevent the baby from coming into contact with the viruses in the sores.

Second, there are now oral medicines available that are safe to take during pregnancy and that decrease the risk of recurrent herpes outbreaks. Your obstetrician may prescribe one of these medicines for you in the weeks leading up to your due date if you are at risk for recurrent herpes.

There are things you can do to decrease your risk of damage to your baby from a herpetic infection. If you have a history of recurrent herpes and have herpes sores present when you go into labor, be sure to tell your doctor about your herpes outbreak so that he or she can deliver your baby via cesarean section in timely fashion. Also, be sure to clarify ahead of time what your obstetrician wants you to do when your bag of waters breaks or you go into labor.

If you have never had herpes, it is imperative that you avoid acquiring it while you are pregnant. If your spouse has a history of genital herpes, you should use condoms during all sexual activity during pregnancy and avoid sexual activity while sores are present. Also, do not have oral sex if your partner has a cold sore because these sores are frequently caused by herpes viruses. If you do get a cold sore, make sure that you carefully wash your hands before using the bathroom or otherwise touching your genital area to prevent "autoinoculation"—self-spread of the virus.

Genital warts: These do not cause miscarriage and their presence at delivery is not harmful to your baby.

Mycoplasma, chlamydia, ureaplasma, and gonorrhea: Although it is clear that chlamydia and gonorrhea can cause miscarriage, the roles of mycoplasma and ureaplasma are less certain. Some experts think that these latter two organisms are normal inhabitants of the vagina. Nevertheless, these four infectious agents are often found together in various combinations and all have been shown in at least some studies to be related to early pregnancy loss. If there is any chance that you have been exposed to any of these organisms, you should be tested for them by having a culture taken of your cervix. If you are infected, these organisms are easily treated with antibiotics. Your partner should be treated as well. Following such treatment, it is important that you and your partner be re-cultured to make sure that the treatment has worked and that the organisms are no longer present.

Syphilis: Syphilis causes miscarriages, birth defects, and fetal death. Fortunately, it is not a common infection in the United States today.

Most states mandate testing for the disease both before getting married and during an initial pregnancy visit. Thus, you no doubt already know that you have tested negatively for it and need not worry. In the rare event that your test comes back positive, the results must be confirmed. Other conditions, such as lupus and other autoantibody diseases can cause "false positive" readings. If subsequent testing shows that you truly are infected with syphilis, you will be treated with antibiotics and followed up until the infection is eradicated.

HIV and AIDS: Women who are infected with the HIV virus and are pregnant are at risk for severe maternal illness, for miscarriage, and for transmitting the HIV virus to their fetuses. If there is any possibility that you have ever been exposed to the HIV virus—either by sexual contact, intravenous drug use, or blood transfusion—make sure you get tested to be certain that you are not infected. Of course, avoid sexual contact that might expose you to the HIV virus. If you do have HIV and are pregnant, new medications are available that can significantly reduce the risk of transmitting the HIV virus to your baby.

Animal- and Food-Borne Infections

Toxoplasmosis: Toxoplasmosis is a disease caused by the parasite *toxoplasmosis gondii*. It is most commonly acquired by exposure to cat feces or raw meat. If a woman is infected with toxoplasmosis for the first time during her pregnancy, she is at high risk for miscarriage. Her fetus is also at high risk of developing neurologic and eye injuries. Although treatment with specific antibiotics during pregnancy can decrease the severity of infection, it is safer and easier to avoid contracting toxoplasmosis in the first place.

There are some things you can do to protect yourself. If your cat is an outdoor cat or has ever caught rodents, avoid exposure to the cat's feces. Have someone else change the litter box. If your cat is an indoor cat, keep it that way, at least for the duration of your pregnancy. Avoid contact with soil where cats may have defecated. Wear gloves while gardening during pregnancy. Make sure that all meat you eat is well cooked.

Listeriosis: Listeriosis is a bacterial infection caused by the consumption of contaminated raw eggs, uncooked meat, or dairy products made from unpasteurized milk. Unwashed vegetables grown in contaminated soil have also been known to be the source of listeriosis infection. If a pregnant woman becomes infected, the organism can pass through her placenta to her fetus and cause miscarriage or stillbirth. Although antibiotics can eradicate the infection in the mother, it is unclear whether such treatment decreases the risk of pregnancy loss. This is because by the time the infection is diagnosed, the listeria organism has already circulated in the mother's blood and presumably into the placenta.

The best treatment is prevention. Avoid eating potentially contaminated foods such as those listed above and make sure you thoroughly wash all vegetables and fruits before you eat them.

Camphylobacter: Campylobacter is another food-related infection that in addition to causing bowel symptoms—diarrhea, cramps, bloody stool—can also cause a pregnant woman to miscarry. It is acquired by eating infected food or by contact with contaminated food utensils. It is most frequently associated with the eating or preparation of chicken. Avoidance is the best approach. Make sure all meat products you eat, especially chicken, are well cooked. Make sure eating utensils and food preparation surfaces you use are thoroughly and regularly cleaned.

Lyme disease: Lyme disease is suspected of causing miscarriage and fetal death. The organism responsible for Lyme disease is a spirochete—the same type of organism that causes syphilis—and is acquired when an individual is bitten by deer ticks, usually while walking in tall grass or in woods. Lyme disease is most commonly seen in the northeastern and central United States.

Antibiotics in both the tetracycline and penicillin families can successfully treat Lyme disease. But because Lyme disease can have many serious and sometimes permanent side effects (arthritis, neurologic damage), it is better and easier to avoid and prevent it than to try to cure it once acquired. The best means for you to prevent contracting Lyme disease is to exercise care when in areas known to be infested with deer ticks. When walking outdoors in such areas, wear long pants and check after each walk for ticks you might have picked up. Call your doctor immediately if after being in an infested area you develop fever, joint aches, or a circular red target-like rash.

Pets

There is no reason not to enjoy pets during pregnancy. It is only rarely that they transmit any infection to humans or that such infections increase the risk of miscarriage in pregnant women. The only conditions of concern during pregnancy that might be acquired from pets are

1. toxoplasmosis, from cat feces;
2. psittacosis—"parrot fever"—a rare viral illness that can be acquired from infected birds such as parrots and pigeons; and
3. brucellosis, an uncommon bacterial infection acquired by contact with the meat, milk, or cheese of infected cattle and goats.

Avoidance of these conditions is relatively straightforward: Don't eat raw meat. Let your spouse clean the cat litter box. Avoid close contact— petting, hand feeding—of animals whose health you do not know.

Anatomic Abnormalities

Congenital uterine defects: As we discussed in Chapter 3, several sorts of congenital uterine defects can lead to miscarriage. The frequency with which such defects cause miscarriage depends on what kind they are. For instance, the total duplication of the uterus, or a uterus with two "horns," increases the miscarriage rate from the baseline rate of 20% to between 30 and 40%. But a uterine septum—a largely fibrous structure that divides the uterus in half—will result in miscarriage rates as high as 80%.

If you have a uterine defect, the decision to have it repaired should be based on two factors. The first one is obvious: What kind of abnormality do you have? Your obstetrician would be more likely to recommend that you undergo surgery to remove a high-risk uterine septum than to advise you to have surgery on a lower-risk arcuate—"two-horned"—uterus.

The second is your own reproductive history. If despite having a uterine abnormality you have had a successful pregnancy, the old adage "If it ain't broke don't fix it" should be followed. If, on the other hand, you have had multiple miscarriages or pregnancies with preterm labors, then repair of your uterine abnormality will increase your chances of having a successful pregnancy in the future.

Currently, most procedures to correct uterine anomalies are performed through the hysteroscope. As we have discussed, the hysteroscope is a telescope-like device with its own light source that is placed into the uterus through the cervix. Long narrow instruments can be placed through channels in the hysteroscope that can cut, burn, or laser the abnormal tissue that protrudes into or divides the uterine cavity. Thus, without an abdominal incision, abnormal uterine anatomy can be corrected.

The average obstetrician-gynecologist performs these sorts of uterine repair operations only rarely. Since the situations requiring such surgery are uncommon, only certain reproductive gynecologists in a given city or region see enough of such uterine abnormalities to be truly adept at their correction. Therefore, if you have a uterine abnormality and have experienced one or more miscarriages, I encourage you to ask your doctor whether any gynecologists in your area have special expertise with these uncommon medical conditions. If so, I recommend that you make an appointment to see this doctor so that you can discuss your options more fully. If you decide to undergo surgery, you will be able to have it done by the surgeon in your area best qualified to do it.

Cervical incompetence: When a cervix is weakened, either congenitally (diethylstilbestrol [DES] exposure during pregnancy) or through trauma (childbirth, biopsies), the growing weight of a fetus can cause the cervix to open prematurely, resulting in the loss of the pregnancy or in preterm delivery. This is called cervical incompetence. Two options for treatment exist for this condition. Both are controversial.

The first is for you to go to bed rest for most of your pregnancy. Why? When a pregnant woman stands or sits, gravity brings the weight of her fetus down against her cervix. The less pressure placed on your cervix, the less chance the cervix will open prematurely.

A couple of problems arise with this seemingly commonsense approach. The first is that there is no data to show that it is effective. Moreover, for young, active women—probably with a job and/or other children—staying at bed rest for six months is both physically uncomfortable and logistically impossible.

The second approach to preventing cervical incompetence is cervical cerclage. This is the placement of a stitch around the cervix to tie it shut. The procedure is usually performed between the twelfth and fifteenth week of pregnancy. This timing is selected so as to be after when the vast majority of sporadic miscarriages will have occurred but before the fetus becomes so big that its weight will initiate cervical dilation. Although strenuous activities are prohibited after placement of the stitch, a woman can generally resume her normal lifestyle. The stitch is removed two to three weeks before her due date.

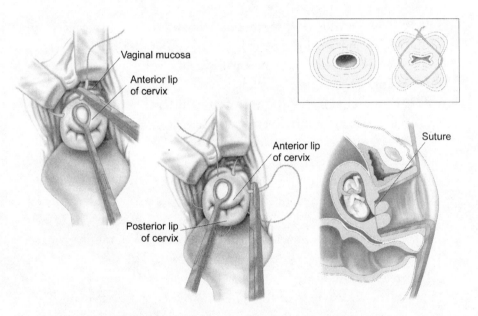

FIGURE 10.1 Cervical Cerclage

There are two techniques for performing cervical cerclage. The McDonald cerclage procedure is the simplest and most commonly used. It involves placing a strong stitch circularly around the cervix at its junction with the uterus to close off the cervical opening mechanically. The second procedure, less often used today, is the Shrodkar technique. In this technique, a half-inch-wide mesh tape is placed around the cervix and buried under the vaginal tissue near the junction of the cervix and uterus. The Shrodkar's supposed benefit is that the mesh is covered so that there is no irritating foreign material in the vagina to increase vaginal discharge and predispose to vaginal infection. But most obstetricians prefer the McDonald procedure because it involves less dissection and disruption of normal tissues.

The data on the effectiveness of cervical cerclage to treat cervical incompetence is not clear-cut. For every study that shows a distinct decrease in the rate of miscarriage following cerclage, there are studies that show no difference in outcome. But this is one of those situations in medicine where "the data" do not match the everyday experience of skilled clinicians. The vast majority of obstetricians who treat women with incompetent cervixes use cervical cerclages and find them extremely effective in preventing miscarriage.

DES (diethylstilbestrol) uterine abnormalities: The abnormal shape of the cervix and uterus in many DES-exposed women has been shown to lead to an increased risk of miscarriage and preterm birth. But as with other uterine defects, not all women with DES-induced abnormalities will have these problems. Most, in fact, will have normal pregnancies and no increase in their risk of miscarriage.

Therefore, if you are diagnosed as having a DES-induced cervical or uterine abnormality, no treatment should be contemplated unless you have already had two or more miscarriages. At such point, it would be reasonable to consider surgical correction of any structural problems. The surgical procedure is similar to that described above for the repair of other sorts of uterine anomalies. Success rates in achieving normal full-term pregnancies have been shown to improve dramatically following such surgery.

Fibroids: Fibroids are benign balls of tissue in the uterus that can range in size anywhere from that of a pea to that of a cantaloupe. They can cause miscarriage by interfering with implantation of the placenta or cause preterm labor by restricting the room available for a fetus to grow. During pregnancy, under the stimulation of the high blood levels of estrogen and progesterone that are present, fibroids often undergo rapid enlargement. Thus, fibroids that in a nonpregnant uterus would not appear large enough to cause complications can, in pregnancy, enlarge to such a degree that miscarriage or preterm labor results.

Fibroids are relatively common and are present in about 25% of all women. Most women who have them go through pregnancy without difficulty. If you have fibroids, therefore, it is prudent to see how you do during a pregnancy before considering treating them. If you go through pregnancy without significant difficulty, nothing should be done. If, however, you experience recurrent miscarriage, preterm labor, or severe incapacitating uterine pain during pregnancy, your fibroids will need to be treated.

This treatment can take three forms. The first is hormonal suppression. As mentioned above, fibroids frequently enlarge during pregnancy under the stimulation of high hormone levels. By the same token, fibroids shrink if deprived of these hormones. Thus, one way to treat fibroids is to cut off their hormonal supply. This can be done (prior to your becoming pregnant, of course) with medications—such as Lupron—that totally suppress ovarian hormone production. Such medicines essentially produce an artificial, temporary menopause. Thus deprived of hormones, your fibroids will shrink by as much as 33 to 50%.

The drawback to such suppressants is that when you stop the medication your fibroids will quickly grow back to their former size. Also, the symptoms you experience while in this artificial menopause are significant: hot flashes, night sweats, vaginal dryness, and loss of calcium from bone.

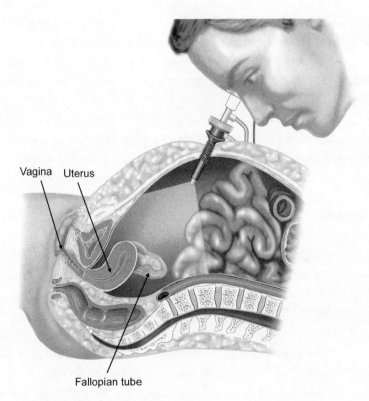

Vagina Uterus

Fallopian tube

FIGURE 10.2   Laparoscopy

The second method of treating fibroids is the one most commonly employed: surgical removal. This can be done either through traditional open abdominal surgery, via laparoscopy, or through the hysteroscope. The method a doctor chooses depends upon the location and size of fibroids and, to a certain extent, on his or her skill and preferences. If, for instance, a fibroid is on a stalk off the main surface of the uterus, it is usually easily resectable and would likely be removed by laparoscopy. Similarly, if a fibroid is on the inside surface of the uterine cavity, it can usually be "shaved off" via hysteroscopy. But if a medium to large fibroid is embedded deeply within the wall of the uterus, it can be extremely difficult to remove. Surgery on such a fibroid entails significant risk of damage to the uterus. In such a situation, the best approach would be open abdominal surgery. No matter which approach is selected, the goal is the same: to remove the uterine-distorting fibroid while at the same time preserving normal uterine anatomy to as great a degree as possible.

The recovery following fibroid-removal surgery depends on the approach used—laparoscopy, hysteroscopy, or open surgery—and the amount of tissue removed from the uterus. After fibroid removal—a procedure technically called *myomectomy*—your obstetrician will probably advise you not to become pregnant for one to three months so that the uterus has a chance to heal completely. If the surgery required incision into the innermost lining of the uterus, you will likely be advised to have a cesarean section for delivery when you become pregnant. The reason for this is that the part of the inner uterine cavity that was opened will heal by scar formation. This part of the uterus is permanently weakened and could possibly rupture during labor.

The third method for treating uterine fibroids is relatively new. It is called uterine artery embolization. Through a catheter placed into the arteries leading to the uterus small balls of a gelatin-like material are released. These partially block blood flow to the uterus, thus diminishing the supply of nutrients, hormones, and oxygen that fibroids need to grow. The fibroids thus stop growing and usually decrease in size.

The removal of fibroids by any of these methods has been clearly shown to reduce the risk of preterm labor and uterine pain in the subsequent pregnancies of women who have had these problems. But whether these procedures can prevent miscarriage in women who have fibroids is less clear. Of the published studies on this question some have shown a reduction in the miscarriage rate while others have not. Thus if you have fibroids and have suffered one or more miscarriages, you will have to discuss this issue and the specifics of your individual situation in detail with your obstetrician.

Asherman syndrome: Asherman syndrome occurs when the lining tissue of the uterine walls has been so badly damaged that the walls actually become stuck together by scar tissue. Since there remains little or no normal lining tissue in which an embryo can implant, infertility and miscarriage often result. The most frequent cause of such damage is excessive tissue removal during one or more D&Cs.

Asherman syndrome can almost always be effectively treated. The first step is to free up the intrauterine scar tissue via hysteroscopy and thus separate the walls of the uterus. Using small scissors on a long handle placed through the hysteroscope, the scar tissue bridges connecting the front and back uterine walls are cut and the scar tissue removed. To prevent reformation of the scar tissue, an intrauterine contraceptive devise—an IUD—is placed into the uterine cavity to keep the walls apart. The final step is to encourage the regrowth of normal endometrial tissue on the walls of the uterus. This is accomplished by having the woman being treated take moderately high levels of estrogen for three to six months, usually via oral estrogen tablets. Over this time, the high levels of estrogen in the blood promote the growth of any islands of normal endometrial tissue left in the uterus until this tissue covers the entire surface of the uterine walls. Once this is accomplished and the IUD is removed, the uterus should be ready to accept the implantation of an embryo.

Hormonal Problems

Corpus luteum deficiency: Corpus luteum deficiency, a controversial entity, supposedly arises when the main source of hormonal support for early pregnancy, the corpus luteum of the ovary, does not produce sufficient progesterone. As discussed in detail in Chapter 3, there is only limited evidence that corpus luteum deficiency is a significant cause of miscarriage.

Those practitioners who treat corpus luteum deficiency to try to prevent miscarriage employ various forms of progesterone therapy. This hormone can be administered either orally, vaginally in the form of suppositories, or via intramuscular injection.

As I have discussed, there is no proof that such treatment decreases the rate of miscarriage. Nevertheless, many reproductive specialists feel that progesterone might help hormonally "support" an early pregnancy and prescribe it to patients with a history of miscarriage so that "no stone is left unturned."

The only situations in which progesterone treatment has been definitely shown to improve pregnancy outcomes is when ovulation has been manipulated with fertility medications. In these pregnancies it has been shown that progesterone production sometimes is inadequate. Only in these pregnancies has the use of progesterone supplementation been shown to decrease a woman's chances of having a miscarriage.

Thyroid over- or underactivity: Diagnosing thyroid over- or underactivity is relatively straightforward. There are simple blood tests that will show whether your body's blood level of thyroid hormone is too high or too low. In addition, the hormone that regulates thyroid production, thyroid-stimulating hormone, can be measured. This shows us whether the body perceives itself as lacking, needing more, or having the right amount of thyroid hormone. If your thyroid levels are abnormal, it is important to find out why. Often the cause involves antithyroid antibodies. You will likely be tested for such antithyroid antibodies as well as for other autoimmune diseases. Sometimes the thyroid gland will contain nodules or tumors. These, of course, have to be evaluated for possible malignancy. Once the cause of the over- or underactivity of the thyroid gland has been established, efforts can be made to treat the problem.

In hyperthyroidism the goal is to decrease the amount of thyroid hormone the gland produces. The usual way of doing this is with medications that interrupt the chemical pathway of thyroid hormone production. Another technique, usually resorted to only if medical treatment fails, is the surgical removal of part of or all the thyroid gland to physically decrease the amount of hormone-producing tissue present. A third technique is the use of radioactive iodine—which gets preferentially absorbed by the thyroid gland—to destroy thyroid tissue without damaging other tissues of the body. Because this method involves radiation, it is rarely used during pregnancy. It might, however, be used following a miscarriage before a woman becomes pregnant again.

Hypothyroidism—under activity of the thyroid gland—is usually treated by supplementing inadequate thyroid production with artificial thyroid hormone in the form of pills. The dose is adjusted until blood tests show that a woman has the appropriate amount of thyroid hormone in her blood.

As was mentioned in Chapter 3, abnormal thyroid hormone levels are not the only thyroid problem that can affect pregnancy. Antibodies to thyroid gland tissues are associated with miscarriage independently of the level of thyroid hormone in the blood. Moreover, women with antithyroid antibodies have an increased chance of having other autoimmune diseases that can lead to miscarriage and stillbirth. The treatment for all these immunologic diseases of pregnancy is discussed below.

Polycystic ovarian syndrome: In polycystic ovarian syndrome, multiple egg follicles develop simultaneously. This produces abnormally high levels of all the hormones these follicles make: estrogen, testosterone, and androgens, which are male-type hormones usually produced only in very small quantities. These higher-than-normal hormone levels interrupt the normal function of the glands that control the ovulation cycle: the hypothalamus, the pituitary gland, and the ovaries. Ovulation is suppressed, menstrual periods are interrupted, and obesity, excessive hairiness, and infertility result.

Fortunately, polycystic ovarian syndrome is almost always amenable to treatment. In between pregnancies, the birth control pill offers an easy-to-take, effective solution. It regulates the menses, decreases male hormone in the blood, and consequently decreases obesity and hairiness. For women with polycystic ovarian syndrome who wish to become pregnant, the main issue is inducing ovulation. There are several techniques for doing this.

The first is a largely outmoded approach called "wedge resection." In this operation, a small section of both ovaries is surgically removed. By suddenly decreasing the amount of hormone-producing ovarian tissue, the high level of hormones in the blood drops, allowing the stalled ovulation cycle to "reboot." Such procedures have a very high rate of success in stimulating ovulation—but at the cost of surgery and potential scarring of the surface of the ovaries and nearby fallopian tubes.

Wedge resection is rarely employed today because several safe and effective medications are available to induce the ovaries to ovulate. Ovulation-stimulating drugs such as clomiphene have an excellent rate of success in producing eggs. If clomiphene fails, more potent medications can be prescribed. These are usually given by injection and can almost always generate ovulation in a woman who has viable eggs.

New research has shown that some of the oral antidiabetes medications such as metformin and troglitazone are able to reverse the suppression of ovulation caused by polycystic ovarian syndrome (PCOS). It seems there is a relationship between the body's ability to handle glucose—the definition of diabetes—and the hormone changes of PCOS. Although the mechanism of this crossover effect has not been fully worked out, treating diabetes with these medications counteracts the PCOS effects as well. The use of these medications may someday become the preferred treatment for PCOS.

Environmental Factors

Reducing risk in your home: Fortunately, neither household cleaners nor common electrical appliances such as the microwave, television, or your computer cause miscarriages. If questions arise about the quality of your water supply, you should contact your local board of health or speak to your doctor to get answers as to its safety. If you are doing a renovation or construction project at home, try to determine whether asbestos and/or lead dust is present. If so, it would be best to avoid the site until the contaminated material has been removed and the dust has settled and been cleaned up. If you engage in activities or hobbies that involve working with potentially dangerous materials—stained glass, jewelry making, or furniture finishing, for example—check with your obstetrician about their safety.

At work: Because of oversight by city, state, and federal regulatory agencies, most work sites in the United States are safe places for pregnant women. Nevertheless, you must be vigilant, especially if you are employed in such industries as manufacturing, electronics, mining, chemical production, or farming. It is perfectly reasonable to ask your employer about air quality and possible chemical exposures at your job site. If you do not receive adequate answers or cooperation from your employer, you can ask your local health department or state department of employment for help.

Radiation exposure: If you work where radiation is employed, make sure you follow all recommended safety instructions. You need to keep track of how much radiation exposure you are getting. Make sure you use a film badge or some other form of radiation exposure measuring device and have it checked at the recommended intervals. If your exposure even approaches maximum safe levels, stop working in that area. If you have questions about this or run into difficulties in obtaining information about radiation safety where you work, let your doctor know. He or she will help you get and interpret that information or will direct you to local or state agencies that will help you.

I discussed medical diagnostic radiation in detail in Chapter 5. Up to five rads exposure is not harmful to pregnancy and does not cause miscarriage. Fortunately, most x-ray procedures involve less than this dose. Nevertheless, whenever an x-ray—medical or dental—is ordered for you, you should:

1. Know for certain whether you are pregnant.
2. If pregnant, avoid unnecessary x-rays.
3. Use lead shielding over areas not directly being examined.
4. Make sure the doctor ordering the x-ray and the radiology technician performing it know that you are pregnant if you are. Remind them that you are not supposed to have more than 5 rads of radiation exposure during pregnancy. They should certainly know this, but reminding them may make them rethink which x-rays absolutely have to be taken and which can be avoided.

Of course, all these general rules about diagnostic radiation exposure do not apply in life-threatening circumstances when your doctors need vital information provided by x-ray examinations in order to treat you.

CT scans are merely another form of x-ray and have a potential for high radiation exposure. They should be avoided during pregnancy if possible. Since MRIs use magnetism and not radiation, they are safe whether you are pregnant or not.

Physical labor and exercise: Pregnant women have performed hard physical labor throughout human history. There is no evidence that such work increases the risk of miscarriage. Exercise, too, is generally safe during pregnancy, but here a bit of uncertainty exists.

The potential dangers of overexertion are

- becoming overheated;
- generating so much "waste material" in your blood from breaking down sugar and fat for energy that your blood becomes acidotic; and
- burning up so much oxygen that your blood-oxygen level decreases.

Raising your core body temperature can damage growing fetal cells and lead to birth defects and miscarriage. Working out or exercising beyond your body's aerobic capacity causes your body to use alternative chemical pathways to produce energy. This excessive exertion changes the content of your blood and can lead to your fetus being exposed to dangerously low levels of oxygen and a more acidotic environment.

Over a long time, excessive physical activity can suppress ovulation and hormonal cycles. This can lead to infertility—no egg, no baby—and potentially alter the hormonal environment of early pregnancy. Thus, if you regularly engage in an extensive exercise program, you should cut back on your level of physical activity while trying to conceive and during early pregnancy, especially if you have previously had one or more miscarriages.

Activities that involve significant risk of physical injury should be avoided before and during early pregnancy. Sports such as ice hockey, skiing, and climbing can result in injuries that, if they do not themselves injure the pregnancy, may require medical intervention and surgery, none of which is good for an early pregnancy.

Security systems: More and more frequently all of us are subject to scrutiny by security systems. Fortunately, the devices used inside these systems involve either very low-dose radiation or harmless electromagnetic fields. None of these pose a threat to you or your pregnancy.

Diet: Except for alcohol and cigarettes, all food products you can buy in a supermarket are safe for pregnancy if cooked well and stored properly. The same applies to food eaten in restaurants, at least in developed countries. The only question about food, which I mentioned in Chapter 5, is whether eating more than one serving a week of oily deep-sea fish could possibly raise the amount of mercury in your blood to dangerous levels. Until there is further clarification about this, I recommend that you heed the FDA's warning and avoid more than one serving of such fish a week.

Travel: Travel by itself does not lead to miscarriage. However, during your early pregnancy it is a reasonable precaution to avoid traveling to areas where medical care is less than excellent. Since miscarriages occur as frequently as they do—one in five pregnancies—you do not want to find yourself bleeding and possibly in need of surgery where safe, sanitary medical facilities are unavailable.

Bed rest: Women who are in *preterm labor* are often placed at bed rest to decrease the pressure of the fetus on the cervix because this pressure can lead to contractions. However, there is no evidence that bed rest helps to prevent *miscarriage*. It used to be thought that if there was an "insecure" attachment of the placenta to the uterine wall, decreased maternal activity would prevent miscarriage while the placenta was "digging in." It is now known that this concept has no validity. Nevertheless, in desperate situations where a woman has had multiple miscarriages despite thorough evaluation and the application of all appropriate therapies, bed rest may be recommended on the grounds that it "can't hurt, might help."

The only time that bed rest is likely to be an effective treatment for miscarriage is if an *incompetent* cervix has been diagnosed, as discussed above.

Sex: Sex is generally safe during pregnancy and does not increase the risk of miscarriage. The only exceptions are when certain pregnancy conditions are present, such as early pregnancy bleeding, cervical incompetence, preterm labor, and placenta previa (where the placenta covers the cervical opening). In all these circumstances, the physical manipulation of the cervix during intercourse might worsen the situation (see Chapters 5 and 7). But a normally growing pregnancy in the absence of these complications will not at all be affected by routine sexual play, intercourse, or orgasm.

Hot tubs, saunas, and jacuzzis: The danger here is that a pregnant woman's core body temperature might rise to levels dangerous for her fetus. Elevated core body temperature has been repeatedly shown in experimental animals to interfere with fetal cell growth and to cause birth defects and miscarriage. Thus, exposure to sources of sustained elevated temperature should be avoided during pregnancy.

Stress and anxiety: Neither of these emotions feels good, but there is no reliable evidence linking them to miscarriage. Stress and anxiety can cause a woman not to ovulate, and thus result in infertility. But if she does ovulate and become pregnant, there is no reason to think that stress and anxiety will cause her to miscarry.

Tobacco: Smoking is definitely linked to miscarriages. If you smoke, you should stop before trying to become pregnant. You should certainly stop if you are pregnant. If you find it impossible to stop smoking, lower the number of cigarettes you smoke each day to an absolute minimum. Various techniques, both medicinal and psychological, are available to help smokers quit. Quitting is not an easy thing to do. However, smoking is one of the relatively few instances in which it can clearly and unequivocally be said that the health of your baby is in your hands. It behooves you, therefore, to make the maximum possible effort to stop or severely curtail your smoking during pregnancy.

Caffeine: Several studies over the last ten years have looked at the effects of caffeine on miscarriage and birth defects. The evidence shows that consuming up to 200 mg of caffeine a day (the equivalent of two cups of regular American coffee) does not increase the risk of either miscarriage or birth defects during pregnancy, but that ingesting over 300 mg a day does. Thus, while you can continue to enjoy coffee, colas, and chocolate during pregnancy in limited quantities, it is important that you not exceed these guidelines. (See the list of caffeine levels in various foods in Chapter 5.)

Alcohol: Alcohol is a definite danger to pregnancy. It causes birth defects and miscarriage. There is no level of alcohol than is known to be safe. However, in many cultures, pregnant women do regularly drink wine or beer without apparent population-wide consequences.

I recommend that you keep your level of alcohol consumption very low during pregnancy: Either abstain entirely or have no more than one glass a week of beer or wine. If you have had previous miscarriages or difficulty becoming pregnant, if would be best for you to drink no alcoholic beverages at all when pregnant or trying to conceive.

Recreational drugs: With the exception of cocaine, the specific effects of most narcotics and mood-altering substances on pregnancy are not fully known. Cocaine has been shown to cause vasospasm, which is why cocaine has been associated with heart disease in so many healthy athletes. It is thought likely that cocaine has similar effects on the blood vessels of the placenta.

Narcotics such as heroin and morphine cause addiction in the babies born of mothers who use them. Other complications linked to the use of illicit or "street" drugs include severe mental retardation, neurologic injury, and smaller-than-normal babies. Pregnancy is not a good time to use or experiment with drugs.

Medical problems

Diabetes: In Chapter 6, we discussed how important it is for diabetic women to have their blood sugar under good control before and during pregnancy. It has repeatedly been shown that women whose blood sugar levels are normal before they become pregnant have a much lower rate of miscarriage and birth defects than women whose blood sugar levels are not well controlled. Control of blood sugar levels is achieved with diet, insulin, or oral diabetes medications.

If you have diabetes and are planning to become pregnant make sure that you are doing everything possible to maintain normal blood sugar levels. Know how to test your sugar levels yourself and keep a record of them. It is especially important to know what these levels are in relation to meals and in the fasting state. Learn the symptoms of excessively high blood sugar—lethargy, confusion, nausea, vomiting—and be in touch with your obstetrician and diabetes doctor if they occur.

You also need to be in the best possible physical shape at the onset of your pregnancy. You should be close to your ideal weight, be in an exercise program, and be under the care of a physician experienced with diabetes in pregnancy. Because diabetes can affect your eyes and kidneys, your vision and kidney function should be monitored regularly as part of your prenatal care.

Asthma: Good control of your asthma during pregnancy is vital for your health and the health of your fetus. However, asthma itself does not lead to miscarriage. Moreover, all categories of asthma drugs currently in use are safe for pregnancy.

Epilepsy: Both epilepsy and antiseizure medications increase the risk of miscarriage and birth defects. Ideally you should be in touch with your obstetrician and your neurologist before getting pregnant to review the medicines you are taking and their doses. Because seizures can cause injury to a pregnant woman and result in decreased oxygen supply to her fetus, antiseizure medications should be continued during pregnancy.

Hypertension: Hypertension is potentially dangerous for pregnancy because it increases a woman's chances of developing toxemia of pregnancy during her third trimester. Hypertension does not, however, cause miscarriage.

Irritable bowel syndrome (IBS): IBS causes diarrhea, cramps, and general abdominal discomfort. Its course during pregnancy is variable, sometimes improving, sometimes worsening. Fortunately, it has not been shown to increase the risk of miscarriage.

Depression and other psychiatric illnesses: Given how common depression, mood disorders, and other psychiatric illnesses are, it is not surprising that the treatment of women with these conditions is a common concern in pregnancy. Depression and psychiatric illness by themselves do not increase the risk of miscarriage. However there has been concern about the safety of medications used to treat these disorders.

Fortunately, more and more research is demonstrating that many of the medicines prescribed for depression, anxiety, and other psychiatric and emotional conditions *are* safe for pregnancy. Some medications remain controversial, such as the use of lithium for manic-depressive illness. Others, such as the popular SSRIs—Prozac, Zoloft, Paxil, and Celexa—are increasingly seen to be safe and effective medications for pregnant women.

But information about drug use in these circumstances changes rapidly. I therefore recommend that, if you are pregnant and are being treated for an emotional or psychiatric disorder, you obtain the advice of a psychiatrist experienced with the use of these drugs during pregnancy. Your obstetrician can help you find the names of such psychiatrists in your area.

Many of my patients, out of fear of the newness and potency of the medications they are on, ask me whether they should discontinue their antianxiety, antidepressant, or other psychiatric drugs when pregnant. My answer is that it depends on how much they need the medications. If a woman can go off them without risk to her mental or emotional well-being, she should do so, but only in consultation with her psychiatrist. But if in order to function comfortably she needs to remain on them, she can do so without fear that she is harming her pregnancy. It is much better for a woman to be psychologically healthy during pregnancy than to stop medications that work well for her when they are not known to cause miscarriage or to pose any other risk to pregnancy.

Immunologic and Hereditary Clotting Disorders

So much is being learned each year by ongoing research in the area of immunologic and hereditary clotting disorders that it is difficult to give advice with authority about how to reduce the risk of miscarriage from these conditions. What we do know for certain is that specific immunologic disorders increase the risk of miscarriage. Antiphospholipid syndrome and lupus, as discussed in Chapter 7, lead to blood clots in the small blood vessels of the uterus and placenta. This often results in miscarriage or stillbirth. Deficiency of factor V Leiden, protein S, and protein C causes similar damage. We discussed how these conditions are diagnosed in Chapter 9.

While medical scientists are beginning to understand what causes these syndromes and how they do the damage they do, not as much is yet known about to how to treat them. Currently, three medications are available: aspirin, steroids, and heparin. Aspirin and heparin work by preventing excessive blood clotting. They counteract the very mechanism by which immunologic and hereditary clotting disorders cause damage: decreased blood flow through the placenta due to clots. Steroids, as anti-inflammatory agents, stabilize chemicals in the blood vessels walls that initiate the blood-clotting process.

How well these three therapies work has not been clearly defined. The best results for preventing miscarriages so far obtained have been with the use of aspirin. It had been thought as recently as 1998 that the use of aspirin in pregnancy carried the risk of causing placental separation— placental abruption. Fortunately, several recent studies have shown that this is not the case. Despite this and other minor concerns, the relative success of aspirin in treating immunologic and clotting disorders in pregnancy and the lack of proven safe alternatives has led to the current recommendation that pregnant women diagnosed as having antiphospholipid syndrome or other blood-clotting disorders take one baby aspirin a day until just prior to delivery.

The use of heparin and/or steroids to treat immunologic and clotting disorders in pregnancy has advocates and critics. Since the studies that have been done show conflicting results as to the success or failure of these agents in reducing the number of miscarriages, their use has to be weighed against their risks: excessive bleeding in the case of heparin and the known steroid complications of elevated blood sugar, loss of calcium from the bones, and suppression of maternal and fetal adrenal glands. As mentioned, this is an area of active research. It is hoped that over the next few years we will have more definitive information about the effectiveness and safety of these treatments.

Surgery

Surgery during pregnancy is sometimes necessary and unavoidable. Appendicitis and accidents requiring emergency surgery can occur whether a woman is pregnant or not. But surgery for many nonemergent conditions could be avoided during pregnancy by taking care of them ahead of time. For example, if you know you have gallstones, discuss with your obstetrician the advisability of having them removed before you become pregnant. If you have an abdominal hernia, have it repaired. If you have orthopedic problems, have them evaluated and have needed x-rays taken before pregnancy. Take care of major dental work if you need it. In this, as in so many things, an ounce of prevention is worth a pound of cure.

The Role of Assisted Reproduction

There may come a point, either because you have experienced recurrent miscarriages or because of difficulty you have had becoming pregnant, that you need the help of a fertility specialist. With the techniques for assisted reproductive therapy now available, problems that in the past kept couples from becoming pregnant are now routinely sidestepped. No longer do scarred fallopian tubes, low sperm counts, or erratic ovulation cycles pose an insurmountable barrier to conception. With the use of ovulation induction medications, intrauterine insemination, and in vitro fertilization, many more infertile couples or couples with a history of recurrent miscarriages can now conceive and carry their pregnancies to term.

So if you have experienced difficulty conceiving or have had multiple miscarriages, or both, talk to your doctor about availing yourself of the services of a reproduction specialist. Even a one-time consultation may be helpful to you by letting you know what your chances are for having a successful pregnancy on your own and by letting you know what assisted reproduction techniques might offer you.

Alternative Medicine

We have very little reliable data by which to evaluate the performance of alternative medicine techniques to help avoid miscarriage. Since these techniques are largely unregulated and unlicensed, they have generally not been studied in any organized way by authoritative bodies. The controlled clinical trials by which the medical community judges the effectiveness of all other treatments and surgical procedures have not been done with alternative medication therapies. With these limitations in mind, let's take a look at some of these alternative therapies and review what we do know about them.

Herbal remedies: It's ironic: Just as herbal medical treatments have become mainstream enough to receive public and private funding for clinical trials, many of the studies that have just been completed show that these treatments are either useless or even potentially harmful. Several studies have shown that herbal drugs actually increase the risk of miscarriage by constricting of blood vessels throughout the body, including those in the placenta.

Over the next few years we should have much more specific information about herbal remedies. For now, however, I urge you to exercise extreme caution when using over-the-counter vitamins, herbal medicines, teas, or other materials thought to influence fertility, pregnancy, or miscarriage. Until we know more about them, I would regard the use of herbal medications to prevent miscarriage with skepticism and I suggest that you avoid them.

Acupuncture: Many physicians are biased against acupuncture because it is not clear how acupuncture works. Nevertheless, acupuncture therapy has been demonstrated to relieve pain in surgery, childbirth, and other circumstances.

Still open to question are claims made for the effectiveness of acupuncture in inducing ovulation and preventing miscarriages. I have not been able to find supporting evidence in the medical literature verifying the usefulness of acupuncture for treatment of these problems.

Chiropractic medicine and massage: Except for the fact that ligaments and joints are looser than normal during pregnancy and thus may be more susceptible to injury, there does not appear to be any danger from skillful chiropractic manipulation or from massage during pregnancy.

Conclusion

Whether miscarriages can be prevented depends upon what kind of miscarriage is being discussed. Miscarriages caused by (1) accidental chromosomal misalignment during the process of egg and sperm formation and (2) their combination at fertilization are not, with our current knowledge, preventable. Miscarriages caused by specific, identifiable medical, hormonal, anatomic, or other problems may well be treatable.

Much research is currently being done in the field of miscarriage. Causes of and treatments for miscarriages are under investigation from a variety of approaches. As we learn more about genetics, embryology, immunology, infectious disease, and blood clotting, we should have more and better tools available to help counteract the causes of miscarriage and to decrease their frequency.

So what now? How can you apply all you have learned thus far about miscarriages toward preparing yourself to try to become pregnant again? That is the subject of Chapter 11.

Moving on to a Successful Pregnancy

MY GOAL IN WRITING *MISCARRIAGE* HAS BEEN TO EXPLORE with you why miscarriages happen and how and when they can be prevented. Thus I have discussed with you the biology of pregnancy, the reasons why miscarriages occur, ways to diagnose the causes of miscarriages, and the various forms of treatment that are available. Together with Alice Domar, I have also sought to share with you some of the emotional responses that are normal for women and men to have following a miscarriage. It is my hope that, after you have read this book, one thing will be abundantly clear to you: The majority of miscarriages are spontaneous events over which you have no control and for which you should feel no guilt or responsibility. By learning the science of why miscarriages happen and the medical options you have to try to decrease your risk of having another miscarriage, you can reestablish for yourself at least some degree of control in your future attempts to have a successful pregnancy.

There is a beautiful poem, probably familiar to you, called the "Serenity Prayer." It was written in 1932 by the theologian Reinhold Niebuhr. Part of it goes like this:

God,
Grant me the Serenity to accept the things I cannot change
Courage to change the things I can
And the Wisdom to know the difference.

I feel this prayer provides a very useful model for thinking about and coming to terms with having had a miscarriage.

Accepting What I Cannot Change

As I discussed in Chapter 1, the first thing most women and men want to know after having a miscarriage is why it happened. The next thing they seek is some way of guaranteeing that they won't have another one.

By reading this book, you have already taken the first step toward addressing these two questions. You have learned why miscarriages happen. You have seen that most miscarriages are spontaneous natural events that come about through random chromosomal miscombination. You can now understand why, at least for the present, medicine can't prevent these sorts of sporadic miscarriages.

The Courage to Change What I Can

You have also seen that some miscarriages are *not* random sporadic events but come about because of specific medical problems. You now know that many of these problems can be treated, and with good results. You have seen when medical testing following a miscarriage is reasonable and, alternatively, when it would be a waste of your time, money, and energy.

You now know about the various treatments available to you that can reduce the risk of your having another miscarriage. With this knowledge you are now in a position to understand, after consultation with your doctor, when such treatments might be useful and when you are better off simply trying to become pregnant again. You have taken the first step in "making a change." You have learned that there are, in many cases, things that you can do to make a difference.

Here is a review of some of those things you can do to help prevent having a miscarriage in the future:

Chromosomal/Genetic/Immunologic

Know your family medical history. Know what hereditary conditions you might be at risk for. Have yourself and members of your family tested for genetic diseases for which you or they are at higher-than-normal risk. If you have had two or more miscarriages, have your own chromosomes tested. Also if you have had two or more miscarriages, be sure that the fetal tissue from the last miscarriage is tested for chromosomal abnormalities. Certainly be sure that tissue from further miscarriages is tested.

Check to see whether anyone in your family has had recurrent miscarriages or whether you have relatives who have had strokes, especially at an early age. If so, you may be at risk for the blood clotting disorders related to protein S and C deficiency or factor V Leiden abnormalities. If you have had more than one miscarriage, make sure you are tested for immunologic disorders such as anticardiolipin antibody syndrome.

Infection

Know your immune status before becoming pregnant. If you are not immune to chickenpox, rubella (German measles), and other infectious diseases for which inoculation is possible, get yourself immunized. Be vigilant at work to avoid close contact with coworkers, customers, and clients known to have an infectious illness. This is especially important if you are a teacher or if you work in the health care field where students or patients might have communicable illnesses. Check ahead when visiting friends or relatives to make sure that no one there is ill with a contagious disease.

Make sure all foods you eat are properly cleaned and prepared. Limit activities and travel to avoid areas where infections—such as Lyme disease, hepatitis, toxoplasmosis, malaria—may be prevalent. Practice safe, monogamous sex.

Anatomic Abnormalities

If you have had more than one miscarriage, make sure you are checked for cervical or uterine structural defects. If you have risk factors or a medical history suspicious for cervical incompetence, have this evaluated. Discuss with your doctor whether a cervical cerclage stitch is warranted. If you have fibroids in your uterus, find out what role they might have played in your miscarriage and whether anything should be done about them before you become pregnant again.

Hormonal Problems

Have your thyroid blood level checked. If you have had several miscarriages, and especially if your periods are irregular, have your doctor evaluate your levels of FSH and progesterone before conceiving again.

If you have polycystic ovarian syndrome, make sure that your hormonal status is normal before you become pregnant. Inquire of your physician to be certain that he or she has evaluated you for treatment with the most up-to-date medications.

Environmental Factors

Make certain that your home and workplace are safe. Know what chemicals are in the air and water around you. Limit your exposure to radiation and carefully monitor the exposure you do get when you are pregnant. Modulate your level of physical activity, whether it be for work or for exercise, to within safe limits. Make sure you eat a healthy, varied diet. If you smoke, stop. Keep alcohol consumption to a minimum. Limit the number of cups of coffee you drink to no more than two a day.

Medical Problems

Make certain that any medical problems you have are being optimally treated before you become pregnant. If you are a diabetic, get your blood sugar levels under the best possible control. If you have asthma or epilepsy, make certain that your medications are appropriate and well adjusted. If you suffer from depression, speak with your physician or therapist about your plans to become pregnant and make sure you are on the best medications both for you and for your soon-to-be fetus.

General Health Issues

Be sure to be up-to-date with physical examinations, Pap smear, mammogram if appropriate, and all immunizations. Have a dental checkup. Try to have dental problems attended to before conceiving.

While attempting to become pregnant, be certain that you are consuming adequate amounts of folic acid. It is recommended that all women trying to conceive take at least 400 mcg of folic acid a day. Although most women get this in their regular diets, almost every over-the-counter multivitamin tablet contains this amount.

The Wisdom to Know the Difference

It's one thing to read an academic description of why miscarriages happen. It's an all-together different matter when the miscarriage is happening to you and you personally experience the shock and grief of losing a much-desired pregnancy.

Yet an understanding of exactly why miscarriages happen will be invaluable to you if you are going to come to terms with the miscarriage you have just been through. It will also be of tremendous practical assistance to you as you move forward to your ultimate goal of having a child. For armed with such information you can now be an informed partner as you work with your doctor to evaluate your pregnancy loss. You can help him or her try to determine whether your miscarriage was a sporadic, spontaneous one—the most likely possibility—or whether it might have been caused by some potentially treatable problem. You are in a position to understand the sorts of testing that you may need to have. You can participate knowledgeably in deciding with your doctor what, if any, treatments you should undergo to help you maintain a viable pregnancy the next time you conceive. The information we have reviewed together in the previous ten chapters will help you deal with all these issues—and will give you, at least to some degree, the "wisdom to know the difference" about what you can change and what you cannot.

Moving On

The majority of couples who have had a miscarriage want very much to become pregnant again. So after all the physical and emotional turmoil resulting from the miscarriage has settled down, the question naturally arises, "What now?"

If this is your first or second miscarriage and there is no obvious medical problem to which the miscarriage can be attributed, there is no reason to wait any fixed amount of time before trying to become pregnant again. You can safely attempt to conceive after your first period following the miscarriage. On the other hand, there is no need to rush. Unless you are on the margins of fertility because of your age, waiting before trying to conceive again is unlikely to affect your ultimate chances of having a baby.

If, however, you have had several miscarriages or if you have reason to suspect that there may be a specific cause for your pregnancy loss (or losses), you need to discuss the situation with your obstetrician. You and your doctor can evaluate potential causes for your miscarriage(s) and, if any treatable causes are uncovered, can plan to deal with any problems thus found.

Getting Pregnant

Some couples are lucky: They conceive within one or two cycles of try-ing. For others, the process can be much more difficult. Month after month may go by without success. These couples not only have to deal with having had a miscarriage but now have new concerns about whether they are infertile.

Fortunately, 75% percent of all couples who have had a miscarriage and are trying to conceive will do so in one to six months. For those who do not, it may well be appropriate for them to consult their physicians to see if there are any factors that may be delaying them from becoming pregnant again.

When to Tell Others

This is a question I am frequently asked by couples whose last pregnancy ended in a miscarriage. They remember how upsetting it was to tell peo-ple to whom they had previously announced their pregnancies that they had miscarried. Although they received support from these family and friends, they also felt pain and a certain embarrassment that such inti-mate personal matters had to be made public.

To avoid having once more to tell their family, friends, and coworkers about a pregnancy loss, such couples often initially wish to withhold the news of their pregnancy from all but their closest relatives or friends. The question is then inevitably "When is it safe to tell the wider world?"

I generally tell my patients that they can feel reasonably sure their pregnancies are viable after we hear the fetal heart beat in the office with the Doptone (a portable sonar-type device) at their ten- to twelve-week visit. Miscarriages can occur after this time but are unusual. Once this milestone of hearing the fetal heartbeat has passed, a couple can announce their pregnancy with confidence.

I have some patients who are even reluctant to share the news of their early pregnancy with the people closest to them—their parents and best friends. Although this is certainly a personal, individual decision, I do remind these patients that even if they were to have a miscarriage, their parents and best friends are exactly the people they would turn to for help and support. Parents and friends are adults. They know that pregnancies sometimes end in miscarriage. They can handle this news and, moreover, would want to share this loss with those they love. Just as you would probably be able to react appropriately and supportively toward one of your friends or relatives if she had a miscarriage, your friends and relatives will be able to and want to do the same for you.

How Do I Know How My Pregnancy Is Doing?

If you have had a miscarriage, the first weeks of your next pregnancy will be an extremely anxious time. You will likely be hypervigilant for signs of bleeding, cramping, or loss of normal pregnancy symptoms. It probably will not be until you have heard the baby's heartbeat—sometime after the ten-week visit—that you will feel a sense of relief since, as noted, it is unusual for a miscarriage to occur beyond this point.

The first step toward knowing how your pregnancy is doing is to establish that you are indeed pregnant and that your pregnancy is in the uterus—as opposed to in the fallopian tube or somewhere else in the pelvis. This is done by your doctor's physical examination and, if necessary, an ultrasound scan.

Next, you should look for physical symptoms that are often seen with a healthy early pregnancy. These include nausea, vomiting, loss of appetite, food aversions, breast tenderness, and fatigue. Not all pregnant women experience these symptoms. But if you do, you can look upon them as a good sign—despite the way they make you feel. At some point thereafter, you will begin to "show" (look pregnant), experience quickening (feeling the baby move), and note progressive abdominal enlargement as your baby grows.

Your doctor will use some of this same information in judging how your pregnancy is going. He or she will inquire whether you are feeling normal pregnancy symptoms. Your abdomen will be examined to note the size of the uterus. If there is a question in early pregnancy about the status of your pregnancy, your pregnancy hormone levels—HCG—will be checked serially. HCG levels should roughly double every forty-eight hours in early pregnancy. Finally, ultrasound examination can tell as early as a gestational age of five and one-half weeks that a live fetus is present in the uterus. More precise findings concerning the fetus can be made as the pregnancy progresses and as fetal features become more easily visualized.

It has been my experience that even if all appears to be going well, couples who have had a miscarriage strongly exemplify the old adage "once burned, twice shy." In fact, it is often not until a woman either sees her baby moving during a detailed second-trimester ultrasound at eighteen weeks of gestation, or feels the baby's squirming in her abdomen at approximately twenty weeks of gestation that she will accept the fact that she is indeed going to become a mother.

Conclusion: Having a Baby

This is, after all, the goal of most people reading this book. It is certainly the goal of the vast majority of couples who have suffered a miscarriage. It is most likely your current goal, too. Fortunately, it is a goal you will very likely attain.

There are some things you should keep in mind as you plan to get pregnant again. Remember—and keep telling yourself—that although miscarriages are a common, natural event, 80% of all pregnancies *do not* end in miscarriage. Remember that the data invariably show that the great majority of women who have had a miscarriage go on to a successful pregnancy the next time they conceive. Remember that most miscarriages are caused by spontaneous events outside of your control. You did not cause yourself to miscarry and there was nothing you could have done to prevent it. Remember, too, that even if your miscarriage was caused by a specific medical problem, usually such problems are either preventable, treatable, or can be bypassed via assisted reproduction technologies.

So once you are at the point where

—you have learned as much as you can about miscarriages in general and your miscarriage in particular

—all necessary diagnostic studies have been performed

—all recommended treatments have been implemented

move on with your life! If for you that means trying to become pregnant again, wonderful. The odds for success are in your favor.

With the understanding you now have about why you had your miscarriage, with a well-justified confidence that your next pregnancy is likely to be a successful one, and with your knowledge of how to prepare yourself for being pregnant the next time, you have every reason to be optimistic about having the baby you so much desire.

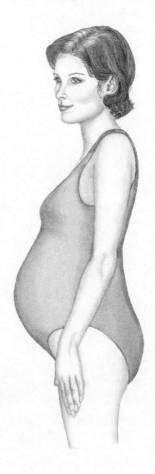

Resources on Miscarriage and Pregnancy

Best General Sites

The American College of Obstetricians and Gynecologists (ACOG)
409 12th Street, S.W.
Washington, DC 20024-2188
(202) 638-5577
www.acog.org

Government Center for the Evaluation of Risks to Human Reproduction (CERHR)
http://cerhr.niehs.nih.gov

March of Dimes Birth Defects Foundation
1275 Mamoroneck Avenue
White Plains, NY 10605
(914) 428-7100
www.modimes.org

Motherisk Program
www.motherisk.org

National Institute for Occupational Safety and Health (NIOSH)
www.cdc.gov/niosh/homepage.html

National Library of Medicine (Medline)
www.nlm.nih.gov/

The National Women's Health Information Center
www.4women.gov

Occupational Safety and Health Administration (OSHA)
www.osha.gov

Pregnancy Environmental Hotline
1-800-322-5014
www.thegenesisfund.org

Other Organizations

National Center for Education of Maternal and Child Health
2000 15th Street N, Suite 701
Arlington, VA 22201-2617
(703) 524-9335
www.ncemch.org

National Society of Genetic Counselors
233 Canterbury Drive
Wallingford, PA 19086-6617
(610) 872-1192
www.nsgc.org

Specific to Miscarriage

Baby Center
www.babycenter.com

The Miscarriage Association—British
01924 200795
www.miscarriageassociation.org.uk

Miscarriage Information
www.silk.net

SHARE Pregnancy & Infant Loss
Support, Inc.
www.nationalshareoffice.com

Infertility and Miscarriage

International Counsel on Infertility
Information Dissemination, Inc.
P.O. Box 6836
Arlington, VA 22206
(520) 544-9548
www.inciid.org

Resolve, Inc.
www.resolve.org

DES Exposure

DES Action
Long Island Jewish Medical Center
New Hyde Park, NY 11040
(516) 775-3450
www.desaction.org

Herpes

The Herpes Resource Center
American Health Association
P.O. Box 100
Palo Alto, CA 94306
(415) 328-7710
www.ibiblio.org/ASHA/herpes

National Herpes Hotline
P.O. Box 13827
Research Triangle Park, NC 27709
(919) 361-8488
www.ashastd.org

Index